THIS little handbook, which has been under constant revision since its first issue in June, 1941, appears in a new edition for which the advance demand has greatly exceeded all possibility of supply on account of paper restrictions. While the Editor laments the Publishers' inability to produce more than a small proportion of the copies for which would-be readers are asking, he is happy to think that, including the present edition, a total of fully 380,000 copies has been provided ; and as many thousands of these will doubtless each have several readers, it is probably no exaggeration to say that the total number of readers who may have profited by this unique assemblage of practical and authentic information about the varied activities of the Royal Air Force might be estimated at near the million mark.

His Majesty King George VI

ABC of the RAF

Handbook for all Branches of the Air Force

Edited by
Sir John Hammerton
Editor "War in the Air,"
"The War Illustrated," etc.

Preface by
Air Chief Marshal Sir Charles Portal, K.C.B., D.S.O., M C.
Chief of the Air Staff

NEW EDITION, 1943

With Special Identification Section of
R.A.F. Aircraft in Service

Five Plates in Full Colour &
266 Photographs and Diagrams

LONDON : THE AMALGAMATED PRESS LIMITED

TABLE OF CONTENTS

*This book is arranged in 4 main Sections with Subsections grouped **under** letters of the alphabet, as here shown. At various convenient points tabular and other reference matter is inserted (see separate list p. 160).*

Preface: by Air Chief Marshal Sir Charles Portal	3
The R.F.C. and the R.A.F. An Historical Note	4

SECTION 1. THE R.A.F. TODAY

	The R.A.F., Its Needs and Opportunities	9	H. Opportunities for Self Education	38
A.	Apprenticeship	10	J. Organization of the R.A.F. at Home and Abroad	39
B.	Entry into the V.R. and Tables of Trades and Pay Groups	12	K. Leaders of the R.A.F.	44
C.	Air Crew Duties	17	L. Women's Auxiliary Air Force	55
D.	Commissioned Branches of the R.A.F. V.R.	18	Princess Mary's R.A.F. Nursing Service	59
E.	Life and Training of Recruit	20	M. The Auxiliary Air Force	60
	The R.A.F. Volunteer Reserve	29	N. The Royal Observer Corps	62
	R.A.F. Authorized Badges	30	O. The Air Training Corps	63
	Airmen V.C.s	32	P. University Short Course	65
	Decorations Awarded to R.A.F. Personnel	32	Q. Air Forces of the Dominions Empire Training Scheme	66 / 70
F.	How to Become a Technician	33	R. R.A.F. Benevolent Fund	71
G.	Reclassification, Remustering, and Leave	36		

SECTION 2. ELEMENTS OF FLYING

A.	Training and Practice in Flying	75	D. I.C.E. Theory	106
B.	Aircraft Employed by the R.A.F.	97	Aeroplane Engines	107
			E. Map Reading	109
C.	'Plane Flight and Structure	101	F. Navigation of Aircraft	110
			G. Signalling Methods	112
			H. Meteorology and the R.A.F.	117

SECTION 3. SPECIAL TRAINING AND EQUIPMENT

A.	Photography in the R.A.F.	121	E. Balloons and Balloon Barrage	129
B.	Aircraft Armament	124	F. Air Sea Rescue	131
C.	Bombs and Bombing	127	G. Work of the Ground Staff	133
D.	Life Saving Parachutes	128	H. Parachute & Air-Borne Troops	136

SECTION 4. ELEMENTS OF AIR FIGHTING

A.	Notes on Tactical Methods	141	C. 'Briefing' the Bomber Crews	149
B.	Methods of Formation Flying	146	D. The Record of the R.A.F.	151
	General Index	159	List of Reference Tables	160

PLATES IN COLOUR AND DUOTONE

H.M. King George VI .... *Frontispiece*

Decorations Awarded to R.A.F. Personnel; Equivalent Ranks in the Three Services; R.A.F. Ensign, Badge, Flags and Target .. *Between pp. 32 and* 33

British & American Aircraft in R.A.F. Service (*Duotone Section*) .. 81-96

PREFACE *by the* CHIEF OF AIR STAFF

Air Chief Marshal SIR CHARLES PORTAL K.C.B., D.S.O., M.C.

This book is an up-to-date guide to the varied and numerous activities of the R.A.F. It is full of accurate information, and will be especially useful to all those who hope themselves to enter the Service.

But there can be few families throughout the Empire who do not feel a personal interest in the R.A.F. because they are connected as relations or as friends with serving members of the Royal Air Force or of the Air Forces of the Dominions. I am confident that the little book will appeal to this wider public, and give them all the information which they must be eager to have.

Portal.

Chief of the Air Staff.

MACHINES THAT MADE HISTORY

This Howard Wright biplane, with its primitive control surfaces and flimsy construction, is typical of the kind of aircraft that flew at Brooklands in 1910.

A B.E.3 biplane and the tail and port wing of a Blériot monoplane are seen in this photograph, taken during the first Royal inspection of the R.F.C. at Aldershot in 1913.

The Vickers "Gun Bus" was a fighter of 1915. Its sole armament was a Lewis gun, mounted in the front cockpit. The 100 h.p. Monosoupape engine drove a pusher airscrew.

In 1916 the D.H.2 single-seat fighter went into R.F.C. service. It had a pusher airscrew and its top speed was about 90 miles per hour.

INTRODUCTORY

The Story of the R.F.C. and R.A.F.
Thirty Historic Years in the Air

On April 1, 1911, Britain's first Air Battalion of the Royal Engineers was formed. A year later the R.F.C. was formed, to be re-born after six years, in 1918, as the R.A.F. Air supremacy and the formation of the world's greatest air force was achieved in those historic years. How is here told in outline.

THE history of Britain's air service is spread over a period of just thirty years. It opens on April 1, 1911, the day when a special Army Order, issued on Feb. 28, 1911, came into force, by which an Air Battalion of the Royal Engineers was created as the first step in building a British army air arm. The commandant of the battalion, which consisted of two companies, one dealing with airships, the other with aeroplanes, was Major Sir Alexander Bannerman. It was arranged that officers should be appointed from any branch of the Army to the Battalion, but all other ranks were men already serving in the Royal Engineers.

The Battalion functioned for one year, and then, by Royal Warrant, was absorbed into the Royal Flying Corps. The Warrant was dated April 13, 1912, and the Corps was actually formed four weeks afterwards. It was split up into two wings, a Naval Wing and a Military Wing; the former, which at a later date became the Royal Naval Air Service, carried out flying training and experiments with seaplanes, airships as well as landplanes, while the Military Wing concentrated on landplanes.

There were in those days few ideas concerning the use of aircraft in warfare other than that they should be employed for observation purposes. There was no standardization of equipment, no set methods in flying training, and no hard and fast rules in operational technique. The art of flying was, in fact, still in its infancy; the aeroplane was at that time only slightly in advance of the original power-driven aircraft which the Wright brothers flew over the sand dunes in North Carolina in 1903.

When the Royal Flying Corps was formed it was planned that the Military Wing should have 182 officers and 182 N.C.O.s, and arrangements were made so that non-commissioned officers could be trained to fly.

Amongst the officers seconded was Viscount Trenchard, Marshal of the Royal Air Force. He was then an officer in the Royal Scots Fusiliers, and he had previously learned to fly at his own expense at Mr. T. O. M. Sopwith's school at Brooklands. On joining the R.F.C. Major Trenchard (as he was then) went to the Central Flying School at Netheravon, passed all his tests and was then appointed an instructor on the staff. The Military Wing was commanded by Major Sykes (now Major-General Sir Frederick Sykes).

Engines Were Only 80 h.p.

The equipment was heterogeneous, consisting of an assortment of Farman biplanes, Blériot monoplanes and other types. None was fitted with an engine of more than 80 h.p. rating, and most of them were structurally unsound, judged by later standards. There were questions asked in Parliament about the new Corps and its aeroplanes, criticism in the Press, and the view which had been held by the War Office only two years before that the aeroplane had no "military significance" was still upheld in many quarters. Yet the pioneers worked on with enthusiasm, and while they learned to fly and evolved new ideas

Brig.-General Sir David Henderson commanded Squadrons 2, 3, 4 and 5 of the R.F.C. when they went to France on Aug. 13, 1914.

In the early part of the war of 1914-18 the bomber pilot dropped his missiles overboard by hand, and no certain aim could be taken.

they laid the foundations of Britain's great Air Force.

Then came the Great War, and the first British pilots went to France on August 13, 1914. Under Brigadier-General Sir David Henderson Squadrons Nos. 2, 3, 4 and 5 established themselves across the Channel and within a short time pilots and observers were in action. On August 19 the first reconnaissance flight of the R.F.C. was carried out, and it is of historic interest to note that the pilot was Captain Joubert de la Ferté (now well known as Air Marshal Sir Philip Joubert). Those early days of the conflict provided abundant opportunities in which was shown the value of the aeroplane in operations before, during, and after a battle. The power of the military reconnaissance aeroplane was made plain to the most sceptical.

Pilots Armed With Pistols

Improvements in equipment in some cases were introduced quickly, and the art of aerial reconnaissance, of artillery observation, rapidly advanced. New wireless apparatus for signalling to the ground forces and systems of intercommunication were adopted; new cameras were designed and fitted to our machines. Few aircraft of 1914 had armament, and pilots and observers carried out patrols armed only with rifles and revolvers. But gradually the machine-gun was adopted, and about the first machine of the R.F.C. to be so equipped was the Vickers F.B.5, a pusher biplane powered with a 100 h.p. Monosoupape Gnôme rotary engine. This aeroplane, with the B.E.2c, the Avro 504, and the French Maurice Farman, formed the main equipment of the squadrons in those early days. All were two-seaters designed and used for army co-operation duties. There were few fighters, or scouts as they were called, because fighting had not entered into the scheme of things.

Air combat swiftly developed, however, when the synchronized gun gear which allowed a machine-gun to be fired through the airscrew was produced by the enemy and then by ourselves. From then on, the struggle for air supremacy went on without respite. In 1915 the notorious Fokker monoplane took heavy toll of the slower and ill-armed aeroplanes of the R.F.C. But in 1916 the Sopwith Pup and the D.H.2 with which new fighter squadrons were equipped helped us to wrest for a time the ascendancy which the Germans had obtained.

The speeds of aeroplanes then steadily rose; for example, the B.E.2c of 1914 flew at 75 m.p.h., but the Sopwith Pup of 1916 vintage could achieve 105 m.p.h. Each year of the Great War both sides brought into the field new types of aeroplane, and while

Used for training and for reconnaissance, the Maurice Farman Shorthorn biplane came into service from 1916 onwards.

the main function of the R.F.C. was reconnaissance, the fighter and the bomber moved forward to occupy places of major importance. The advantage in the air was held first by one side and then by the other. From the Sopwith Pup, fighter squadrons changed to the Sopwith Camel, a two-gun single-seater of 130 h.p. with a speed of about 120 m.p.h. Other squadrons were equipped with the S.E.5, another single-seater fighter which had a speed of 130 m.p.h. These aeroplanes, with the Bristol Fighter two-seater, were outstanding in helping the R.F.C. to gain the mastery of the air from 1917 until the Armistice.

In 1916 and onwards a colossal effort was put out by Britain to expand and strengthen her air services. A standardized system of instruction had been evolved by Colonel Smith Barry, Commandant of the Instructors' School at Gosport, so that pilots were trained efficiently and the standard of flying was high. Men poured into the R.F.C. to train as pilots, observers, and air mechanics to fill the ranks of newly-formed fighter, artillery-observation and bomber squadrons.

Then, as now, it was recognized that mastery of the air was essential for victory. At home, in France and in the Middle East the R.F.C. and the Royal Naval Air Service fought with unsurpassed gallantry, and the service which had been regarded with wondering suspicion by some Service chiefs and politicians but two years before was gathering honours and great distinction in every major operation on all fronts. The building up of the service into a vast and extremely powerful arm was not carried out without difficulties. With meagre experience a gigantic aircraft industry had to be established to provide the ever-expanding Air Service with fighters, bombers, army cooperation machines, and training aircraft. Aero engines in their thousands had to be manufactured, with multitudinous parts, accessories and auxiliaries, and aerodromes had to be prepared. Supplies of aircraft were, in fact, accompanied by serious obstacles, one of which was the rivalry between the War Office and the Admiralty when dealing with the manufacturers.

The Royal Air Force is Born

On April 1, 1918, the R.F.C. and the R.N.A.S. merged to become one great fighting force, the Royal Air Force, and from that date this country went from strength to strength in the air war. In France and in every other seat of the war our airmen began to drive the enemy out of the sky. Squadrons which in their early days had fought against tremendous

Capt., later Lt.-Col. Bishop, V.C., D.S.O., hero of a hundred combats, is here seen with his single-seat Nieuport Scout (1917).

odds when they were ill-equipped and heavily outnumbered, often carried out patrols without meeting a single German machine.

When the Armistice was signed the R.A.F. had 188 operational squadrons at home and abroad. In addition to these there were no fewer than 56 training stations, each one of which contained three training squadrons, and apart from the stations there were 19 training squadrons. In that memorable November of 1918 the R.A.F. strength stood at **27,333 officers** and **263,410 other ranks**. There were **22,647 aeroplanes** on charge and **103 airships**, and at home and abroad there

INTRODUCTORY R.F.C. and R.A.F.

The Bristol Blenheim (2 840-h.p. Mercury engines) has been employed as an escort fighter and for night work Armed with 4 Browning machine-guns

were close on 700 R.A.F. aerodromes England possessed the biggest air force in the world.

But in the early post-war years this great and mighty service was cut and whittled down to such an extent that by March 1920, only 25 squadrons were in existence. Eight were in process of formation and only half of the total were stationed in the British Isles. We know now that the policy that brought about this immense reduction in our Air Force was ill-advised From 1920 until 1933 the R.A.F. remained a small service, and in the latter year our Home Defence squadrons numbered only 40

In 1935 the big scheme for air expansion was formulated and put into practice Woven into the scheme was the formation of the R.A.F. Volunteer Reserve in 1936. Through this Reserve the strength of the Air Force was very considerably increased during the four years preceding the outbreak of war. At the same time the shadow factory scheme gathered momentum to answer in some measure the urgent and vital demands of the R.A.F

The period of the present war has provided irrefutable evidence that the plan has not failed. At the outbreak of war Britain was far behind the enemy in numerical strength and in aircraft production. In the quality of personnel and equipment the R.A.F. has been, is, and will continue to be, superior to the enemy. In every form of air operations British pilots and air crews have shown again and again a matchless skill and courage. Squadrons are manned by men from all parts of the Empire as well as from the Home Country. Some are regulars, some received their training as members of the A.A.F., others in the R.A.F.V.R., and many have come to Britain from New Zealand, South Africa, Australia and Canada, after being trained under the Empire Air Training Scheme.

All are imbued with the same magnificent spirit, no doubt intensified by the fact that the R.A.F. aircraft are definitely superior to those of the enemy, and for that we have to thank the brilliant designers and craftsmen who have produced the Vickers-Supermarine Spitfire, the Hawker Hurricane, the Hawker Tornado, and other fighter aircraft. In the bomber class, too, it is conceded that the Vickers-Armstrong Wellington, the Bristol Blenheim, the Handley Page Hampden, the Halifax, and the Short Stirling are unexcelled by any machine in the service of the Luftwaffe.

Now new machines that far exceed our present best are on the way and the ever-growing quantity of new equipment is being rapidly augmented by aircraft from the United States By day and by night, over the land and far out over the seas, the R.A.F. will continue the fight until undisputed supremacy in the air is secured.

The Royal Air Force Today
Its Imperious Needs and the Opportunities it Offers

In this Section, after the prefatory note below, we consider in outline the whole organization of the R.A.F., the conditions of entry, with tables of Trade Groups and their Pay, Apprentices, Aircrafthands, Air Crews, and so forth. These are followed by special articles on the training of recruits and technicians, the Commands, the Leaders of the R.A.F. and the Auxiliary and other Services.

"MORE men—more men!" That is the call of the Royal Air Force today. Never before have the requirements of this country been more vital, more incessant, and because the grim struggle in which we are engaged is inseparably woven with the battle for the skies the demand of the R.A.F. will continue.

Conquest, victory and peace cannot be secured unless superiority in the air is achieved, and that means quality and quantity. The unsurpassed deeds of British airmen ever since the war began have shown conclusively that the former is not lacking. It never will be lacking. Now the drive forward is to obtain an unending growth in numerical strength. So the R.A.F. needs men. They are required not only to serve as pilots, observers, airgunners and wireless operators and navigators, but in dozens of different capacities in which skill, efficiency and specialized knowledge are essential qualifications.

Heroic Tradition of the R.A.F.

To serve in the R.A.F. is to serve in one of the finest forces that has ever been evolved. Though young in comparison with other of His Majesty's Forces, it has nevertheless built up a grand tradition in its 23 eventful and heroic years. And with this tradition there is a spirit, the spirit of the R.A.F.

It was born of and nurtured by those early pilots of the R.F.C. and R.N.A.S., some of whom crossed the Channel on August 13, 1914, the vanguard of a force which inaugurated a new form of warfare. Through the months and years of the Great War that spirit was sustained and in later years continued when a new generation filled the ranks of the Service.

At the R.A.F. College at Cranwell, which was established in 1920, until the outbreak of war necessitated its being temporarily closed down, the self-same spirit was upheld. From Cranwell have come many successors of Albert Ball, Barker, Rees, Leefe Robinson and a host of others. From the Auxiliary squadrons and from the Volunteer Reserve there have emerged many officers and men, many pilots, observers, gunners, navigators, wireless operators and aircraftmen whose gallantry has stirred the world.

Fifty Crafts to Follow

Old squadrons with a famous history and new squadrons whose stories have yet to be inscribed are striving now and all the time with a superlative will, determination and *esprit de corps*. Every man who joins the R.A.F. today joins it as a member of the Volunteer Reserve and for the duration of hostilities. Apart from Air Crews and the Medical Branch there are five trade groups covering more than fifty different crafts.

These range from blacksmith to pigeon keeper, from winch driver to parachute repairer, from armourer (bombs) to teleprinter operator. There is no job which is without interest, no duty that must be learned and carried out which is valueless to the individual. There is much that a man experiences, learns and executes in the R.A.F. which builds up the character and will help him on his return to civil life when the war ends. Many who are now serving will doubtless wish to continue when "the job is finished."

Meanwhile the R.A.F. fights on, resolute and with growing might. For those who serve in it now there are, as there have been always, hardships and dangers and vicissitudes. Yet in helping in the defence of freedom, in playing his part in the struggle the R.A.F. man finds a deeply satisfying life.

SECTION 1. A

Apprenticeship in the R.A.F.
Starting a Career Second to None

For boys under military age, i.e. from 15½ to 17 years, vacancies for apprentices in the R.A.F. (regular force) are available from time to time. Here are details.

AIRCRAFT Apprenticeship in the Royal Air Force is the first and most important step in a career which has been proved second to none.

Almost every boy is sufficiently a man to realize that truth, and any youngster with a fair record of school work to his credit need not despair of piloting an aircraft or helping by means of his acquired trade to keep that same aircraft in the air as evidence of Britain's supremacy in aviation and craftsmanship.

Boys have no need to be told such things, but parents sometimes require reminding of this splendid alternative to a black coat and bowler hat for the son who is about to start life away from his immediate family circle or school.

Medical attention, good and plentiful food, clothing, general welfare, liberal leave, and adequate pocket money are all given to the boy whose parents have decided that he shall also be given highly skilled and continuous instruction until he becomes equally skilled in one of the many trades which are necessary to the maintenance of the Royal Air Force.

Fitters, Armourers, Wireless Operator Mechanics, and Instrument Makers are among trades which are mentioned as callings for the boy who has received an education good enough to profit by his training after entry at no less an age than 15½ years. There are two methods of entry:

(a) Success in a competitive examination.
(b) Direct Entry.

Those applying under the second heading must produce School Certificate showing "credit" standard in mathematics and an approved science subject.

The Entrance examination must usually be undertaken 12 weeks before the month of actual entry and candidates must not have attained 17 years on the first day of the month of entry. The normal number of entries has had to be reduced since the beginning of the war, but it is anticipated that there will be entries in both February and August each year.

Space does not permit of the inclusion of all conditions and circumstances which are likely to govern a boy's life before and after successful candidature; such are widely embraced in Air Ministry Pamphlet No.15 issued gratis from the Air Ministry. A few extracts of general interest are given below. Changes

A satisfying and progressive career is assured to these lucky youngsters serving an apprenticeship in the Royal Air Force. Should they desire to study any appropriate subject they can do so in the reading room of this well-stocked library. (Inset is the Badge for Apprentices and Boy Entrants.)

Apprenticeship in the R.A.F. SECTION 1. A

Practical instruction of the highest grade is given to apprentices, and this future mechanic is learning details about a radial engine in actual use.

are liable to occur and they are to be considered subject to the detailed regulations issued from time to time by the Air Council.

What the Service Offers

1. The Royal Air Force aircraft apprentice scheme provides educational and technical training for boys aged 15½ to 17 years at entry with a view to their becoming skilled tradesmen in the service. Aircraft apprentices receive pay and free food, housing, clothing and medical attendance.

2. The trades open to aircraft apprentices are:
(i) Fitter, (ii) Fitter (armourer), (iii) Wireless operator mechanic, (iv) Electrician, and (v) Instrument maker.

3. The period of apprenticeship is normally two years, but general and technical education continue throughout service life.

4. An aircraft apprentice on joining is attested for a period covering his apprenticeship and twelve years' regular service from the age of 18, that is, from the date of joining until he reaches the age of 30.

5. On attaining the age of 27 an airman may be selected to be re-engaged from the age of 30 to the age of 42; if re-engaged he becomes eligible for pension.

6. The health and general welfare of aircraft apprentices receive careful and continuous attention. Special attention is paid to games and outdoor exercises and to suitable employment of leisure time.

7. Apprentices are accommodated separately from men.

8. Towards the end of his training the apprentice will be examined and, if successful, will be posted to a unit for duty in his trade. After posting, provided he has attained the age of 17½, he will be granted the classification of leading aircraftman (L.A.C.), aircraftman 1st class (A.C.I) or aircraftman 2nd class (A.C.II) according to his passing-out marks.

9. After his classification an airman is eligible for promotion to non-commissioned rank when a vacancy occurs. An ex-apprentice airman who volunteered before passing out to be trained as an airman pilot may later be selected for that training.

10. Apprentices may be granted leave for approximately six weeks in the year, and during leave will receive pay and an allowance in lieu of rations. For the two main leave periods free return railway tickets are supplied, and for shorter leave periods half-price tickets.

Entry Abroad

In a country where there is an R.A.F. Command sons of British residents, including Service personnel, may apply

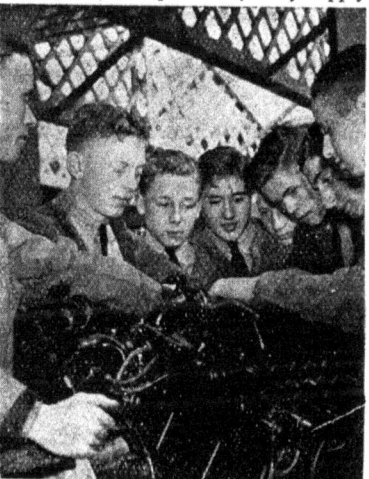

Keen as can be, these apprentices are having explained to them the intricacies of a liquid-cooled engine.

to the Air or other Officer Commanding for a nomination to an apprenticeship.

Experts at the Air Ministry are very ready both to advise and direct parents, guardians and school teachers, who are prompted to discover a career for boys whose spirit and character render them deserving of every help to approach the future in the right way, time and place.

SECTION 1. B

Entry into the R.A.F. Volunteer Reserve
How to Become an Airman

Apart from apprenticeship and a limited number of special commissions, the only means of entry into the R.A.F. is by enlistment in the Volunteer Reserve. The Trades open, with rates of pay, are listed in the following pages.

A RECRUIT may be accepted for enlistment in the Royal Air Force Volunteer Reserve provided :

(a) he is within the age limits.
(b) he is suitable for an existing vacancy in a trade appropriate to his civil employment.
(c) he is not a naval or army reservist.
(d) if in a reserved occupation his application is approved by the Ministry of Labour.
(e) his medical grade is appropriate to the trade.

Tradesmen able to pass a trade test for the trade for which they are accepted are normally entered in the appropriate trade group in the classification of aircraftman, 2nd class. After necessary training they are reclassified according to standard attained.

In certain trades semi-skilled men with some technical experience or experience in a corresponding civilian trade, or unskilled men with the necessary aptitude, are entered for trade training. They are entered as aircraftmen 2nd class, Group V. On successfully completing training they receive pay appropriate to the group and classification for which they qualify.

The table below shows trade and pay groups of the R.A.F. These are subject to amendment from time to time, and the latest information, including trade vacancies, can be obtained at any R.A.F. Recruiting Office or at The Information Bureau, Adastral House, Kingsway, W.C.2.

TRADES AND PAY GROUPS OF THE R.A.F.

Group I
Airfield controller
Architectural draughtsman
Blacksmith and welder
Carpenter
Carpenter (boat builder)
Clerk of works
Civil engineering assistant
Compass adjuster
Coppersmith and sheet metal worker
Draughtsman
Draughtsman (mechanical)
Electrician, grade I
Fitter, grade I
Fitter, grade II (airframe)
Fitter, grade II (engine)
Fitter (armourer)
Fitter (general)
Fitter (marine)
Fitter (M.T.)
Fitter (stationary engine)
Instrument maker
Instrument repairer, grade I
Link trainer instructor
Machine tool setter and operator
Metal worker
Navigation instructor
R.D.F. mechanic
Wireless and elec. mechanic
Wireless mechanic
Wireless operator mechanic

Group II
Acetylene welder
Aerial erector
Armoured car crew
Armourer
Armourer (bomb disposal)
Balloon operator
Blacksmith
Bricklayer
Carpenter
Coppersmith
Driller
Electrician, grade II
Electrician (works)
Flight mechanic (airframe)
Flight mechanic (engine)
Foreman of trades
Grinder
Instrument repairer, grade II
Interpreter (technical)
Mechanic (stationary engine)
Meteorologist
Miller
M.T. mechanic
Pattern maker (architectural)
Photographer
Plant operator
Plumber
Quarryman
*R.D.F. operator
Safety equipment worker
Sheet metal worker
Steel erector
Turner
Wireless operator
  On completing training radio operators are placed in Group IV, and after 6 months satisfactory service in Group II.

Group III
Concreter
Cook and butcher
Drainlayer
Fabric worker
Hydrogen worker
Motor boat crew
Shoemaker
Tailor

Group IV
Clerk (accounting)
Clerk (equipment accounting)
Clerk (pay accounting)
Clerk (general duties)
Clerk (provisioning)
Clerk (signals)
Clerk (special duties)
Equipment assistant
Radio telephony operator
Radio telephony operator (Balloons)
Teleprinter operator

Group V
Aircrafthand
Armament assistant
Barber
Batman
C.W. Fighter
Driver (M.T.)
Ground observer
Groundsman
Gunner
Maintenance assistant
Motor cyclist
Musician
Packer
Physical training instructor
Pigeon keeper
R.A.F. Police
Safety equipment assistant
Station police
Telephonist
Works hand

Group M
Chiropodist
Dispenser
Laboratory assistant
Masseur
Medical orderly u/training
Mental nursing orderly
Nursing orderly
Operating-room assistant
Optician orderly
Radiographer
Sanitary assistant
Special treatment orderly
Trained nurse
Dental clerk orderly
Dental mechanic
Dental orderly u/training

DAILY RATES OF PAY FOR TRADESMEN AND AIR CREW

Rank	Group I	Group II	Group III	Group IV	Group V	Group M	Airman Pilot	Navigator other than Navigator (radio)	Air Bomber	Navigator (radio)	Wireless operator (A.G.)	Wireless op'tor mechanic (A.G.)	Air gunner	Fligh engineer
	s. d.	s. d.	s. d.	s. d.	s. d.	s. d.	s. d.	s. d.	s. d.	s. d.	s. d.	s. d.	s. d.	s. d.
Aircraftmen														
Aircraftman, 2nd class	4 9	4 6	4 0	4 3	3 0	3 0	—	—	—	—	—	—	—	—
Aircraftman, 2nd class (over one year)	—	—	—	—	3 9	4 0	—	—	—	—	—	—	—	—
Aircraftman, 2nd class (over two years)	—	—	—	—	4 0	4 3	—	—	—	—	—	—	—	—
Aircraftman, 1st class	5 6	5 3	4 9	5 0	4 6	4 9	—	—	—	—	—	—	—	—
Leading aircraftman	6 6	6 0	5 3	5 6	5 0	5 3	—	—	—	—	—	—	—	—
Leading aircraftman (over three years)	7 0	6 6	5 6	6 0	—	5 9	—	—	—	—	—	—	—	—
Non-Commissioned Officers														
Corporal	8 6	7 6	6 0	6 6	5 6	6 3	—	*Note. The conditions and rates of pay for Air Crew given below are those in operation on Jan. 1, 1943. They were then under review.*						—
Corporal (over three years)	—	—	—	—	—	7 0	—							—
Corporal (over four years)	9 0	8 0	6 6	7 0	6 0	—	—							—
Sergeant on probation	—	—	—	—	—	—	—	—	—	8 5	—	—	—	—
Sergeant	10 6	9 6	7 6	8 0	7 0	8 0	13 6	13 6	13 6	13 6	10 0*/9 0	12 0	8 0/8 9†	12 0
Sergeant (over three years)	—	—	—	—	—	9 0	—	—	—	—	—	—	—	—
Sergeant (over four years)	11 0	10 0	8 0	8 6	7 6	—	14 6	14 6	14 6	14 6	—	—	—	—
Flight sergeant	12 6	11 0	9 0	9 6	8 9	10 6	16 0	16 0	16 0	16 0	10 6*/10 0	13 0	9 0/10 0†	13 0
Flight sergeant (over three years)	—	—	—	—	—	11 6	—	—	—	—	—	—	—	—
Flight sergeant (over four years)	13 0	11 6	9 6	10 0	9 0	—	16 6	16 6	16 6	16 6	—	—	—	—
Warrant Officers														
Warrant officer	15 0	13 6	12 6	12 6	12 6	14 6	17 6	17 6	17 6	17 6	—	—	—	—
Warrant officer (over five years)	17 6	16 0	14 6	15 0	14 6	—	—	—	—	—	—	—	—	—

† Applicable only to air gunners in Group I and Group II.
* Rates shown for air gunners Grade I and II.
War pay at the rate of 1s. 0d. a day is included in the rates of pay set out above. A further sum of 6d. a day is set aside as a post war credit.

Additional Pay.—Non-substantive pay at daily rates varying from 3d. to 1s. is issuable as follows .
    (a) Qualification pay granted for definite qualifications.
    (b) Duty pay for performance of specific duties.
Full details in R.A.F. Form 1306.

Flying Instructional Pay.—Airmen under actual flying instruction are eligible for an allowance at the following daily rates: Navigators (all categories) and air bomber, Link trainer instructors, pilots, 2s.; flight engineers, wireless operator mechanics (air gunner), wireless operators (air gunners) and air gunners 1s. per day.

Bonus for Drivers.—Drivers (M.T.) not above the rank of flight sergeants are eligible, under certain conditions, for bonus at the rate of 3d. a day.

Good Conduct Badges and Pay.—Badges are awarded for very good conduct after 3, 8 and 13 years' qualifying service rendered after attaining the age of 18 years. Good conduct pay of 3d. a day is awarded for each badge.

Table of Trades for Aircrafthands in Training
With Conditions of Entry and Pay Groups

Note.—The Groups shown in the following Table are those in which men will be placed on satisfactorily completing their course. Medical grades are indicated. These notes do not include every trade in the R.A.F., but only those in which vacancies occur.

AIRCRAFTHAND (Group V).
Age limits 18-38. Medical grades I, II (a) Feet, II.
No special qualifications are required.

ARMOURER (Group II).
Age limits 18-42. Medical grades I, II (a) Feet, II. Colour vision must be Normal or Safe.
Good education required. Preference is given to men with some mechanical knowledge. Men enlisted in this trade will be required to maintain bombing and gunnery equipment on aircraft and must be of good intelligence.

BARBER (Group V).
Age limits 18-50. Medical grade II.
Recruits should have had at least one year's experience in their trade.

BATMAN (Group V).
Age limits 18-50. Medical grade II.
Candidates should have had some experience as Waiters, Valets, Batmen, etc.

BLACKSMITH
ACETYLENE WELDER
COPPERSMITH } (Group II).
SHEET METAL WORKER
Age limits 18-50. Medical grades I, II (a) Feet, II.
Skilled men or men suitable for training from such trades as : Plumbers' Mates, Blacksmiths' Mates, Blacksmiths' Strikers, Forge Hands, or any Metal Worker except heavy industries and turners.

CLERK PAY ACCOUNTING
CLERK EQUIP. ACCOUNTING } (Group IV).
Age limits 18-50. Medical grade II.
Applicants for this trade must be fully qualified. An extensive knowledge of accountancy and book-keeping is necessary, together with a good education and ability to spell and write clearly. Typing is an asset but not essential.

CLERK G.D. (Group IV).
Age limits 18-50. Medical grade II.
Must have sound clerical experience. Knowledge of typing and shorthand is an advantage.

CLERK S.D. (Group IV).
Age limits 18-50. Medical grades I or II (a) Feet only ; II. Must not be " defective unsafe colour vision."
Typewriting experience is not essential, although men with shorthand-typing experience are preferred. Applicants must be of good education, intelligent, steady, and not inclined to get flustered under pressure.

*COOK AND BUTCHER (Group III).
Age limits 18-50. Medical Grades I, II (a) Feet, II.
Applicants should be skilled Cooks or Chefs in civil life, but semi-skilled cooks capable of being trained may be accepted.

DENTAL MECHANIC (Group M).
Age limits 18-50. Medical Grades I, II (a) Feet, II.
Applicants for this trade must be fully skilled and experienced Dental Mechanics in civil life.

*ELECTRICIAN (Groups I and II).
Age limits 18-50. Medical grades I, II (a) Feet, II.
Applicants must be skilled with at least 3 or 4 years' experience in the trade. They must be skilled wiremen and understand the care of accumulators and preferably have some theoretical knowledge.
Semi-skilled men of bright and intelligent type, with a certain amount of previous experience, may be entered for training as electrician (Group II). The Housewireman or Electrician's Mate is the type required.

EQUIPMENT ASSISTANT (Group IV).
Age limits 18-42. Medical grade II.
Applicants for this trade should be men whose occupation in civil life is that of Storekeeper, Shopkeeper, Stores Clerk, Warehouseman. A bright and intelligent type is required.

FITTER, grade I ; FITTER,
grade II (Airframe) ; FITTER,
grade II (Engine) ; FITTER } (Group I).
(Armourer) ; FITTER (Marine) ;
FITTER M.T.
Age limits 18-50. Medical grades I, II (a) Feet, II.
These trades are the most highly skilled in the R.A.F. trade groups, and men will be employed in maintaining aero engines, armament and torpedo gear, etc. They should have had practical fitting experience, be able to use a micrometer, read a vernier, and file to fine limits.

FLIGHT MECHANIC (E) or (A) (Group II).
Age limits 18-42. Medical grades I, II (a) Feet, II.
Applicants should be men of some mechanical experience but who do not quite come up to the standard of skilled fitters. The garage mechanic is the type required, but anyone capable of dismantling and re-assembling the internal combustion engine is suitable. Bright and intelligent young men suitable for training with an interest in this trade may be accepted.

GRINDER (Group V).
Age limits 18-50. Medical Grades I, II (a) Feet, II.
Universal grinding ; able to set up own machine, use micrometer and work to English and Metric measurements.

*INSTRUMENT REPAIRER (Groups I and II).
Age limits 18-50. Medical grades I, II (a) Feet, II.
Men who are accustomed to very fine work are required for this trade. Watchmakers and jewellers are the most suitable since the work

* *Men for training in trades so marked may be accepted up to 43rd birthday.*

Table of Trades — SECTION 1. B

entailed will embody the maintenance of Aircraft Instruments, which is' work of a very fine nature. Men without previous experience in the trade but capable of assimilating the necessary instruction, and with a mechanical bent and liking for fine work, may be entered for training as Instrument Repairer, Group II.

LINK TRAINER INSTRUCTOR (Group I).
Age limits 32-45. Medical grades I, II (a) Feet, II.
Must be of good educational standard and likely to prove good instructors.

METEOROLOGIST (Group II).
Age limits 18-50. Medical grade II.
This trade calls for Meteorological qualifications in civil life or thorough knowledge of maths. and physics.

MILLER (Group II).
Age limits 18-50. Medical grades I, II (a) Feet, II.
Candidates must be able to set up and operate a milling machine.

MOTOR-BOAT CREW (Group III).
Age limits 18-42. Medical grades I or II (a) Feet only. Colour vision must be Normal or Safe.
Men with seafaring experience, amateur yachtsmen and men who express keenness and have had experience with motor-boats may be accepted. They must be able to swim.

M.T. MECHANIC (Group II).
Age limits 18-50. Medical grades I, II (a) Feet, II.
Men for training may be accepted up to 46th birthday.
Recruits must have had some mechanical experience. The garage mechanic is the type required.

MOTOR CYCLIST (Group V).
Age limits 18-38. Medical grades I, II (a) Feet, II.
Recruits for this trade must be able to ride a motor-cycle and have a current driving licence for at least six months. Required to do running repairs as well as drive a motor-cycle.

***PHOTOGRAPHER (Group II).**
Age limits 18-50. Medical grades I, II (a) Feet, II.
Applicants for this trade must have a good knowledge of commercial photography and be of an intelligent type.

PHYSICAL TRAINING INSTRUCTOR (Group V).
Age limits 25-40. Medical grades I.
Applicants should, if possible, have done a Physical Training course at one of the recognized schools, but any man who has been keen on gymnastics or Physical Fitness in a professional or private capacity might be suitable. Candidates should have personality, intelligence and possess ability to take charge of a class.

R.D.F. MECHANIC (Group I).
Age limits 18-50. Medical grades I, II (a) Feet, II.
Highly skilled radio men are necessary for this trade. They should be Radio Engineers who are capable of servicing modern radio superhet sets. Men who have held an amateur transmitting licence may be accepted. Candidates of School Certificate standard, or who have attended evening classes in mathematics or physics, may be accepted for training in this trade, provided they have not attained their 35th birthday. Men over this age who are exceptionally suitable can be accepted.

R.A.F. POLICE AND STATION POLICE (Group V).
Age limits 21-45. Medical grades I, II (a) Feet.
Men who are mentally and physically alert must be selected for these trades. A good standard of physique is required and applicants must be of 5 ft. 8 ins. minimum height.

SHOEMAKER AND TAILOR (Group III).
Age limits 18-50. Medical grade II.
These men must all have had at least 1 year's experience in their trades in civil life.

SPECIAL TREATMENT ORDERLY (Group M).
Age limits 18-50. Medical grades I, II (a) Feet, II.
Should have experience in nursing and miscellaneous duties in special hospitals.

TORPEDOMAN (Group V).
Age limits 18-42. Medical grades I, II (a) Feet.
Recruits enlisted for training in this trade should be of good elementary educational standard, and must be capable of assimilating technical instruction. Technical knowledge and experience are not essential, but practice in the handling of tools would be an advantage.

TURNER (Group II).
Age limits 18-50. Medical grades I, II (a) Feet, II.
Men for this trade should have civil experience, and be capable of using all types of centre lathe.

WIRELESS MECHANIC (Group I).
Age limits 18-50. Medical grades I, II (a) Feet, II. Colour vision need not be normal or "safe."
Applicants must have a good practical and theoretical knowledge of radio, but will not be required to know or at a later date to learn Morse. Candidates of School Certificate standard or men who have attended evening classes in mathematics or physics, may be accepted for training provided they have not attained their 35th birthday, but men of exceptional suitability may be accepted over this age.

WIRELESS OPERATOR (Group II).
Age limits 18-25 for men with no previous knowledge of the trade; 18-32 for suitable applicants with some knowledge of the trade; 18-50 for fully skilled wireless operators; 17½ for candidates capable of transmitting Morse at a speed of 20 words per minute, or in possession of P.M.G. Certificate. Medical grades I, II (a) Feet, II.
No previous knowledge of wireless is necessary, but candidates must possess keenness for training in this trade. They should have sufficient intelligence to be able satisfactorily to complete their course of training, but need not necessarily have had a Secondary School standard of education. Candidates must be able to spell and read clearly ; a knowledge of Morse is an asset, but is not essential.

* Men for training in trades so marked may be accepted up to 43rd birthday.

CONVERSION FACTORS

Example—
Column 1 × Multiplier = Column 2   Inches × 25·4 = millimetres.
Column 2 × Reciprocal = Column 1.   Millimetres × ·039 37 = inches.

Column 1	Column 2	Multiplier	Reciprocal
Acres	Hectares	0·405	2·47
Centimetre	Inch	0·3937	2·5399
Inches	Mms.	25·4	·039 37
,,	Metres	0·0254	39·37
Feet	,,	·304 8	3·280 8
Yards	,,	·914 4	1·093 6
Miles	Kms.	1·609 3	·621 37
Miles per hour	Knots (6087 ft.)	·867 4	1·152
Square ins.	Square mms.	645·16	·001 55
,, ins.	,, cms.	6·451 6	·155
,, ft.	,, metres	·092 9	10·764
Cubic ins.	Cubic cms.	16·387	·061
,, ins.	Litres	0·0164	61·0
,, ft.	Cubic metres	·028 32	35·314 8
,, metres	,, yards	1·308	0·7646
Grains	Grammes	0·0648	15·432
Grammes	Ounces	0·03527	28·35
Lb.	Kgs.	·453 59	2·204 62
Cwt. (112 lb.)	,,	50·802	·019 68
,,	Quintals	0·508	1·97
Tons	Tonnes (metric)	1·016	·984 2
Kilogrammes	Ounces	35·27	0·02835
Lb. per yard	Kg. per km.	496·06	·002 02
Lb. per sq. in.	Kg. per sq. cm.	·070 31	14·223
,, ,, ,,	Atmospheres	·068 03	14·706
,, ,, ,,	Miles per hour	·681 82	1·466 7
Ft. per second	Metres per sec.	·3048	3·280 8
,, ,, ,,	Km. per hour	1·097 28	·911 33
Ft. per minute	Miles per hour	·011 363 6	88·0
,, ,, ,,	Metres per sec.	·005 08	196·85
,, ,, ,,	Km. per hour	·018 288	54·68
Metres per min.	Feet per sec.	0·0547	——
Miles per hour	Metres per sec.	·447 04	2·236 9
,, ,, ,,	Km. per hour	1·609 34	·621 37
Kms. per hour	Metres per sec.	·227 78	3·6
Square kilom.	Square mile	0·3862	2·589
Square metres	,, yards	1·197	0·8361
Pints	Litres	·568	1·76
Gallons	,,	4·546	·22
Gallons (water)	Cubic feet	0·161	——
,, (Imperial)	Gallons, U.S.	1·205	0·830
H.P. (British)	*H.P. (metric)	1·013 85	·986 3
,, ,,	Ft.-lb. per sec.	550·0	·001 818 2
,, ,,	Kg.-m. per sec.	76·04	·013 15
Force de Cheval	Horse-power	0·986	1·014
Centigrade	Fahrenheit	C × 9/5 + 32	(F−32) × 5/9
Joules	Gramme calories	·238 8	4·186
,,	B.Th.U.	·000 948	1055·36
Joules per sec.	Horse-power	·001 340 3	746·08
Watts	,,	·001 340 3	746·08
,,	B.Th.U. per sec.	·000 948	1055·36
Watt-hours.	Ft.-lb.	2654·0	·000 376 8
kW. (kilowatt)	Horse-power (Br.)	1·340 3	·746 08

*The metric H.P. = 75 kg. metres per sec.

Air Crew Duties

How Candidates are Selected for Flying and Air Fighting

FLYING personnel are provided by enlistment in the R.A.F. Volunteer Reserve. Vacancies in the General Duties (commissioned) branch (see page 18) are filled by promotion from the ranks.

Candidates for air crew duties must be men who desire to fly and fight in the air, with a reasonable standard of intelligence and good standard of alertness and character. They must be up to the necessary standard of physical fitness. No prescribed educational standards are laid down except for elementary mathematics.

Air crew applicants will undergo a preliminary medical examination at the Recruiting Centre at which they applied for enlistment. They will then proceed for interview by the Aviation Candidates Selection Board, which will decide whether the applicants are suitable for air crew training and the category in which they should be trained. Applicants may, however, indicate their order of preference for training as Pilot, Observer, Observer (radio) and Wireless Operator (air gunner). If passed by the Aviation Candidates Selection Board, candidates will have a further medical examination to determine fitness for flying training.

The ages for enlistment are: Pilot must be 17¼ and not yet 31, Observer and Wireless Operator (air gunner) must be 17¼ and not yet 33. Observer (radio) may in exceptional cases be accepted up to 41st birthday and need not have so high a visual standard as the other categories of air crew.

Men enlisted for air crew will not be called up for flying training until they attain the age of 18¼, and will not be called up for ground duties until they attain the age of 18.

Air Crew Training, Remustering and Promotion

Pilots and Air Observers undergo ground training at an Initial Training Wing, being mustered as Aircrafthands, Group V, on completion, and re-classified as Leading Aircraftmen, Group II, with flying instructional pay during actual flying training at Flying Training School or at Air Observer Navigation School

Wireless Operators (air gunners) are mustered as Aircrafthands, Group V, until their training is complete as Wireless Operators, and then remustered to Wireless Operator, Group II, during actual flying training at Bombing and Gunnery

Inside this aeroplane is held a practical lesson in air crew duties, and the pupils are clad as in actual flight.

School, and re-classified as Leading Aircraftmen with flying instructional pay.

On successful completion of training course Airmen are remustered to the aircrew category for which they have qualified and promoted Sergeant. Promotion of air crew, to Warrant Officer, N. or Flight Sergeant, is by selection (six months' service in an air crew category). For further notes on remustering see p. 36.

Daily rates of pay for air crew Non-commissioned or Warrant Officers and flying instructional pay are given in p. 13. For officers' pay see p. 18.

AIR CREW : TRAINING, REMUSTERING and PROMOTION

Candidates Selected as	Ground Training At	Classification and Group	Pay*	Flying Training At	Classification and Group	Pay†
Pilot	I.T.W.	AC2 V	2/6	F.T.S.	LAC II	7/6
Air Observer	I.T.W.	AC2 V	2/6	A.O.N.S.	LAC II	7/6
Wireless Operator (Air Gunner)	Wireless School	AC2 V	2/6	B. & G.S.	LAC II (Wireless)	6/6

Notes. *Includes 6d. a day war pay. †Includes 6d. war pay and flying instructional pay.

Commissioned Branches of the R.A.F. Volunteer Reserve

Notes of qualifications for commissions in the R.A.F.V.R. Direct entry from civil life with very few exceptions (mainly technical and professional) is discontinued.

THE following are brief details of the qualifications required of candidates for commissions in the Volunteer Reserve subject to Air Council regulations. Direct entry from civil life to commissioned rank in the R.A.F.V.R. has been discontinued except for entry to the Technical Branch, the Medical, Dental and Chaplain Branches and to the appointments in the Administrative and Special Duties Branch for Marine Craft, Physical Training and Catering duties.

The branches of the R.A.F.V.R. are:

General Duties (Flying)	Accountant
Technical Engineering, Electrical Engineering, Armament, Signals.	Medical

Administrative and Special
  Duties
  Administrative, Intelligence, Marine Craft, Photographic. Physical Training, Operations Room, Defence, Catering, Mechanical Transport.
	Dental

	Chaplain
	Equipment

There are, of course, identical branches to the above list already in existence from the pre-war Regular R.A.F., and it is only certain personnel already serving on regular engagements, i.e. Warrant Officers and Airmen, who may be, in due course, granted commissions in the regular R.A.F.

The active list, as published, covers all forms of entry to commissioned service.

For G. D. (Flying) see page 17.

TECHNICAL BRANCH

Divided into three sections—Engineer, Armament and Signals. Minimum qualifications are:

Engineer
Engineering degrees, or
Engineering certificates, or members of engineering institutes of two years' practical experience, or
Practical engineers who have served an apprenticeship followed by a number of years' experience in erecting or overhauling internal combustion engines or aeroplane structures, and with knowledge of the properties of engineering materials.

Electrical Engineer
Electrical engineering degrees, or
Electrical engineering certificate, or membership of appropriate engineering institution, with two years' practical experience, or
Practical electrical engineers (apprenticed) with a number of years' experience in erecting, maintaining or overhauling electrical equipment and knowledge of the properties of engineering materials.

Armament
University degree which includes as one subject engineering, physics, or chemistry, or an equivalent diploma or certificate, or
Member of an engineering, physics, or chemistry institution, with at least two years' practical experience, particularly experience in armament manufacture, or
Practical engineers, physicists or chemists (apprenticed), with a number of years' practical experience, and knowledge of materials used in armaments.

Signals
Engineering or science degrees, or
Technical college or approved institute diplomas and two years' experience in telecommunications engineering (preferably radio side).
From time to time posts are available for those possessing a sound theoretical knowledge of elementary electricity and magnetism, of the principles of wireless, telegraphic and telephonic communications, transmitter circuits and wireless receiving apparatus, etc., etc. Practical experience an asset.

ADMINISTRATIVE AND SPECIAL DUTIES BRANCH

Administrative duties
Administrative and managerial experience in civil life, preferably with some knowledge of service procedure. Previous commissioned service in the forces is an advantage.

Intelligence duties
Ability to collect and collate information and to appreciate its military values.
The personality and ability required to interrogate officers and others. (Previous commissioned service, particularly as pilot or observer, also an advantage.) A good knowledge, including fluent speech, of one or more foreign languages. Posts also exist for interpreting photographs; good powers of observation required and ability to study fine detail.

Minimum Daily Rates of Pay

Rank on Entry	Acting Pilot Officer	Pilot Officer	Flying Officer	Flight Lieutenant	Squadron Leader
	s. d.	s. d.	£ s. d.	£ s. d.	£ s. d.
Branch and age limits					
Gen. Duties (Flying)	11 10	14 6	0 18 2	1 1 9	1 10 10
Technical (19-60 yrs.)	11 10	14 6	0 18 2	1 1 9	1 10 10
Admin. and Special Duties (32-50)	10 0	11 10	0 13 6	0 19 0	1 9 0
Equipment (32-55)	10 0	11 10	0 13 6	0 19 0	1 9 0
Accountant (32-55)	11 0	13 6	0 17 2	1 0 0	1 9 0
Medical (up to 50)	—	—	1 1 8	1 3 6	1 15 4
Dental (up to 50)	—	—	0 18 2	1 1 8	1 11 8
Legal (32-50)	—	—	—	1 3 6	1 15 6

Chaplains. On entry, 15s. 4d.; after 3 years, 18s. 2d.
Ranks on entry are indicated by lowest rank with rate of pay stated.

Commissioned Branches

Marine craft duties
First class coxswain's or naval watchkeeping certificate; Master's, First Mate's, or Second Mate's certificate (foreign going or home trade); or Yacht Master's certificate (age limits 23 to 38 years). Practical marine craft experience, including good knowledge of navigation, charts and seamanship may also be accepted subject to satisfactory completion of training course. Candidates having good qualifications and otherwise suitable, who are above the age limits, will not be ruled out.

Physical training duties
Service or civilian experience in supervising and organizing physical training games and recreational facilities, and the personality and ability to encourage all forms of outdoor and indoor activity for physical development and fitness. A diploma of a recognized physical education college or its equivalent is an advantage. (The ability solely to organize and conduct ordinary service drill is not sufficient.)

Operations Room
Intelligence and alertness of a high standard. Ability to make quick decisions; clear speech. Previous flying experience an advantage.

Defence
Aptitude for leadership. Sound knowledge of defence weapons, particularly light automatics. Ability to impart knowledge. Previous military training an advantage.

Catering
Extensive experience of catering for large numbers, probably commencing with kitchen apprenticeship. Knowledge required of kitchen equipment, lay-outs, storage and handling of foodstuffs and its preparation for large numbers, and staff supervision.

Mechanical Transport
Extensive practical experience of maintenance, overhaul, and repair of motor vehicles, starting with apprenticeship. Thorough understanding of principles of automobile engineering. Operating experience and map-reading an advantage.

EQUIPMENT BRANCH. Business or industrial experience preferably in administrative or managerial capacity in one or more firms of standing. Knowledge of stores records and handling of stores also an advantage.

ACCOUNTANT BRANCH. Practical accounting or financial experience; and experience in an executive post, or educational and personal qualities which would fit candidates to assume responsibility after training.

MEDICAL BRANCH. Fully qualified to practise medicine and surgery and registered under the Medical Act in force in the U.K.

DENTAL BRANCH. Fully qualified to practise dental surgery and must possess a degree or licence in dental surgery of a British University or recognized licensing body, and be registered under Dentist or Medical Acts in force in the United Kingdom.

Allowances. Officers are provided with free accommodation and rations, or cash allowances in lieu. Provision is made for other allowances and these are given in more detail in A.M. Pamphlet 101 and A.M. Pamphlet 106.

Applications. Applications for commissions in the Technical, Chaplain and in the Administrative and Special Duties Branches for those duties mentioned in the first paragraph of this section should be submitted on Form 1020 to the Under Secretary of State, Air Ministry, S.7 e., Department Q.J., Kingsway, London, W.C.2. Candidates for direct entry commissions are now required to enter by initial enlistment in the ranks and undergo a cadet training course at an O.C.T.U., on successful completion of which they are appointed to commissioned rank.

Candidates for commissions in the other Branches should apply in the first instance to the following:—

Medical Branch. The Central Emergency Committee, British Medical Association, Tavistock Square, London, W.C.2.

Dental Branch. The Central Emergency Committee, British Dental Association, 13, Hill Street, Berkeley Square, London. W.1.

THE CHAPLAINS' BRANCH (R.A.F., V.R.)

In the words of King's Regulations "The reverent observance of religion will be regarded as of the highest importance," and the Air Council have seen to it that officers, Airmen and Airwomen of the R.A.F. may have access to a chaplain and be given full opportunity to go to church.

All the better known denominations have their own commissioned chaplains. Smaller Stations employ the services of the local clergymen and ministers.

The larger Stations have their own churches on the camp itself. Here the chaplain takes parade services in addition to voluntary services at other times.

Almost invariably the chaplain has an office where officers and airmen may come to see him to receive his guidance and counsel, not only religious and moral, but also personal and domestic. He visits the sick quarters regularly: he "looks up" men commended to his care by their local civilian clergymen: he writes letters to anxious parents, and is, in fact, a "guide, philosopher and friend."

A chaplain has a number of other channels of contact with the airmen. He is usually to be found, for instance, on the aerodrome when a Squadron takes off on a flight over enemy territory, and again is there to welcome them on their return. Many chaplains are in charge of all the station games and sports. Others, again, run the entertainments on the camp. In fact, a chaplain is usually the Officer i/c "Comforts."

It is fully recognized by the Air Council that the work of the chaplains on their different camps is an indispensable side of the life of the R.A.F.

SECTION 1. E

Life and Training of the Recruit
How New Pilots and Air Crews are Made

This is the story of the candidate chosen by a Selection Board from the day he enters an Initial Training Wing to that happy time when, as Pilot or Air Crew, he puts up his flying badge, a trained man. See also Section 2, A (pages 75–80).

NOT all can emulate the wonderful fellows who, as members of air crews, have performed deeds which have thrilled the world and added fresh glory to Britain's history. But it is safe to say that in the hearts of the majority of the young men who come forward to join the R.A.F. there is the urge, the longing, to serve their country in the air. The qualifications required for entry into the R.A.F. as a member of an aircraft crew are not exceptional ; a young man should have a good general education, and if he has a " mechanical background," so much the better. He should have a fair working knowledge of mathematics, including the use of simple formulae, of the metric system, averages, vulgar and decimal fractions, and so forth.

Such knowledge is important, for it enables the candidate to absorb the necessary technical training, which is very thorough indeed. Physical fitness, of course, is essential, but apart from this a candidate must be bright, alert, and more than keen to learn.

The Fighting Temperament

Many years of experience enable officers serving on the Selection Boards who interview Air Crew candidates to gauge accurately the suitability of a man appearing before them. Flying is not purely a matter of fitness and intelligence. That strange thing temperament plays a governing part in the making of a fighting airman. And the fighting airman is not a " type." The great pilots of the last war differed widely in temperament, manners, physical build, likes and dislikes. The first airman to be decorated with the Victoria Cross was Second-Lieutenant W. B. Rhodes Moorhouse. Slight in build, and with a thin, light voice, his appearance and manner gave little inkling of the great spirit which lay within him. In no way, save in his indomitable courage and his skill, did he resemble the big and boisterous Canadian, Major W. G. Barker, the last to win the V.C. with the R.A.F. in the war of 1914-1918. In the present conflict the same variety of types is to be found amongst those British airmen who have won the V.C. and other decorations for gallantry.

As has been said, the training of air crews is extremely thorough. Such thoroughness breeds confidence, and it is absolute confidence—the confidence a pilot has in himself, his comrades, and his aircraft—that gives this nation superiority in the air.

First Steps in the Service

The airman receives his first introduction to service life at the Aircrew Receiving Centre. Here he is fitted out with uniform and given his first lectures on service procedure, barrack room equipment, kit inspection, squad drill, inoculation, vaccination, etc. At this centre he is tested for his educational standard in mathematics and general knowledge. He also receives certain psychological tests to determine his aptitude for pilot, observer, air gunner, etc.

Subject to his reaching the necessary standard at this centre he then proceeds to the more serious side of training via the Initial Training Wing. The training at these I.T.W.s, as they are called in service language, deals exclusively with ground subjects, so important to the pilot and observer.

First in importance in the making of a fighting airman come physical fitness, discipline, esprit de corps, and the rousing of the aggressive spirit which is lying dormant. All these things are dealt with at the I.T.W.

These I.T.W.s are the departments into which flows the raw material, the young men who, coming straight from civil life, feel for the first time the growing meaning of comradeship and pride in the service. Day after day these recruits drill, march, and attend lectures. It is a strenuous time, in which muscles, nerve and brain are brought up to concert pitch. The syllabus of training at these units, intensive though it is, is carefully balanced, so that while the embryo airman retains his air enthusiasm and his individuality, he acquires a sense of discipline and develops the team spirit. Individuality is a necessary quality for making war in the air, but there must be discipline and the "crew spirit."

Goal of the Cadet

No doubt, to the fellows who have entered the I.T.W.s, the time when they will fly seems distant, for while they learn the finer points of service conduct, of drill, saluting, R.A.F. administration, Morse, aircraft recognition; while they attend lectures on anti-gas measures, mathematics, gunnery and air navigation, they are kept away from aerodromes and aeroplanes.

This is deliberately arranged, for experience has shown that in the initial stages it is a mistake to bring the recruit into contact with flying. The keenness to fly overshadows everything else, and the basic and less enthralling duties are affected in consequence. And so the cadet works on with each day, each drill, each lecture and each parade bringing him nearer his goal—to fly and then to fight.

In the instruction and training at the I.T.W.s moving pictures play a

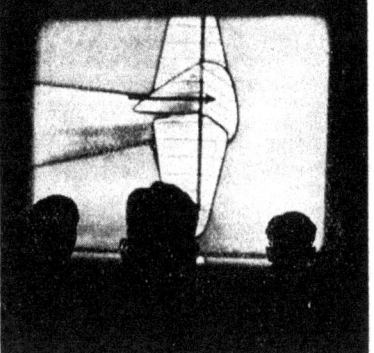

Here, in the cinema of an Elementary Flying Training School, R.A.F. pupils are being shown the effect of airflow on tail surfaces.

notable part. These films are used to demonstrate air gunnery, the principles of flight, and blind flying.

Elementary Flying Training School

The day comes when the cadet passes out of the I.T.W. and is posted to an Elementary Flying Training School (E.F.T.S.). It is a great moment which none forget easily.

With others who have been his comrades from the day when he packed away his mufti and donned his uniform he reports to the new station. The sky above is alive with Tiger Moths or Miles Magisters. The place echoes to the sound of aero engines, of motor transport and other busy noises. His pulse quickens as he takes in the scene. Then he is given his flying kit, his parachute, and he meets his instructors. And within a few hours he is in the air, taking his first real lesson in the art of flying. In classrooms his studies continue. He must increase his knowledge of navigation, he must grasp the points required in working out courses, and must learn about air photography, armament and bombs.

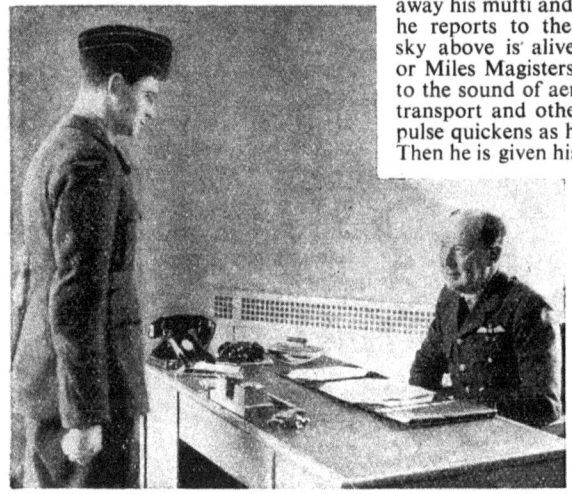

The Chief Flying Instructor has a word with a new arrival at the Elementary Flying Training School, where pupils come after a period at an Initial Training Wing.

There is an enormous amount to be learned in the classroom, but it is done with the underlying knowledge that soon he will be up in the air again, applying what he has learned on the ground. For instance, the first cross country, successfully completed, is a terrific thrill and justifies all those hours at the desk.

Apart from the actual desk work which navigation, etc., involve, there are many interesting lectures and practical exercises. "Rules of the Air" are learned at the E.F.T.S. These are very similar to "Rules of the Road," inasmuch as they comprise a "Highway Code" or "Safety First" of the air. For instance, not all aerodromes have the same circuit. Some are clockwise, whereas others are anti-clockwise. A pilot approaching a strange aerodrome must fly over the signals area and read the code sign before he knows which way to circle prior to landing. This is important, because if there are several aeroplanes waiting to land they must fly around in a circle until their turn comes, and great confusion would occur if some were flying one way and some another.

Then the cadet must learn care of the aeroplane. This is much more important than care of a car, for if you break down in the air you cannot get out and push the plane to the nearest garage—you may crash and des-

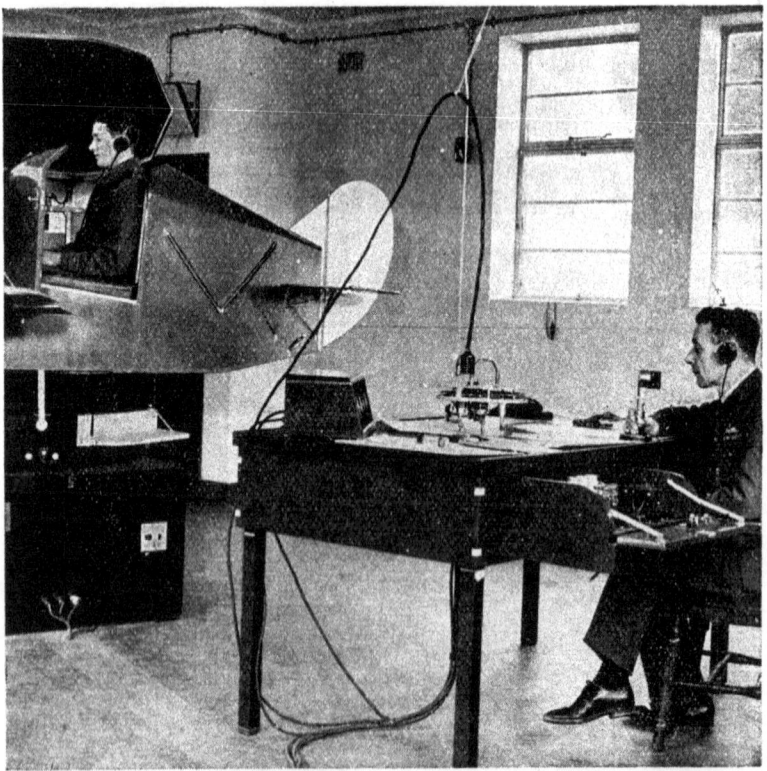

In the Link Trainer pilotage is taught. Pupil and instructor—the latter seated at the instrument table in foreground—are connected by 'phone, and the track of the pupil's make-believe course is traced out on paper by the "crab" and compared with the course set by the instructor.

SECTION 1. E

PUPILS AT WORK IN FLYING TRAINING SCHOOLS

Pupil at a Bombing and Gunnery School about to begin a practice shoot with power-operated gun turret.

Instructional course on the rear gunner cockpit. The aircraft is the Fairey Battle, a training machine.

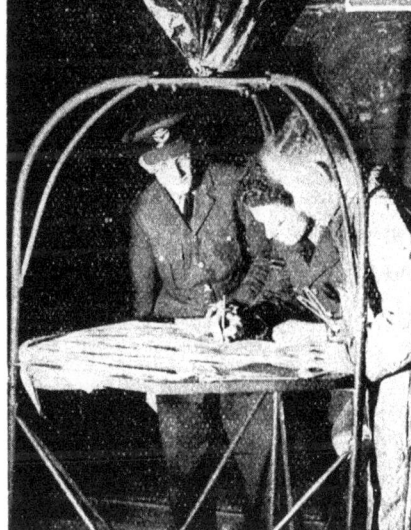

Left, an aspect of training for night-flying: after a practice " bombing run " with a camera obscura the pupils check up results. Right, practice on the ground with a bomb sight; this is followed by instruction during flight.

troy the machine. Cleanliness is a primary factor in maintenance. How, for instance, are you going to see that one of the hinges on your elevator is cracked if it is coated with a film of slime or caked with mud?

Then there is much to be learned about moving an aeroplane in and out of hangars. Quite serious damage can be caused if this is done clumsily. Picketing aircraft in the open also requires skill and knowledge. Starting an engine, too, is not easy at first. Tuition in airscrew swinging is very important. If you try to crank a car unskilfully you may find yourself with a broken arm, but if you tackle an

connected with electrically driven bellows, and any movement of the controls in the cockpit reproduces faithfully the motions of actual flight.

In this Trainer the pupil is shown the primary effect of the elevator, the ailerons and the rudder. The cockpit is fitted with a set of instruments which work in a similar way to those in real flying. Thus, as the Trainer is "climbed" or "dived," so does the air speed indicator (A.S.I.) show a change in speed. The engine revolution indicator works realistically in a similar way, as does the Sperry artificial horizon (a blind-flying instrument) and other devices.

In the dispatch room of an R.A.F. Bombing and Gunnery School these air gunners are waiting their turn to go out for firing exercises. On the wall are parachute packs, ammunition drums and other equipment.

airscrew lightheartedly there may be little of you to find.

All this, together with the lectures and demonstrations on the principles of the 4-stroke internal combustion engine (see page 106), makes the E.F.T.S. course one that is packed with interest and valuable information.

The Link Trainer

Instrument and blind flying technique is taught with the Link Trainer. This ingenious apparatus, which has been developed over a number of years, consists of a stub fuselage with miniature wings, ailerons, elevator, tailplane and rudder. The controls are

The pupil in the Link Trainer receives his instruction via headphones from an instructor who is seated at a desk near by. Words come through as in the "real thing"—"Too much rudder, too much rudder! You are swinging badly. Steady, steady." And as the raw hand moves the controls this way and that, groping and clumsy at first, but gradually gaining skill in this make-believe flying, the course of his "flight" with every turn is faithfully plotted by an electrically operated "crab," which traces in ink all the sequences.

So his time is spent: now he is

Training the Recruit

trying to master the technique of a steep turn with the horizon streaking by the Tiger's nose; half an hour later he is bent over a desk working a Course and Speed Calculator. Inside the classrooms and in the corridors and halls are posters with slogans, apt words that form golden rules for the new men of the R.A.F. "Beware of the Hun in the Sun"; "Will Your Guns Fire?"; "Temper Dash with Discretion."

One, two, three weeks go by, and then the pupil makes his first solo flight. The weekly total of flying hours rises steadily.

In "synthetic" training the bomber crew is briefed as if for an actual operation. These men are being briefed in navigation. Left, fighter pilots learn to load their guns.

Another stage in his ripening career as an airman has been reached, and he is due to be transferred to a Service Flying Training School (S.F.T.S.).

Service Training School

The object of the S.F.T.S. course is to convert the pupil to modern types of aircraft and to the seemingly complicated controls and instruments they contain. Also, this is the first time that the pupil flies in a service machine. The "Moths and Maggies" of the E.F.T.S. are nothing more than conventional club flying machines, and are very easy to handle when compared with the more advanced types. Another point of interest is that now the pupil is flying in a closed cockpit for the first time. The elementary types are both open.

The first glimpse of an instrument panel in an Oxford or Master is a formidable one. It must seem at first to many pupils impossible that so many dials and gadgets are necessary, but each has its own individual and combined part to play in the functioning of these modern, vastly efficient machines. Perhaps the most radical change is for the pupil who goes on to the Oxford with twin engines. He soon gets used to it, though, and in a short time has complete confidence in this excellent machine, besides appreciating the splendid view which can only be got from a multi-engined aircraft where the engines are out on the wings.

It is well known that nearly all the operational aircraft have retractable undercarriages, and it is at the S.F.T.S. that the pupil must get into the habit of raising and lowering these as he takes off and lands. This is most important, because if a pilot lands with his undercarriage up, not only does he run the risk of personal injury, but he may severely damage a very expensive aircraft. There are times, however, when aircraft have to be landed with the undercarriage up, in the event of engine failure or other causes which may result in a forced

SECTION 1. E — Training the Recruit

landing. This is never done at the S.F.T.S., but the technique of doing it is taught, so that the pilot is fully prepared for this contingency should it ever arise at a later date. Similarly, he is taught to fly the aircraft on one engine only. However, if the pilot is careful he will not find himself landing with his undercarriage up, because that is what another of those gadgets in the cockpit is for. A warning device shows the position of the undercarriage. A great deal of instrument flying is done at S.F.T.S. and many cross-countries are flown. Also, so greatly has instrument and radio flying been developed that it is possible for an experienced pilot to do a 300-mile cross-country flight completely blind, and only looking outside the cockpit to land. Naturally, to attain this high state of efficiency requires a lot of work and a great deal of skilful tuition. It cannot all be effected at the S.F.T.S., but great strides towards this goal are made during the course.

There are also many other interesting things to be learned at the S.F.T.S., but they all go to fit the pupil for his next course, at the O.T.U. (Operational Training Unit), where, having learned thoroughly how to fly a Service aircraft, he now learns to use it as a weapon.

Intermingled with this work in the air are lectures on organization, discipline and administration. Armament, signalling, engine maintenance, and photography have their allotted time also.

Night-Flying Work

Night-flying too now comes into the curriculum, and a new and thrilling stage is reached by the budding airman.

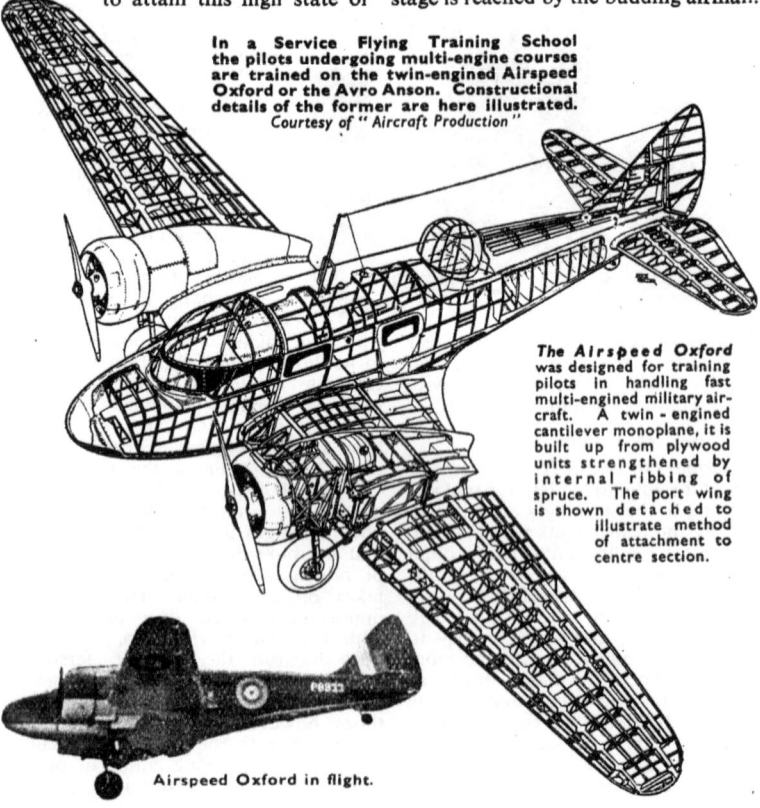

In a Service Flying Training School the pilots undergoing multi-engine courses are trained on the twin-engined Airspeed Oxford or the Avro Anson. Constructional details of the former are here illustrated.
Courtesy of "Aircraft Production"

The *Airspeed Oxford* was designed for training pilots in handling fast multi-engined military aircraft. A twin-engined cantilever monoplane, it is built up from plywood units strengthened by internal ribbing of spruce. The port wing is shown detached to illustrate method of attachment to centre section.

Airspeed Oxford in flight.

A great moment: young airmen at an Elementary Flying School going to the 'plane for their first flight.

Activity on the aerodrome, busy throughout the day, does not cease with nightfall. Across the great, open expanse the yellow flare path is spread, while red, white and green lights, cowled from above, mark the taxying post. The edge of the landing ground is marked by small, discreet red lights. The thunder of engines, the stab and flicker of exhaust flames, signal that the night's work in the air is about to begin.

Human figures move hither and thither, and aircraft, with navigation lights switched on, lumber out to the leeward end of the flare path. Aldis lamps flash signals and the machines roar away into the night. Often in the midst of all this busy scene the sirens sound, the searchlights sweep the sky. But the training of Britain's airmen goes on, so that soon they too will be flying over enemy territory to strike back and strike hard.

While the pupil pilot has thus progressed, others who have been selected to train as observers, gunners and navigators are flying too. At the Air Observers' Schools men are trained in map reading, in the use of navigational instruments, and their instruction is carried out on the ground and in the air. In Avro Ansons the budding observer practises locating targets, and these are "bombed" and photographed. Throughout the training course the work is intensive and thorough, and at the end the cadet sits for an examination in which he must reach a high standard. For an observer is a key man in a bomber crew and his efficiency is essential.

The weeks pass and these men who are learning to be fighter pilots or bomber pilots move on to the final stage of training at an Operational

---

FITNESS AND THE HUMAN MACHINE

For long-term results *and* sudden emergency, physical fitness is vital. Only attained and maintained by self-discipline and individual keenness.

On an operational flight, what one man does may be a decisive war incident—a dump blown up—a marshalling yard disorganized—a key man killed—may depend not only on reasonable fitness, but on the instant brain-muscle reaction of perfect training.

Relaxation helps training and avoids staleness—but anything beyond strict moderation in alcohol, tobacco, etc., is a danger. Alcohol never made an "ace" out of a moderate pilot.

On the job think of nothing else; off it occupy the mind and body with everything except flying and fighting. An hour of leisure is then as effective as an hour of leave.

Courage is much easier if you are on the top line—"fighting fit." The body is a machine, *but* brain, nerves, emotions are all interdependent. You may suffer more harm by worrying about the "girl friend" than by any small physical defect.

FIRST-AID NOTES

Flying Accidents.—If occupant is pinned beneath wreckage do not drag him out, except in case of fire; the wreckage should be cut away from him. If possible, examine position of the injured occupant to determine quickest and safest method of approach and release. Further injury, such as conversion of a simple into a compound fracture, may thus be avoided

If the injured occupant is conscious, ask him to move gently each limb in turn. If there is pain, the limb is probably broken. Apply splints (struts can be used) and pad with clothing. Remove boots and cut away if necessary.

Even though the occupants may appear uninjured, they should be removed by ambulance to sick quarters. The shock may cause a subsequent collapse (faint).

Burns from Petrol. Cover *minor burns* on face or hands with gauze or lint impregnated with sterilized vaseline. On other parts of body, dress with tannic acid jelly or gentian violet jelly, 1 per cent. Keep clothing away from burnt area. Before applying jelly cleanse area with soap and water. *Serious burns*: cover exposed portions with sterile vaseline on gauze or lint; if patient can shortly be transferred to near-by hospital, do not remove more clothing than needed for first aid.

Filing, Dust, etc., in the Eyes. If object loose in eye, remove with corner of handkerchief. If object does not move, put a few drops of castor oil in eye and see a medical officer as soon as possible.

Normal Pulse, Respiration & Temperature
Pulse ... ... 72 per minute
Respiration ... ... 15 to 18 per minute
Temperature ... ... 98·4° Fahr.

Training Unit. It is here that those who are training as bomber pilots join pupils who have been posted from the air-gunnery, navigation and wireless schools, to form and train as teams. Each member of the crew—pilot, air-gunner, wireless operator, observer—works in the type of aircraft in which he will fly under active service conditions.

This training is sometimes amplified by synthetic means. In buildings at the training station "cubicles" may be installed in which each member of an air crew carries out his task as he would in an actual operational flight. The pilot watches his air speed and compass bearing; the navigator plots his course; the wireless operator gets "fixes." On the wall pictures are projected to add to the illusion of flight.

In other buildings pupils learn how to work bomb-release gear and how to use the latest automatic course-setting bomb-sight. Air gunners practise operating gun turrets and aim at moving images of enemy machines projected on a screen. Theory and practice, simulation and the " real thing"; by such means are Britain's fighting airmen being made.

Out of the R.A.F. Schools, each one

In an advanced stage of training, these pupils are about to take part in actual bombing practice from the air. *Cecil Beaton*

of which is a hive of high-pitched yet unhurried industry, pour an endless stream of new pilots and new air crews. Each man retains his individuality, yet he is trained and disciplined and conscious that he is one of a great unconquerable team. The success of the Royal Air Force is due to the fact that every man engaged in flying duties has been " hand-picked " for his desire to serve his country in the air. And he has been trained in the best school in the world.

Ground Work Technicians

There can be, of course, no reduction in the standard required for admission to the R.A.F., and there are therefore some candidates who are disappointed at being rejected for flying duties. Yet it must never be forgotten that the ground personnel of the R.A.F. are key men, and without their skill and devotion to duty all the courage of the air crews would be of no avail. And so when an air crew candidate is turned down he need not despair, and the Selection Board will consider whether he has a trade or hobby which may make him useful to the R.A.F. There is wide scope for intelligent men in a variety of trades and technical jobs in the Service. For details of the trades in the R.A.F. open to men of a mechanical turn of mind see pages 33-35. The trade groups are listed in pages 14-16.

Whatever a man is doing on the ground, he is not just a cog in the wheel. Aircraftmen, Electricians, Radio Mechanics, Instrument Repairers, Wireless Operators—all play a vital and essential part in the Struggle for Freedom.

As they watch the fighters roaring off into the sky, or see the bombers return in the dim light of dawn, or watch the trainers land and take off, the whole day through, they know that they are " in it." They know that by their work, their service, Victory and Peace are being brought nearer. Life in the Royal Air Force, one of the finest services that has ever been created, is a life for men. In the comradeship and the feeling that one is doing one's duty to one's country there is a deep and lasting satisfaction.

THE ROYAL AIR FORCE VOLUNTEER RESERVE

THIS Reserve was announced by the Secretary of State for Air in July, 1936. It was only open to men in civil life and no experience of flying was necessary. The Reserve was originally formed for pilots, and the number required annually was 800, as compared with 60 from civil life before the expansion of the Royal Air Force began. Later, sections were formed for most other categories of airmen.

Men received flying training at aerodrome centres which were established in the vicinity of important towns and areas with a large population. There was a network of centres throughout the country with several in the neighbourhood of London. Ground instruction was provided at town centres at which lectures on the theory of flight, airmanship and other essential subjects were given. The lectures were arranged mainly during winter evenings when opportunities for flying were necessarily restricted.

The aerodrome centres were organized on similar lines to the then existing Civil Flying Schools at which reserve flying training and the initial training of pilots for the regular Air Force were carried out. They were operated by firms under contract with the Air Ministry.

Volunteers were recruited from the neighbourhood of the aerodrome at the centres, and candidates had to be between the ages of 18 and 25. The minimum period of service was five years.

The flying instruction was arranged to allow pilots to train at week-ends, in the evenings, or at any time that would be most convenient. In addition, volunteers had to attend an annual flying course of fifteen days' duration.

At first, training took place in elementary types of light aircraft and, later, in service types. Candidates received a retaining fee of £25 a year and appropriate allowances while under training.

The Reserve also provided facilities for a continuous period of 8 to 10 weeks for initial instruction. Members of the R.A.F. Reserve who entered from civil life were afforded the opportunity of transferring to the new Reserve.

As noted in page 12 the Volunteer Reserve has been employed in wartime as the principal means of entry into the R.A.F. today, all enlisted men being entered through it. All commissions in the General Duties (Flying) Branch are now given to men from the ranks of the V.R. Commissions in the Branches listed in the present section are granted direct, and they also are V.R. commissions.

BADGES AUTHORIZED IN THE R.A.F.

1. Cap badge for Officers of Air Rank
2. Medical Officer, Collar
3. Air Gunner
4. Navigator
5. Bomb Disposal Squad
6. Chaplain, Collar
7. Cap badge, Officers below Air Rank
8. Bomb Aimer
9. Dental Officer, Collar

For the badges of ranks in the R.A.F. and their equivalents in other services see Colour Plates between pages 32 and 33. For Royal Observer Corps see page 62, and A.T.C. page 63.

BADGES AUTHORIZED IN THE R.A.F.

10 Pilot's Wings
11 Education Officer (lapel)
12 Radio Operator (Air)
13 Officers, Auxiliary Air Force
14 Officers, Royal Air Force Volunteer Reserve
15 Officers below Air Rank (Field Service Cap)
16 Warrant Officer
17 Central Band, Musician
18 Physical Training Instructor
19 Airman (Cap Badge)
20 Leading Aircraftman

For Apprentice Badge see page 10 and for Wireless Operator see page 35.

Airmen Who Have Won the V.C.

In the War of 1914-18

Rhodes-Moorhouse, 2/Lt. W. B. ; R.F.C. 22/4/1915. Mortally wounded over Courtrai.
Warneford, Flt. Sub-Lt. R. A. J. ; R.N.A.S. 7/6/1915. Destroyed Zeppelin.
Hawker, Major L. G., D.S.O. ; R.E. and R.F.C. 25/7/1915. Brought down 2 aircraft out of 3.
Liddell, Capt. J. A. ; A. & S. H. and R.F.C. 23/8/1915. Bravery on reconnaissance.
Insall, Lt. G. S. M., M.C. ; R.F.C. 7/11/1915. Bravery on patrol.
Davies, Sqdr.-Cmdr. R. Bell, D.S.O., A.F.C. ; R.N. and R.F.C. 19/11/1915. Rescued fellow pilot.
Rees, Major L. W. B., O.B.E., M.C., A.F.C. ; R.A. and R.F.C. 8/5/1916. Engaged 10 enemy aircraft, though wounded.
Robinson, Lt. W. Leefe ; Worcs. Regt. and R.F.C. Gaz. 5/9/1916. Destroyed airship.
Mottershead, No. 1396. Sergt. T. ; R.F.C. Gaz. 12/2/1917. Though set on fire, brought back aircraft and observer. (Posthumous.)
McNamara, Lt. F. H. ; A.I.F. and R.F.C. Gaz. 8/6/1917. Rescued another pilot, though severely wounded.
Bishop, Capt. W. A., D.S.O., M.C., D.F.C. ; Canadian Cavalry and R.F.C. Gaz. 11/8/1917. Attacked 7 aircraft, engaging 4 and destroying 3.
Ball, Capt. A., D.S.O., M.C. ; Sherwood Foresters and R.F.C. Gaz. 11/9/1917. In 11 days in 26 combats destroyed 11 enemy 'planes.
McCudden, Major J. T. B., D.S.O., M.C., D.F.C. ; R.F.C. Gaz. 4/4/1918. Accounted for 54 enemy aircraft.
Jerrard, Lt. A. ; R.F.C. Gaz. 1/5/1918. Bravery on an offensive patrol.
McLeod, Lt. A. A. ; R.F.C. Gaz. 1/5/1918. Bravery when attacked by 8 enemy aircraft.
West, Capt. F. M. F., M.C. ; R.F.C. Gaz. 8/11/1918. Outstanding bravery in combat.
Barker, Major W. G., D.S.O., M.C. ; R.F.C. Gaz. 30/11/1918. Exceptional bravery (50 enemy machines destroyed by this date).
Beauchamp-Proctor, Capt. A. W., D.S.O., M.C., D.F.C. Gaz. 30/11/1918. Victor in 26 decisive combats during two months.
Mannock, Major E., D.S.O., M.C. ; R.F.C. Gaz. 18/7/1919. Destroyed 50 enemy aircraft.

In the Second World War

Garland, Fl. Off. D. E. ; R.A.F. 12/5/1940. Led formation of five aircraft to attack vital bridge over Meuse. Observer/navigator Sgt. T. Gray (below). Despite intense opposition, his leadership enabled formation to dive-bomb target with success. (Posthumous.)
Gray, Sgt. T. ; R.A.F. 12/5/1940. For skill, coolness and resource in most difficult conditions (see above). (Posthumous.)
Learoyd, Act. Fl. Lt. A. B. ; R.A.F. 12/8/40. Resolutely attacked Dortmund-Ems canal at 150 ft. in face of point-blank fire.
Nicolson, Fl. Lt. J. B. ; R.A.F. 16/8/40. Wounded over Southampton by shell which set fire to tank, instead of baling out he shot down an enemy fighter, sustaining serious burns.
Hannah, Sgt. J. ; R.A.F. 5/9/40. As wireless operator/gunner showed conspicuous courage and devotion to duty at Antwerp in extinguishing fire in cockpit, while ammunition exploded.
Edwards, Act. Wing Comm. H. I., D.F.C. ; R.A.A.F. and R.A.F. 4/7/41. Planned and led successful daylight raid on Bremen, attacking at about 50 ft. against hail of fire, all his machines being hit ; withdrew surviving aircraft.
Ward, Sgt. J. A. ; R.N.Z.A.F. 7/7/41. Over Zuider Zee volunteered to extinguish fire near starboard engine, climbed through astro-hatch, descended 3 ft. to wing, and, in great danger of being blown off, smothered flames Action saved aircraft and crew.
Campbell, Fl. Off. K., R.A.F. 6/4/41. Made daring torpedo raid on battle-cruiser at Brest at point-blank range. (Posthumous.)
Nettleton, Sq. Ldr., J. D., R.A.F. 17/4/42. Led section of Lancasters in daylight raid on Augsburg, flying many miles at 25-30 ft. altitude. His was only machine of section to return.

DECORATIONS AWARDED TO R.A.F. PERSONNEL

V.C. (Victoria Cross). Instituted 1856, to reward exceptionally marked individual acts of bravery. Conferred on all ranks. Takes precedence before all other awards and decorations.

G.C. (George Cross). Instituted 1940, for deeds of valour by civilians (men and women). Ranks first and immediately after the V.C. There is a Military Division also.

E.G.M. (Medal of the Order of the British Empire for Gallantry). Instituted 1917 and awarded to civilians and Services. Ranks (with G.C.) next after the V.C. No longer issued.

D.S.O. (Distinguished Service Order). Instituted 1886 for commissioned officers specially mentioned for meritorious or distinguished service in field or before the enemy.

D.F.C. (Distinguished Flying Cross). Instituted 1918. Awarded to commissioned and warrant officers for acts of gallantry when flying in active operations against the enemy.

A.F.C. (Air Force Cross). Instituted 1918. Awarded to officers and civilians for acts of courage and devotion to duty when flying.

G.M. (George Medal). Instituted 1940. Awarded to civilians for valour and may be won by both men and women. Also Military Division.

M.M. (Military Medal). Instituted in 1916. Awarded to warrant officers, n.c.o.s and men for individual or associated acts of bravery in the field. Under special circumstances women are also eligible for it.

D.F.M. (Distinguished Flying Medal). Instituted in 1918. Awarded in the same circumstances as the D.F.C., but to n.c.o.s and men.

A.F.M. (Air Force Medal) Instituted in 1918. Awarded in the same circumstances as the A.F.C., but to n.c.o.s and men.

L.S. & G.C.M. (R.A.F. Long Service and Good Conduct Medal). Awarded after eighteen years' exemplary service.

M.S.M. (Meritorious Service Medal). Instituted in 1845. In the R.A.F. it is awarded to warrant officers, n.c.o.s and men for valuable services in the field as distinct from flying services. (Distinctive R.A.F. ribbon.)

A.E.A. (Air Efficiency Award). Instituted 1942. For long and meritorious service in Auxiliary Air Force and R.A.F.V.R. Green ribbon, 2 central pale blue stripes. To be issued after the war.

Decorations Awarded to R.A.F. Personnel

Other medals seen on R.A.F. tunics are usually those won in the war of 1914–18.
1. D.F.C.
2. V.C.
3. D.S.O.
4. A.F.C.
5. A.F.M.
6. G.C.
7. G.M.
8. D.F.M.
9. M.M.
10. L.S. & G.C
11. E.G.M.
12. M.S.M.

13. Order of ribbons as worn on tunic — V.C., G.C., D.S.O., D.F.C., A.F.C.
Nos. 5, 7, 8, 9, 10 and 12, reverse shown; No. 11, obverse. A similar medal to No. 11 without palm leaf and with words 'For Meritorious Service' is now the B.E.M.

[*To face page* 32

Equivalent Ranks in the Three Services: (1)

Equivalent Ranks in the Three Services: (2)

RAF	Navy	Army
Group-Captain	 Captain	 Colonel
 Wing-Commander	 Commander	 Lieutenant-Colonel
 Squadron-Leader	 Lieutenant-Commander	 Major
 Flight-Lieutenant	 Lieutenant	 Captain
 Flying-Officer	 Sub-Lieutenant	 Lieutenant
 Pilot Officer	 A/Sub. Lt., Commd Officer Warrant Rank	 Second-Lieutenant

R.A.F. Ensign Badge Flags and Targets

The Royal Air Force Ensign

Marshal of the Royal Air Force

Air Chief Marshal

Air Marshal

R.A.F. Badge

Air Vice Marshal

Air Commodore

Group Captain

Wing Commander

Fuselage Marking on British Aircraft

Squadron Leader

Against each flag are set the distinguishing lamps for use by night

Upper Surface Marking on British Aircraft

R.A.F. Armoured Car Commander

Under Surface Marking on British Aircraft

How to Become a Technician in the R.A.F.
Important Trades Open to Amateur Mechanics

Supplementing the Tables of Trades in pages 14 to 16 these notes give fuller details of conditions and advantages of service in six of the more important and interesting trades normally open to both trained and amateur mechanics.

FEW bombers would fly to smash the Nazi war machine, however brave the men ready to fly them, without the aid of the technicians, who, by their skill and loyal service, ensure that fighters and bombers are fit to fly fast and far to destroy the enemy.

There is a big demand and consequently wide scope for intelligent men in a variety of Royal Air Force trades, in which they not only enjoy comfortable living conditions, good pay and a full and interesting life, but acquire much knowledge and skill which will be most valuable to them when they return to civil life.

Here are some of the trades in which there are big opportunities for both skilled and unskilled men.

Flight Mechanic

MEN between 18 and 50 years of age, with a mechanical turn of mind, may find an opening in the R.A.F. Even a man merely interested in machines or the handling of tools as a hobby may have sufficient knowledge to be trained as a Flight Mechanic, ((E) Engine or (A) Airframe). Recruits in this trade begin as aircraft hands under training and are paid at the rate of 21s. a week. At the end of their training course they become Flight Mechanics (Group II), which means that their pay is increased to a minimum of 31s. 6d. a week.

The Flight Mechanic may then undertake a conversion course to Fitter II (E) or (A) (Group I), which carries a minimum pay rate of 33s. 3d. a week for an Aircraftman Second Class. As he acquires further skill or even on completion of his course he may become an Aircraftman First Class and be paid 38s. 6d. a week, or Leading Aircraftman at 45s. 6d. a week. Skilled fitters from civil life may become Fitters II (E) or (A), without first serving as Flight Mechanics and are put in Group I while under training.

These rates of pay compare very favourably with civil life when it is remembered that clothes, food, living quarters, recreation, medical services, and many other amenities are provided in the R.A.F. free of charge. For married men also there are married and family or dependants' allowances which considerably increase the rates of pay quoted above.

Instrument Repairer

A TRADE of particular interest to watchmakers, magneto repairers, opticians, and men whose hobby it is to do fine and delicate work with their fingers is that of Instrument Repairer.

Recruits are accepted between the ages

At a West Country Training School a class of Flight Mechanics (Airframes) listens intently to a lecture on the Spitfire, delivered from the cockpit of the famous fighter aircraft

How to Become a Technician

With deft fingers the Instrument Repairer adjusts an indicator on the instrument panel of an aircraft.
(British Official)

of 18 and 50. Like the Flight Mechanic they begin training as aircraft hands (Group V) at 21s. a week, and on completion of training become Group II tradesmen and are paid 31s. 6d. a week (minimum), with similar chances of conversion to a Group I trade at a minimum of 33s. 3d. a week.

Armourer

To those who are interested in guns, explosives and projectiles the trade of Armourer is a job of absorbing interest. The Armourer maintains and tests the machine-guns and cannon of our fighters, and the guns and turrets of our bombers, fuses and loads the bombs and ensures the efficiency of the bomb-release gear.

Men between the ages of 18 and 50 are eligible for training as Armourers, and no special qualifications are required. They are trained under similar conditions to Flight Mechanics and Instrument Repairers. They too may convert to a Group I trade as Fitter (Armourers) and similar conditions of pay apply.

Electrician

A HANDY man about the house repairing electric irons, or radiators, may be able to serve as an Electrician in the Royal Air Force. Would-be electricians should be between the ages of 18 and 50, and should preferably have a certain amount of knowledge in the elementary theory of electricity, such as a clear knowledge of Ohm's Law. An applicant of the right type without electrical knowledge would be considered.

The Electrician joins the service with similar conditions of pay to the Flight Mechanic. He may also undergo a conversion course to become an Electrician I (Group I).

Most of his work will be done in aircraft on the ground, but, like the Flight Mechanic, Instrument Repairer and Armourer, he may be required to fly to test in the air the efficiency of his work.

Wireless and R.D.F. Mechanics

THE preliminary training for these two grades is identical during a 24 weeks' course. By then the men under training have shown their aptitude either as specialized R.D.F. (i.e. Radio) Mechanics or more generalized Wireless Mechanics. Age limits 18 to 35 years.

They are then remustered from aircrafthand under training wireless/R.D.F. mechanic to aircrafthand under training wireless mechanic, or aircrafthand under training R.D.F. mechanic, and undergo a further fourteen weeks advanced training as wireless mechanic or eighteen weeks as R.D.F. mechanic.

They begin training at the usual rate of 21s. a week, but immediately they have completed their full course are graded as Group I tradesmen, and are paid a minimum of 33s. 3d. a week.

Whichever branch of the trade he follows the work is fascinating to the radio enthusiast. As a R.D.F. Mechanic, he will work with apparatus which is far in advance scientifically of anything which commercial radio has to show today.

Budding Mechanics at work on an engine during instruction at a Technical Training School of the R.A.F. *(British Official)*

How to Become a Technician

This group of eager youngsters at a Technical Training School is being taught the principles of the hydraulic brake. The R.A.F. offers a wonderful opportunity to keen tradesmen.
(British Official)

As a Wireless Mechanic, whilst the above also applies, he deals with wireless installation in aircraft and on the ground, and on his work the tactical efficiency of our bombers and fighters and the safety of the men who fly them largely depend.

There are also openings for skilled R.D.F. or Wireless Mechanics to enlist in the R.A.F. They enter the service as Group I tradesmen with pay at the rate of 4s. 3d. a day if they have a good practical and theoretical knowledge of servicing wireless apparatus.

They avoid the 24 weeks' initial training and only undergo the 14 weeks course for wireless or the 18 weeks course for R.D.F. mechanic. They are acceptable up to 50 years of age.

Wireless Operator

THERE are openings for Ground Wireless Operators in the R.A.F. They need have no previous knowledge of wireless to be eligible, but applicants should be intelligent and alert.

The conditions of trade grouping and pay during training for Wireless Operators are the same as those for Flight Mechanics. (See page 33.)

The chief duties of the Ground Wireless Operator are wireless inter-communication between R.A.F. stations and between the station control room and aircraft in the air.

The Wireless Operator may be recommended to take a conversion course of 25 weeks' training in preparation for remustering to Wireless Operator Mechanic, which is a Group I trade with minimum pay of 33s. 3d. a week.

Semi-Skilled Men Taken.—Semi-skilled Wireless Operators such as amateurs accustomed to reading Morse will be accepted for service in this trade between the ages of 18 and 30.

Wireless Operators entering as unskilled or semi-skilled men between the ages of 18 and 30 will be given an opportunity during their training to volunteer as Wireless Operator (Air Gunners), thus transferring to flying duties.

Vacancies in Other Trades

Other R.A.F. trades in which there are usually vacancies include :

Photographer	Coppersmith	M.T. Mechanic
Blacksmith and Welder	and Sheet Metal Worker	Physical Training Instructor
Clerk		Station Police
Cook	Driver (M.T.)	R.A.F. Police

Badge, Wireless Operator.

SECTION 1. G

Reclassification, Promotion and Remustering
With a Short Note on Leave

Including an explanation for the recruit of the rather puzzling terms, reclassification—transition between the three classes of Aircraftman; and remustering—a change of trade.

Reclassification, although normally an advancement, should not be confused with or interpreted as promotion. There are three classifications:

Aircraftman second class: A.C.2
Aircraftman first class: A.C.1
Leading Aircraftman: L.A.C.

and reclassification refers to transition from one classification to another.

In skilled and semi-skilled trades, including certain trades in Group V, reclassification is determined not by length of service but by the results of an examination by a Trade Test Board. These Boards are held at frequent intervals and reclassification is effective from the first day of the month following trade testing, irrespective of the time the airman has served. The A.C.2 requires 60 per cent. of the marks obtainable to be reclassified A.C.1, and 80 per cent. for reclassification to L.A.C.

An airman who enters the service as an Aircrafthand or in a trade in Group V in which reclassification is not by trade test is, providing his service has been satisfactory, eligible for reclassification to A.C.1, after a certain period of service as an A.C.2 (at present 9 months). Reclassification to L.A.C. is limited to vacancies and may be authorized on merit irrespective of seniority.

Promotion refers to advancement to N.C.O. rank, *i.e.* above L.A.C. On attaining the classification of L.A.C. an Aircraftman becomes eligible for consideration for promotion to N.C.O. rank to fill establishment vacancies. Selection for promotion is made on merit, but seniority may also be taken into account.

Remustering. All airmen are eligible, subject to vacancies, for remustering to a more highly skilled trade for which they can qualify by their own efforts. In addition, opportunities exist for suitable airmen to receive training for trades in the higher groups. Where an airman qualifies for remustering to a trade in the same or higher trade group, but fails to qualify for the retention of his existing classification, he may retain his former rate of pay so that an L.A.C. in, say, Group III, who is remustered to a trade in Group II, but is only able to attain the classification of A.C.2, retains the rate of pay he was receiving in Group III until he qualifies for a higher rate in the new Group.

While the greatest care is taken by interviewing officers and Boards to see that new recruits to the Service are mustered in trades most suitable to their qualifications, it is inevitable that occasionally airmen find themselves training for trades for which they are not wholly suitable. In these circumstances an airman may always apply to his C.O. to be remustered to another trade.

Leave. Leave is granted as a privilege and is dependent on the exigencies of the Service. Every effort, however, is made to grant leave to airmen on the basis of 7 days every three months in the case of ground staff, and up to 61 days every twelve months in the case of air crew personnel. Additional leave to airmen is granted only in exceptional compassionate circumstances at the discretion of the Commanding Officers.

Sick leave and, in certain circumstances, compassionate leave, do not count as ordinary leave, and compassionate leave in any circumstances may be granted wherever justified even though the annual allowance of privilege leave has been exhausted. Railway warrants are issued free four times yearly to all airmen.

Passes are in addition granted four times a year wherever possible. Trainees on courses of instruction are not normally granted passes or leave until the successful completion of their course.

SHORT GLOSSARY OF R.A.F. SLANG

Balbo, A	A large formation of aircraft.	Office	Cockpit of aircraft.
Bale out	To take to one's parachute.	Organize	To " win " a wanted article.
Bind, A	People who obstruct one.	Pack up	Cease to function.
Black, A	Something badly done, a " bad show."	Peel off, To	Break formation to engage enemy.
Blitz, A solid lump of	Large formation of enemy aircraft.	Play pussy	Hide in the clouds.
Blonde job, A	Young woman with fair hair.	Pleep	A squeak, rather like a high note klaxon.
Bomphleteers	Airmen engaged on the early pamphlet raids.	Plug away	Continue to fire. Keep after target.
Brassed off	Diminutive of " browned off."	Pukka gen.	Accurate information.
Brolly	Parachute.	Pulpit	Cockpit of aircraft.
Browned off, To be	" Fed up."	Quick squirt	Short sharp burst of machine-gun fire.
Bumps and Circuits	Circuits and landings.	Quickie	Short for above.
Bus driver	A bomber pilot.	Rang the bell	Got good results.
Buttoned up	A job properly completed, " mastered."	Rings	Rank designation on officer's cuffs.
Completely Cheesed	No hope at all.	Ropey	Uncomplimentary adjective. " A ropey landing," " A ropey type," " A ropey evening," etc.
Cope	To accomplish, to deal with.		
Crabbing along	Flying near the ground or water.	Screamed downhill	Executed a power dive.
Deck, Crack down on	To " pancake " an aircraft.	Scrub	To washout.
		Second Dickey	Second pilot.
Dog Fight	Aerial scrap.	Shooting a line	Exaggerated talk, generally about one's own prowess.
Drill, The right	Correct method of doing anything.		
Drink, In the	To come down into the sea.	Shot Down in Flames	Crossed in love. Severe reprimand.
Dud	Applied to weather when unfit to fly.	Snake about	Operational aerobatics.
Duff gen.	Dud information.	Spun in	A bad mistake. Analogy from an aircraft spinning out of control into the ground.
Dust bin	Rear gunner's lower position in aircraft.		
Erk, An	A beginner in any job.	Stationmaster	Commanding Officer of Station.
Fan	The propeller.		
Fireworks, Mr	Armaments Officer.	Stooge	Deputy, i.e. second pilot, or any assistant.
Flak	Anti-aircraft fire.		
Flap	A disturbance, general excitement.	Stooging about	Delayed landing for various reasons. Flying slowly over an area. Patrolling.
Fox, To	To do something clever, or rather cunning.		
Gen. (pron. jen)	General information of any kind whatever.	Synthetic	Not the real thing. Also applied to ground training.
George	The automatic pilot.		
Get Cracking	Get going.	Tail End Charlie	Rear gunner in large bombing aircraft or rear aircraft of a formation.
Gong, To collect a	To get a medal.		
Greenhouse	Cockpit cover.		
Hedge-hopping	Flying so low that the aircraft appears to hop over the hedges.	Tear off a strip	To reprimand, take down a peg.
		Touch bottom	Crash.
Hurryback	A Hurricane fighter.	Toys	A great deal of training equipment is termed toys.
Jink away	Sharp manoeuvre. Sudden evasive action of aircraft.		
		Train, Driving the	Leading more than one squadron into battle.
Kipper Kite	Coastal Command aircraft which convoy fishing fleets in the North and Irish Seas.	Type	Classification — usually referring to people. Good, Bad, Ropey, Poor type.
Kite	An aeroplane.	View	R.A.F. personnel always take a " view " of things. Good view, Poor view, Dim view, Long-distance view, Lean view, Outside view, " Ropey " view.
Laid on, To have	To produce anything, such as supplies.		
Mae West	Life-saving stole, or waistcoat, inflated if wearer falls into sea.		
Mickey Mouse	Bomb-dropping mechanism.		
Muscle in	To take advantage of a good thing.	Wizar	Really first class, superlative, attractive, ingenious.

Opportunities for Self-Education in the R.A.F.
Facilities for Individual Study

In addition to the daily training, general and technical, of recruits in the R.A.F. Education Officers at every station are ready to assist students in almost any way suited to their capacities and ambitions. Here are brief details:

THE high value of the educational part of the training given to entrants to the Royal Air Force is well known, but it is not so well understood that there are wide facilities for the continuance of individual study by men actually serving. At every R.A.F. station classes are arranged by an Education Officer for remustering men to other trades, according as they show aptitude or preference. Over and above these there are other courses in general educational subjects, and further classes held by arrangement with the local Education Authorities.

Private study is aided in many ways, and guidance afforded. There is a reference and text-book library at the station, to which students have access, and it is possible for men to enrol for Tutorial Courses provided by the R.A.F. or Correspondence Courses by approved outside bodies. When a man takes up an approved course with an outside body part of the cost may be met from public funds. All through the scheme the student has the help and guidance of the Education Officer, behind whom is an organization leading up to the Command Education Officer at Command Headquarters and the Directorate of Educational Services at the Air Ministry.

Ground Training Establishments

At establishments such as Initial Training Wings and Schools of Technical Training for Apprentices there is a staff of Education Officers, and the instruction given is on the lines of that furnished by a civil Technical School of the highest standard and cannot fail to be of lasting value. Trade and craft training—practical and theoretical—is given which will fit the man to take up civil life later with confidence in his knowledge and ability in the chosen pursuit. Only the best of workmanship is good enough for the R.A.F., backed up by a sufficiently thorough acquaintance with the basic theory.

Pre-War Activities of the R.A.F. Educational Service

A general view of the work of the Education Service is given in the following brief review of normal activities. For apprentices there were the schools for Aircraft Apprentices and Apprentice Clerks. For men there were the following examinations, each with its appropriate course:

(a) Promotion examinations (compulsory): Corporal to Sergeant and reclassification to L.A.C.
(b) Elementary Air Navigation (voluntary).
(c) Higher Education Test (3 parts; voluntary). This covered a wide range of subjects, up to quite a high standard.

For officers there was a separate scheme, comprising:

(a) *For individuals.* Help with the Specialization Exam. for Short Service Officers wishing to obtain a Permanent Commission.
Officers' Promotion Exams.
Exam. for entry to Staff College.
(b) *Training Establishments.* Tuition for potential Officers provided by Education Officers on the staff of the R.A.F. College.
R.A.F. School of Aeronautical Engineering (for Officers).

Oversea Opportunities

There are ample educational facilities at many oversea R.A.F. stations, and, in addition to the usual range of studies outlined earlier, men will be able to learn the local languages.

AIR FORCES OF OUR ALLIES

Polish Air Force. Largest of the allied air forces in England, it has several fighter and bomber squadrons serving with the R.A.F. Bombers have made many raids over Germany and German-occupied territory; fighters greatly distinguished themselves during "Battle of Britain," Sept. 1940. The famous Squadron 303 alone then shot down over 100 German 'planes. To July 1942 Polish fighters had destroyed 464.

Czechoslovak Air Force. Has its own fighter and bomber squadrons. Soon after it was constituted, the fighters of the Force took part in the big air battles of Sept. 1940. By July 1942 bag of the fighters was a certain 118 enemy 'planes.

Fighting French pilots are flying with Hurricane and Spitfire squadrons, where they have earned the praise of their British colleagues.

Belgian fighter pilots have scored notable successes with R.A.F. Many Belgians are working with R.A.F. as wireless mechanics and in other trades.

Dutch. Units of the Dutch Naval Air Service operate with the R.A.F. in Coastal Command. A number of pupil pilots from the Dutch Army have entered the R.A.F. for training.

Norwegian Air Force have formed and trained units in Canada to operate with the R.A.F.

The Organization of the R.A.F.
Air Commands at Home and Abroad

The organization of the R.A.F. as laid down in the appropriate King's Regulations and Air Council Instructions is first outlined here, and is followed by brief statements of the work of the Home Commands

THE Royal Air Force at home is divided into nine commands as follows :

Bomber Command   Flying Training
Fighter Command   Command
Coastal Command   Technical Training
Army Co-operation   Command
        Command   Maintenance
Balloon Command   Command
        Ferry Command

The following brief notes indicate the nature of the work of each command.

Bomber Command. The main long-range striking force of the home Air Force is known as Bomber Command. Its function is to attack and undermine the enemy's whole war organization wherever an opportunity presents itself. This may mean attacking a naval dockyard on one occasion, an oil refinery on another, and an explosives factory on a third ; it may also entail direct action against warships, troop concentrations and aerodromes ; but in the long run it is the enemy's " will to win " which forms the final objective.

Whatever their target, the crew of a bomber have to fly long distances in every type of weather, and in the face of every form of opposition. When over enemy territory, they represent a mere handful of British in the midst of millions of Germans ; in such circumstances the highest degree of tenacity and courage is essential, backed up by training of a very high order.

The successful bomber crew have the privilege of knowing that, in addition to the destruction of an important element in the enemy's war organization, they have kept a large number of A.A. guns, searchlights, balloons (and all the other elaborate paraphernalia of air defence) fully manned and equipped over thousands of square miles. A bomber force makes itself permanently felt throughout the whole vast area which it may or may not visit, and this is one of the major advantages of offensive action in the air.

Bomber Command is divided into a number of Groups. These comprise various stations with an aerodrome attached to each, and on every station there are a number of bomber squadrons, each equipped with aircraft of such well-known types as the Lancaster, Halifax, Stirling, Wellington, and Boston.

Fighter Command. Fighter Squadrons provide the air-borne element of the defence of this island against air attack. Into the headquarters comes all information concerning air war over this country and out of them go the orders and the warnings that set the air defence system in motion. It co-ordinates not only the operations of the Fighter Squadrons, but

All ready for a bombing raid, the crew of this machine take a brief rest seated on the deadly missiles which will soon fill the bomb racks of the aircraft in the background.

every other weapon used against the Luftwaffe, including the A.A. guns, balloon barrage, searchlights and the warnings that go to the Civil Defence system.

Between September, 1939, and September, 1942, the Fighter Command was responsible for the destruction of some 5,000 aircraft.

The aerodromes under the Command are ranged in sectors which are under the control of Group Headquarters, the Groups themselves being under Command H.Q. An elaborate system of communication connects the whole, and by radio telephony each sector can control the movements of all fighter pilots in the air.

Operations Rooms at Sector, Group and H.Q. plot all information about hostile machines and at Command H.Q. provide a

SECTION 1. J **Organization of the R.A.F.** 40

complete picture of the entire air battle front, there being present representatives of Bomber and Coastal Commands in direct communication with their own H.Q.

In all Operational Stations a squadron is kept in readiness with pilots waiting, able to be in the air three minutes after receiving an order from the Controller.

Fighter Command shares with Coastal Command the duty of protecting shipping, patrolling Hurricanes and Spitfires looking after coastwise vessels.

In 1941 Fighter Command, having cleared the British skies of the enemy in daylight, carried the war across the

The pilot of a night fighter climbs into his cockpit before taking off

Channel in a constant series of daylight offensive operations and also provided escorts for bombers attacking targets in enemy territory. These offensives were continued in great strength in 1942. In the Dieppe raid alone Fighter Command pilots destroyed 96 enemy aircraft.

Coastal Command. This Command has the primary tasks of reconnaissance and of protecting the merchant shipping that brings the war supplies to Great Britain. To these tasks have been added many others, such as the attack on enemy shipping and the continuous bombing of his docks and U-boat bases and fortified zones on the coasts of occupied territory.

The varied work of the Coastal Command is best illustrated by some records. In the three years aircraft of the command flew approximately 60,000,000 miles on operations over the sea.

More than 10,000 convoys, most of them deep sea, were given air escort; involving some 35,000 operational sorties on this task alone. Enemy naval units or supply ships were attacked 1,350 times, and the total of enemy tonnage sunk or so damaged as to be permanently unserviceable amounted to over 200,000 tons. Enemy aircraft destroyed while approaching convoys numbered 108, and more than 700 were driven off.

The principal task of Coastal Command during the year was anti-submarine work. To the end of the third year of war well over 500 U-boats were attacked.

Highlights in Coastal Command history during the first three years of war include finding the prison-ship Altmark; attacks on the Scharnhorst; location of the Deutschland; protection of the B.E.F. at Dunkirk; torpedoing of the Lutzow; capture from the air of a U-boat; attack in the Channel against the Scharnhorst, Gneisenau and Prinz Eugen, protecting of North African invasion convoys.

Awards to personnel of Coastal Command during the first three years of war were as follows: V.C., 1; D.S.O., 14; D.F.C., 244; D.F.M., 121; 1st Bar to D.F.C., 6; 2nd Bar to D.F.C., 1; D.S.C., 8; D.S.M., 4; C.B., 3; C.B.E., 9; O.B.E., 24; M.B.E., 33; B.E.M., 28; E.G.M., 1; A.F.C., 12; G.M., 11; M.M., 8; M.C., 1; Norwegian M.C., 3; Mentions in Dispatches, 1,063.

Aircraft now in use in Coastal Command include Sunderland and Catalina flying boats, and Northrop sea-planes. Land aircraft are Lockheed Hudsons, Wellingtons, Beaufighters, Beauforts, Hampdens (equipped to carry torpedoes), Liberators, Flying Fortresses and Whitleys.

Army Co-operation Command. The Army Co-operation Command of the R.A.F. was established on December 1, 1940. It comprises all squadrons allotted to Army formations in the United Kingdom, together with the associated training units, and its primary function is to organize, experiment and train in all forms of co-operation between the two services.

The main purpose of an Army Co-operation reconnaissance squadron is to obtain information required by military commanders—information which only an air reconnaissance will reveal. Upon the pilots' skill and initiative, accuracy and speed may depend decisions of Army chiefs.

Many pilots are Army officers seconded to the R.A.F., and a sound knowledge of land warfare is essential to them in the missions given them by Army commanders through the Air Liaison Officers—Army officers attached to each A.C. squadron.

In the A.C. Command is a Training and Development Group, whose activities include the training of British parachute troops. (See page 131.)

At one station new and successful methods of artillery observation have been tried by R.A.F. pilots whose task it is to " spot " for the gunners from the air.

Various anti-aircraft co-operation units provide practice for men training for the anti-aircraft artillery, with target-towing fights which are " attacked " by anti-aircraft gunners during " live-shoots."

Organization of the R.A.F.

In the gallery of the Haskard Range pilots and ground staff are trained for Army Co-operation Command work. Below is a realistic sand map of the terrain.

At Operational training establishments of the Command pilots are trained in the types of work required in an Army Co-operation squadron, and Army Intelligence officers are instructed how to become Air Liaison Officers.

Flying Training Command. In this Command all pilots, air observers, and air gunners are given their training. It is organized in six groups. One group deals with initial training (I.T.W.); two with elementary flying training (E.F.T.S.); two with service flying training (S.F.T.S.), and the sixth with air observation, air gunnery and bombing schools. For details of the selection of air crew and the progress of recruits' training, see pages 20-29.

The Central Flying Schools, at which R.A.F. flying instructors must qualify, are also in this Command.

Technical Training Command. This Command is in number of personnel the largest in the Royal Air Force. It trains all officers and men destined for ground duties. From the administrative point of view it is also the most complex, for at its training schools more than eighty different trades and divisions of trades are taught, and its stations are spaced throughout England, Scotland and Wales. The Command is divided into four

This Air Gunner of a Coastal Command aircraft is on his way to the 'plane, his weapons all in readiness.

Miles Master aircraft are used by the Training Command in actual flying, and here four are seen in the air during formation practice. Another of the same type stands ready.

SECTION 1. J **Organization of the R.A.F.** 42

Groups. Two of these Groups undertake specialized training of various kinds in the trades which appertain to the maintenance and servicing of aircraft and R.A.F. stations, and the second two are Signals Groups dealing with the training for all forms of communication by wireless, radio telephone, telegraph, teleprinter, and telephone.

All recruits, other than flying personnel, pass through Technical Training Command. In the training wings of their Recruits' Centres they receive their "parade ground" instruction. They learn drill, discipline, handling of arms, ground defence, and the military knowledge which is essential for an aircraftman.

In the schools of technical or signal training to which recruits are posted trade instruction is given. The capability of every recruit is judged on entry to the R.A.F., and he is drafted for instruction in the trade for which he shows aptitude.

Practical work alternates with lecture room work in all training courses. Classes are reasonably small so that there are direct contact and fellowship between instructor and pupils.

Instruction is carefully "phased." For example, an aircraftman who is to be a flight mechanic begins by being taught how to handle tools. He learns to file accurately; to work simply in metals; to use precision instruments, and so step by step to more difficult tasks. The instruction is so sympathetically graded that the trainees become efficient tradesmen in what is actually a short time considering all they have to learn.

Every man must pass a trade test at the end of his training course. His future classification in the Service—Leading Aircraftman, Aircraftman 1st Class, or Aircraftman 2nd Class—depends on how well he does at the passing out test.

Apart from technical trades this Command has training establishments for every section of R.A.F. ground duties. Newly commissioned officers do initial training in the Command, and there are officers' schools for accountancy, administration, engineering, equipment and security, as well as other specialist schools.

Further, there are instruction courses for bandsmen, bayonet fighting, fire fighting, and physical training.

In addition, recruits to the W.A.A.F. are received and trained under this Command. There are now more than thirty R.A.F. trades open to the W.A.A.F.

Maintenance Command. This Command exists to supply and maintain the R.A.F. Like all the others it is divided into a number of Groups, each containing numerous units whose task is to issue the vast multitude of items without which the R.A.F. cannot survive for long. A few of these items are mentioned to illustrate their variety:

Aircraft	Ammunition	Cameras
Engines	Machine-Guns	W/T
Balloons	Petrol	Equipment
Clothing	Oil	Torpedoes
Furniture	Oxygen	Electrical
Instruments	Lorrries	Equipment
Bombs	Motor Boats	Hydrogen

The provision and salvage of aircraft and their equipment are the responsibility of the Ministry of Aircraft Production, and not of the Air Ministry. Those units in Maintenance Command which are concerned with the issue, storage and salvage

Short Sunderland flying boats of the Coastal Command at anchor after escorting a convoy into harbour.

of aircraft are under the general direction of the M.A.P.

Balloon Command. The function of this Command is obvious, for everyone has seen balloons floating in the sky, but it is not generally realized what a large organization is required to look after them. Great Britain is divided into geographical areas, each with a Balloon Group and the appropriate number of squadrons, together with the communications necessary for their effective control. (See further under Section 3 (E).)

Ferry Command. The A.O.C. - in - C., Royal Air Force Ferry Command in Canada, is directly responsible to the Air Council for taking over American types of aircraft from the Ferry Command of the U.S. Army Air Corps and delivering them by air to the United Kingdom.

Certain aspects of the work of Home Commands are dealt with in greater detail in Section 3, Special Training.

THE TREE OF COMMAND AT HOME
THE AIR MINISTRY

THE AIR COUNCIL
Secretary of State
Parliamentary Under-Secretary of State (Lords)
Parliamentary Under-Secretary of State (Commons)
Chief of the Air Staff
Air Member for Personnel
„   „   „ Supply and Organization
„   „   „ Training
Vice Chief of the Air Staff
Three Additional Members
Permanent Under-Secretary of State

THE AIR STAFF
Chief of the Air Staff
Vice Chief of the Air Staff
Assistant „ „ „   General
   „   „ „ „   Operations
   „   „ „ „   Intelligence
   „   „ „ „   Technical
   „   „ „ „   Policy

Department of Chief of Air Staff
Directorate of Plans
   „   „ Military Cooperation
   „   „ Bomber Operations
   „   „ Fighter Operations
   „   „ Operations (Overseas)
   „   „   „   (Naval Cooperation)
   „   „ Intelligence (Operations)
   „   „   „   (Security)
Assistant Directorate of Photographic Intelligence
   „   „   „ Scientific Intelligence
Directorate of Allied Air Cooperation and Foreign Liaison
   „   „   „ Ground Defence
Directorate-General of Air Safety
   „   „   „ Signals
Directorate of Signals
   „   „ Radio
   „   „ Telecommunications
   „   „ Operational Requirements
   „   „ Air Tactics
Deputy Directorate of Photography

Department of Air Member for Personnel
Directorate-General of Postings
   „   „   „ Personal Services
   „   „   „ R.A.F. Medical Services
Directorate of Postings
   „   „ Personal Services
   „   „ Educational Services
   „   „ Manning
   „   „ Women's Auxiliary Air Force
Chaplain in Chief

Department of Air Member for Supply and Organization
Deputy Air Member for Supply and Organization
Directorate-General of Organization
Directorate of Organization
   „   „ War Organization
   „   „ Organization (Establishment)
   „   „ Movement
Deputy Directorate of Organization (Mechanical Transport)
Assistant Directorate of Organization (Ferrying)
Civilian Liaison Officer(Ferrying)
Directorate-General of Equipment
Directorate of Servicing and Maintenance
Directorate-General of Works
Directorate of Hydrogen Production
Controller-General of Economy

Department of Air Member for Training
Directorate of Operational Training
   „   „ Flying   „
   „   „ Technical   „
Director of Air Training Corps

Department of Permanent Under-Secretary of State
Secretariat
Finance Branches
Directorate of Contracts
   „   „ Accounts
   „   „ Public Relations
Directorate-General of Civil Aviation
Meteorological Office
Chief Inspector of Accidents

THE COMMANDS OVERSEAS

THE A.O.C.-in-C. *Middle East* is directly responsible to the Air Council for the command and operational employment of all R.A.F. units in North and East Africa, Malta, Persia, Iraq, Palestine and Transjordan, and Aden. Operational control and local administration of R.A.F. units in these areas are delegated as necessary by the A.O.C.-in-C. Middle East to the Air or other Officers commanding.

The A.O.C.-in-C. *India* is directly responsible to the Commander-in-Chief in India for the command and administration of all units in his Command.

The Overseas Commands also include *Air H/Q West Africa.* Technically the Ferry Command (p. 42) is an overseas Command.

The *Overseas Commands* of the R.A.F. are composite and their organization differs from those in the United Kingdom in that the Commands abroad contain elements of any or all of the units which at home are grouped into separate Commands according to their specialized functions. Thus, a Command such as the Middle East Command may contain Bomber, Fighter, General Reconnaissance, Army Cooperation, and Balloon Squadrons. In addition, it will contain its own organization for repair and maintenance and flying and operational training.

The organization of units under Wings, Groups and subordinate Air Headquarters is sufficiently elastic to permit units to be moved and re-grouped in accordance with changes in the strategical situation. This elasticity extends to movements of units between one overseas Command and another.

LEADERS OF THE ROYAL AIR FORCE
Brief Biographies Alphabetically Arranged by Ranks

SINCLAIR, Rt. Hon. Sir Archibald, Bt., P.C., C.M.G. ; M.P. for Caithness and Sutherland. Secretary of State for Air.

Born 1890 ; educated at Eton and the Royal Military College, Sandhurst ; entered the Army in 1910 and became a Major, 2nd Life Guards. In 1912 he succeeded to the Baronetcy of Ulbster, Caithness, on the death of his grandfather. From 1919 until 1921 he was Personal Military Secretary to the Secretary of State for War ; then he became Private Secretary to the Secretary of State for the Colonies (1921–22). In the latter year he was returned as (Liberal) M.P. for Caithness and Sutherland, and has represented that constituency since. Sir Archibald was Chief Liberal Whip, 1930–31, and in Aug., 1931, became Secretary for Scotland in the National Government. He resigned in 1932. In Dec., 1935, he was chosen Leader of the Liberals in the House of Commons.

When Mr. Churchill formed his Government in May, 1940, he chose Sir Archibald to be Secretary of State for Air.

SHERWOOD, Baron. *Parliamentary Under-Secretary of State for Air (Lords).*

Born 1898 ; educated at Cheam and Eton. He became Lieut. in the Grenadier Guards in 1917, serving until 1919 ; from 1920 until 1923 he held a commission in the South Notts Hussars. He represented East Norfolk (L.) from Dec., 1923, until Oct., 1924. Became High Sheriff for Nottinghamshire in 1925. On the death of his father next year he succeeded to the Baronetcy as Sir Hugh (Michael) Seely. Returned to Parliament in 1935 as M.P. (L.) for the Berwick-on-Tweed division of Northumberland.

In 1937 Sir Hugh became Squadron Leader commanding No. 504 (County of Nottinghamshire) (Bomber) Squadron of the Auxiliary Air Force. His Squadron went to France in May, 1940, and, though soon withdrawn, it shot down seven enemy aircraft, and may have accounted for a total of twenty. Returning the same month, it later played a brilliant part in the Battle of Britain : Sir Hugh was released from active service to become Parly. Private Secry. to Sir Archibald Sinclair. In July, 1941, he was appointed an additional Under-Secretary of State for Air (Lords) and created a Baron.

BALFOUR, Capt. Harold Harington, M.C., M.P. for Isle of Thanet. *Parliamentary Under-Secretary of State for Air (Commons).*

Born 1897 ; educated at Chilverton Elms, Dover, and R.N. College, Osborne. 2nd Lieut., 60th Rifles, Nov., 1914 ; Lieut., Dec., 1915. Took his R.Ae.C. ticket (No. 1399) in July, 1915. Appointed Flying Officer, R.F.C., May, 1916 ; Flt. Comdr., Nov., 1916. Apptd. Capt. "A," R.A.F., April, 1918 ; Tempy. Major, Sept., 1918. Wounded while Flt. Cmdr. in No. 43 Squadron, R.F.C., and invalided to England in 1917. Later posted to Central Flying School and to School of Special Flying, Gosport. Returned in Nov., 1917, to No. 43 Sqdrn., where he served until March, 1918. Awarded M.C. in May, 1917, and bar in April, 1918.

In 1921, after service as a Flying Instructor at Cranwell, he became Personnel Asst. to A.O.C., Cadet College, Cambridge, with perm. commission in R.A.F. Flying Instructor at H.Q., Inland Area, Nov., 1922–April, 1923.

Captain Balfour has been M.P. for Isle of Thanet since 1929. Appointed Under-Secretary of State for Air in May, 1938. An early private owner of a light aeroplane, he takes an active practical interest in flying.

STREET, Sir Arthur William, K.C.B., K.B.E., C.M.G., C.I.E., M.C. *Permanent Under-Secretary of State for Air.*

Born 1892 ; educated at the County School, Sandown, and at King's College, London. During the war of 1914–18 he served in the Hampshire Regt. (T.F.) and the Machine Gun Corps. He was mentioned in dispatches and received the M.C. Was Principal Private Secretary to the Minister of Agriculture and to the First Lord of the Admiralty, 1919–22 ; later he became in succession Assistant Secretary and Principal Assistant Secretary to the Ministry of Agriculture and Fisheries. Appointed Second Secretary in 1936, he became First Deputy Under-Secretary of State for Air in 1938 and next year was made Permanent Under-Secretary of State.

Marshals of the Royal Air Force

ELLINGTON, Marshal of the Royal Air Force Sir Edward Leonard, G.C.B., C.B.E., C.M.G.

Born 1877; educated at Clifton College and the Royal Military Academy. Commissioned in 1897 to the Royal Artillery; later promoted to Lieut. and Capt. At Staff College, Camberley, 1907-8; graduated as pilot, 1912. Appointed to R.F.C., 1913.

Went to France Aug., 1914; on staff, Sept., 1915, to Feb., 1916. Then posted to a staff appointment at the W.O., returning to France at end of 1916. Towards end of 1917 he went to the W.O. again, to be D.D.G. of Military Aeronautics, and was promoted Director-General in Jan., 1918. In 1917 he had been promoted to Brigadier-General. On April 1, 1918, he became Major-General in the Royal Air Force. Appointed Controller-General of Equipment in Aug., 1918. In Feb., 1919, he became Director-General of Supply and Research. For his war services he received the C.B., C.M.G., and C.B.E., and was three times mentioned in dispatches. Awarded the K.C.B. in 1920.

In 1922 Sir Edward took over the Middle East Command of the R.A.F.; next year he became A.O.C., R.A.F., India. In Nov., 1926, he was appointed A.O.C., Iraq, relinquishing this to become A.O.C., Air Defence of Great Britain in Jan., 1929. Became Air Member of Council for Personnel, Sept., 1931; iu May, 1933, he was appointed Chief of the Air Staff. Was Inspector-General of the R.A.F, 1937-40. In Aug., 1919, Sir Edward Ellington had received a permanent commission in the R.A.F. with the rank of Air Vice-Marshal. He was promoted Air Marshal in July, 1929; Air Chief Marshal in Jan., 1933; and Marshal of the Royal Air Force in Jan., 1937. In 1935 he had been made a G.C.B.

NEWALL, Marshal of the Royal Air Force Sir Cyril Louis Norton, G.C.B., O.M., G.C.M.G., C.B.E., A.M. *Governor-General of New Zealand.*

Born 1886; educated at Bedford School and the Royal Military College, Sandhurst. Entered Royal Warwickshire Regt., 1905, transferring to the 2nd K.E.O. Gurkha Rifles, I.A., in 1909. Qualified as a pilot while on leave in England in 1911. Selected by the I.A. to receive special flying instruction at Upavon in 1913. On return to India, was engaged in the formation of a central flying school until, on the outbreak of war in 1914, he joined the R.F.C. in England as a Flight Comdr. (No. 1 Squadron).

In 1917 commanded the 41st (Bombing) Wing formed near Nancy to bomb German objectives. The 41st Wing was the forerunner of the Independent Air Force, created in 1918, in which he commanded the 8th Brigade. Three times mentioned in dispatches. In 1916 he won the Albert Medal when in charge of a small party which put out the flames when fire broke out inside a large R.F.C. bomb store. He received the C.B.E. and C.M.G. in 1919, K.C.B. in 1935, and G.C.B. in 1938.

After the war of 1914-18 he was Chief Staff Officer, South-Eastern Area, and D.D. of Personnel at the Air Ministry. In 1926 he became Director of Operations and Intelligence, and Deputy Chief of the Air Staff. Promoted to Air Vice-Marshal in 1930, he took over the Middle East Command of the R.A.F. the following year. Returning to England in 1934, he was appointed to the Air Council (early 1935) as Member for Supply and Organization, and later in the year was made Air Marshal. Promoted to Air Chief Marshal in April, 1937, and became Chief of the Air Staff in Sept.

In Oct., 1940, he was appointed Governor-General of New Zealand (sworn in in Feb., 1941). Became a Marshal of the Royal Air Force on relinquishing his post as Chief of the Air Staff. Sir Cyril received the O.M., and, in Feb., 1941, the G.C.M.G.

SALMOND, Marshal of the Royal Air Force Sir John Maitland, G.C.B., C.M.G., C.V.O., D.S.O.

Born 1881; educated at Wellington College. Commissioned in the K.O. Royal Lancashire Regt. in 1901. In 1912 became instructor in the Central Flying School of the R.F.C. as Flight Commander; promoted to Squadron Commander in 1913.

Commanded 5th and 6th Brigades in France in 1916. Appointed D.G. of Military Aeronautics at the W.O. in 1917, and a Member of the Air Council. Became Major-General, R.A.F., in 1918 and G.O.C. R.A.F. in the field. Several times mentioned in dispatches. Received the D.S.O. in 1915, the C.M.G., in 1917, and the C.V.O. in 1918. He was at Rhine H.Q. in command in 1919, and later appointed to permanent commission in the R.A.F. as Air Vice-Marshal.

SECTION 1. K R.A.F. Leaders 46

Sir John became A.O.C., Southern Area, R.A.F., and A.O.C., Inland Area, in 1920. In India in 1922 and later became A.O.C., Iraq, remaining in Iraq until 1924. In 1923 he was promoted Air Marshal. In 1924 he was at the Air Ministry, and next year was appointed A.O.C.-in-C., Air Defence of Great Britain. Visited Australia and New Zealand in 1928 to report on Air Forces and made recommendations for future development. Appointed Air Member for Personnel on the Air Council in 1929, becoming Air Chief Marshal. Next year appointed Chief of the Air Staff. Retired in 1933 with rank of Marshal of the Royal Air Force. Received the K.C.B., 1919, and G.C.B. in 1930.

TRENCHARD, Marshal of the Royal Air Force The Viscount, G.C.B., G.C.V.O., D.S.O. 
Born 1873; entered Army as 2nd Lieut., Royal Scots Fusiliers, in 1893. For some time in India, and then served in South Africa from 1899 till 1902. With West African Frontier Force from 1904 to 1906, and later commanded North Nigeria Regiment. Graduated as a pilot in 1912. Instructor at Central Flying school, and in 1913 became Asst. Commdt. In August, 1914, apptd. O.C., R.F.C. (Military Wing) at home, with rank of Lt.-Colonel.
Transferred to France as Wing Commander in Nov., 1914, on the creation of the First Wing of St. Omer; in Aug., 1915, he became O.C. 1st Brigade. The following March saw his promotion to G.O.C. the R.F.C. in France, with rank of Major-General. On formation of Royal Air Force and Air Ministry, in Jan., 1918, he became Chief of the Air Staff. Formed and commanded the Independent Air Force.
Returned to the Air Ministry early in 1919 as Chief of the Air Staff (a post he relinquished in 1929) and took up task of reorganizing the R.A.F. Later that year he was granted a permanent commission as Air Marshal; in April, 1922, he became Air Chief Marshal; on Jan. 1, 1927, he became the first Marshal of the Royal Air Force. Chief Commissioner of the Metropolitan Police, 1931–35.
Created a Baronet in 1919, a Peer in 1930, and a Viscount in 1936. He had been awarded the D.S.O. in 1906 and received the C.B. in Jan., 1914. Created a G.C.B., 1924.

Air Chief Marshals

BOWHILL, Air Chief Marshal Sir Frederick William, K.C.B., C.M.G., D.S.O. 
Born 1880; educated at Blackheath School and in H.M.S. "Worcester." Midshipman in the R.N.R., 1898–1904 (acting Sub-Lieutenant, 1904; Lieutenant, 1911). Flying Officer in R.F.C. (Naval Wing), April, 1913. Served with distinction in the R.N.A.S. Commands included Aircraft Carrier "Empress," whence seaplanes raided Cuxhaven on Dec. 25, 1914. In 1916 was in Mesopotamia, and later commanded Air Unit in East Africa. For his "invaluable services" as C.O. of the R.N.A.S. here he received the D.S.O. Shortly after formation of Royal Air Force in 1918 he was appointed to command No. 62 Wing in Aegean Group. In 1919 received a bar to D.S.O., and was awarded C.M.G. Given permanent commission as Wing Commander in R.A.F. in 1919, and appointed Chief Staff Officer to secret "Z" expedition against Mad Mullah in Somaliland. Twelve times mentioned in dispatches.
Subsequently served in Egypt and Iraq. In 1929 became Director of Organization and Staff Duties at Air Ministry. In May, 1931, was appointed A.O.C., Fighting Area, Air Defence of Great Britain. Two years later he became Air Member for Personnel. Sir Frederick Bowhill became A.O.C., Coastal Command, in Aug., 1937. He had received C.B. in 1935 and K.C.B. in 1936. Promoted Air Commodore, 1928; Air Vice-Marshal, 1931; Air Marshal, 1936; and Air Chief Marshal, 1939. G.B.E. in 1941.

BROOKE-POPHAM, Air Chief Marshal Sir Robert, G.C.V.O., K.C.B., C.M.G., D.S.O., A.F.C. 
Born 1878; educated at Haileybury and the Royal Military College, Sandhurst. Commissioned in the Oxfordshire Light Infantry in 1898. In 1911 he qualified as pilot, and in 1912 joined the Air Battalion, Royal Engineers. When the R.F.C. was formed he was posted to Salisbury Plain as instructor. In Nov., 1914, he became Wing Commander, R.F.C., and Tempy. Lieut-Colonel. Served in France between 1915 and 1918. Commanded a Wing, and was later employed on Staff duties. In 1918 he became Tempy. Brigadier-General, R.A.F. Appointed Controller, Technical Dept., Ministry of Munitions (Aircraft Production) in 1919 (Group Captain in the R.A.F.). Later promoted Air Commodore and appointed Director of Research.

In 1921 he became first commandant of R.A.F. Staff College. In 1924 was promoted Air Vice-Marshal, and in 1926 became A.O.C., Fighter Area. Took over Iraq Command in Nov., 1928. In 1931 became Commandant of Imperial Defence College, with rank of Air Marshal; appointed A.O.C.-in-C., Air Defence of Great Britain, 1933. Promoted Air Chief Marshal in 1935, and became Inspector-General of the R.A.F. Retired, 1937, to become Gov.-Gen. of Kenya. Sept., 1939, rejoined as chief R.A.F. member of Air Mission to Canada. Later, Air Mission to S. Africa. C.-in-C., Far East, Nov., 1940–Dec., 1941.

BURNETT, Air Chief Marshal Sir Charles Stuart, K.C.B., C.B.E., D.S.O. 
Born 1882; educated at Bedford Grammar School. Enlisted Imperial Yeomanry, 1900; 2nd Lieut., Highland Light Infantry, 1901: served with I.Y. and West African Frontier Force (Lieut., 1907). Commission in R.F.C. in 1914. Flight Commander, 1915 (posted to No. 17 Squadron, Middle East). Became Squadron Commander, 1916 (posted to Nos. 40, 36 and 12 Squadrons). Promoted Wing Commander (posted to H.Q., No. 5 Wing, Palestine, in 1917), serving until 1919, when he was apptd. Acting Brig.-General and granted a perm. commission as Wing Commander (posted to H.Q., Middle East, to command). D.S.O. in 1918; C.B.E. in 1919. Given command of Palestine Brigade H.Q., No. 31 Wing, Mesopotamia, in 1920. Next year promoted Group Captain and posted to No. 29 Group H.Q. to command. D.D. of Operations and Intelligence in 1923; apptd. 1927 to command Central Flying School (awarded C.B.). In 1929 Air Commodore and Chief Staff Officer, H.Q., Iraq. Air Vice-Marshal, 1931. Apptd. A.O.C., Iraq, 1932–35; 1935, A.O.C.-in-C., Inland Area. Air Marshal, 1936; A.O.C.-in-C., Training Command. Awarded K.C.B. Inspector-General, July, 1939; Chief of Air Staff, R.A.A.F., 1940. Air Chief Marshal. Returned England, April, 1942.

COURTNEY, Air Chief Marshal Sir Christopher L. See page 50.

DOUGLAS, Air Chief Marshal Sir Sholto. See page 51.

DOWDING, Air Chief Marshal Sir Hugh Caswall Tremenheere, G.C.B., G.C.V.O., C.M.G. 
Born 1882; educated at Winchester and Royal Military Academy, Woolwich. Entered Army as 2nd Lieut. in 1900 and served with Royal Artillery until 1914, when he was attached for duty to the R.F.C., having qualified as a pilot in 1913. Served with the Air Force in France, 1914–18, and commanded various squadrons. Mentioned in dispatches and received the C.B. and C.M.G. Group Captain, R.A.F., in 1919, commanding No. 16 and No. 1 Groups. After promotion to Air Commodore, was Chief Staff Officer in the Inland Area (1922) and in Iraq (1924). Director of Training at the Air Ministry, 1926. Promoted Air Vice-Marshal and appointed Tempy. A.O.C. in Transjordan and Palestine, 1929. Later appointed to command the Fighter Area, Air Defence of Great Britain. Member of the Air Council for Supply and Research, 1930–36. Promoted Air Marshal in 1933, and received the K.C.B. In July, 1936, Sir Hugh was appointed A.O.C.-in-C., Fighter Command post held till 1940. Early 1937 promoted to Air Chief Marshal, and later received G.C.V.O. and for war services the G.C.B. On retired list Oct. 21, 1941. From Nov., 1941, to July, 1942, reviewed R.A.F. Establishments for economics and then retired.

FREEMAN, Air Chief Marshal Sir Wilfred Rhodes, G.C.B., D.S.O., M.C. 
Born 1888; educated at Eastbourne, Rugby, and Royal Military College, Sandhurst. 2nd Lieut., Manchester Regt., 1908 (Lieut., 1912). Flying Officer R.F.C., April, 1914. Went to France in Aug. with 2nd Squadron; Flight Commander, 1915, and Capt. in Manchester Regt. Promoted Squadron Commander, R.F.C., later in 1915 and Wing Commander in 1916. Commanded No. 10 Wing in France. Promoted Brevet Major (early 1917) and later commanded No. 9 Wing. Lieut.-Colonel, April, 1918, and Group Commander i/c No. 2 Training Group, S.E. Area. Three times mentioned in dispatches, gaining M.C. and D.S.O. In 1919 was given perm. commission as Lieut.-Colonel (Wing Commander). Promoted to Group Captain (1923). Apptd. D.D. of Operations & Intelligence, 1927. Became Air Commodore, 1929. Commander, H.Q., Transjordan & Palestine, 1930. Air Vice-Marshal, 1933; Commandant of R.A.F. Staff College, 1934. Air Member for Research & Development in 1936. Air Marshal, 1937, and Tempy. Air Chief Marshal, 1940. Vice Chief of Air Staff, 1940–42. Received C.B., 1932, K.C.B., 1937, G.C.B., 1942. Chief Executive Ministry of Aircraft Production. Oct., 1942.

R.A.F. Leaders

JOUBERT DE LA FERTÉ, Air Chief Marshal Sir Philip Bennet, K.C.B., C.M.G., D.S.O.
Inspector-General of the R.A.F.

Born 1887; educated at Harrow and the Royal Military Academy, Woolwich. Served nearly 6 years in R.A. before being seconded for flying duties in 1913 with rank of Flying Officer. During war of 1914–18 he saw service in France and Egypt (promoted Flight Commander) and later in Italy. Awarded D.S.O. and C.M.G., and mentioned in dispatches seven times.

Granted perm. commission in R.A.F. as Wing Commander, 1919. Promoted Group Captain, 1922, and following year became D.D. of Personnel; was Director of Manning, 1924. From 1926 until 1929 was on special duty list as instructor at Imperial Defence College. Promoted Air Commodore (1929) and apptd. to command No. 23 Group H.Q. In 1930 was apptd. Commandant of R.A.F. Staff College, and as Air Vice-Marshal became A.O.C. H.Q., Fighting Area, in 1934. Promoted Air Marshal and became A.O.C.-in-C., Coastal Command, in 1936; A.O.C. in India, 1937; created K.C.B., 1938. In Feb., 1940, was attd. to Dept. of Chief of Air Staff as Adviser on Combined Operations. Promoted Tempy. Air Chief Marshal in 1941; A.O.C.-in-C., Coastal Command, June, 1941–Nov., 1942. Appointed Inspector-General of the R.A.F., Nov., 1942.

LONGMORE, Air Chief Marshal Sir Arthur Murray, G.C.B., D.S.O.

Born 1885; educated in H.M.S. "Britannia." Commissioned Sub-Lieut. in R.N., 1904; in 1912 he joined the Naval Wing of the R.F.C. as Squadron Commander, having qualified as pilot in 1911. Instructor at the Central Flying School, 1912. Placed in command of No. 1 R.N.A.S. Squadron, Dunkirk, he continued with the R.N.A.S. until 1916, reverting then to sea service (H.M.S. "Tiger"). Later that year he returned to the R.N.A.S. and, after promotion to Wing Captain in 1917, joined staff of the C.-in-C., Mediterranean. In May, 1918, was given command of Adriatic Group. Received high commendation for work at Flying School and great ability as pilot and instructor. Awarded D.S.O., appointed C.B. in 1925, and promoted K.C.B. in 1935. In March, 1941, he received the G.C.B. After the war of 1914–18 Sir Arthur saw service in Iraq and as Commander of No. 7 Group in Britain. In 1925 he became Director of Equipment. Appointed, in 1929, A.O.C., R.A.F., Cranwell, where he remained until, in 1933, he became A.O.C., Inland Area. In 1934 he was placed in command of the Coastal Area. Promoted Air Marshal in 1935, he was Commandant of the Imperial Defence College until, in July, 1939, he took over the Training Command. Nov., 1939, promoted Air Chief Marshal. May, 1940, became A.O.C.-in-C., Middle East Command. July, 1941, Inspector-General, R.A.F. Retired March 1, 1942.

LUDLOW-HEWITT, Air Chief Marshal Sir Edgar Rainey, K.C.B., C.M.G., D.S.O., M.C.
Inspector-General of the R.A.F.

Born 1886; educated at Radley College, Eastman's School and the Royal Military College, Sandhurst. Appointed to the R.F.C. from the Royal Irish Rifles in Aug., 1914, having qualified as a pilot in the same month (R.Ae.C. certificate No. 887). Served in France with intervals from March, 1915, until the end of the war. Received the C.M.G., D.S.O. and M.C., and mentioned in dispatches on a number of occasions. Permanent commission in the R.A.F. with the rank of Wing Cmdr. in 1919.

Subsequently he was employed at the Air Ministry for several years (D.D. of Training and Organization; Air Secretary to the Secretary for Air; President of the Aerodrome Board). He was Air Aide-de-Camp to King George V from 1921 to 1923. From May, 1926, until Sept., 1930, he was Commandant of the R.A.F. Staff College. Received the C.B. in 1928, and the K.C.B. five years later. In Oct., 1930, he was appointed to the Iraq Command.

Sir Edgar Ludlow-Hewitt was appointed Director of Operations and Intelligence, and Deputy Chief of Air Staff at the Air Ministry in Feb., 1933. He commanded the R.A.F. in India from March, 1935, until Sept, 1937, leaving India to come to England as A.O.C.-in-C., Bomber Command. He had been promoted to Air Commodore in 1923; to Air Vice-Marshal in 1930; to Air Marshal in 1934; and became Air Chief Marshal in 1937. In April, 1940, he left the Bomber Command to become Inspector-General of the R.A.F., with the rank of Air Chief Marshal.

R.A.F. Leaders

PORTAL, Air Chief Marshal Sir Charles Frederick Algernon, G.C.B., D.S.O., M.C. Chief of the Air Staff.

Born 1893; educated at Winchester and Christ Church, Oxford. Enlisted in Royal Engineers as dispatch rider in Aug., 1914, and in September was mentioned in the first dispatches of Sir John French; later gazetted 2nd Lieut. Seconded to R.F.C. as observer in 1915, with rank of Flying Officer, he graduated as pilot at the Central Flying School a year later, and on one flight he encountered the machine of the German Air Ace, Immelmann; taking a pot shot with a Winchester automatic rifle, he hit the aircraft. Lieut. Portal served with many Squadrons both at home and abroad. Awarded M.C. and D.S.O. in 1917, and next year received a bar to D.S.O. At the age of twenty-five he was made a Colonel.

Granted a permanent commission in the R.A.F. in 1919, with rank of Squadron Leader, his first squadron won the Laurence Minot bombing trophy, he himself aiming. In the same year he assumed command of No. 59 Wing, Cranwell. In 1923 he was posted to the Air Ministry for Staff duties. He commanded No. 7 (Bomber) Squadron in 1927. In 1930 he was again posted to the Air Ministry for Air Staff duties, remaining until he assumed command at Aden in 1934. Promoted Air Vice-Marshal in July, 1937, in August he became Director of Organization. In Feb., 1939, he was appointed Air Member for Personnel, and became Air Marshal. Apptd. A.O.C.-in-C., Bomber Command, in March, 1940, receiving the K.C.B.; in Oct. he was promoted Air Chief Marshal and Chief of the Air Staff. G.C.B., June, 1942.

TEDDER, Air Chief Marshal Sir Arthur William. See page 53.

Air Marshals

BABINGTON, Air Marshal Sir Philip, K.C.B., M.C., A.F.C. A.O.C.-in-C., Flying Tr. Comd.

Born 1894; educated at Eton. Gazetted 2nd Lieut. in Hampshire Regt., 1914, and later seconded to the R.F.C. Commanded Nos. 46 and 141 Squadrons in France, 1914-18. Awarded M.C. in 1916 for distinguished service in the field, and the A.F.C. in 1919. Twice mentioned in dispatches.

In 1919 he was granted a permanent commission in the Royal Air Force, with the rank of Squadron Leader, and served in the Middle East both on operational and air staff duties. On his return to England in 1922 he was posted to the Air Ministry for Personnel Staff duties. Commanded No. 19 (Fighter) Squadron in 1924. Promoted Wing Commander in 1925, and commanded No. 5 F.T.S. (Sealand) from that date until 1928. Went to H.Q., Inland Area, for Personnel Staff duties, 1928, and next year took up a similar post at H.Q., Middle East. Asst. Commandant, R.A.F. College, Cranwell, 1931; apptd. Group Captain in 1932. In 1936 he was appointed Director of Postings; promoted Air Commodore later that year. Promoted Air Vice-Marshal, 1939; Air Member for Personnel, 1940; Air Marshal, Aug., 1942. C.B., 1941. K.C.B., 1943. A.O.C.-in-C. Flying Training Command.

BABINGTON, Air Marshal Sir John Tremayne, K.C.B., C.B.E., D.S.O. A.O.C.-in-C., Technical Training Command.

Born 1891; educated at Osborne and Dartmouth, entering Royal Navy as Midshipman in 1908. Commissioned Sub-Lieut., 1911; attached to Naval Wing of R.F.C. in 1913, serving during the war of 1914-18 in the R.N.A.S. and R.F.C. Won the D.S.O. for his part in attack on Zeppelin sheds at Friedrichshaven in November, 1914. Mentioned in dispatches, 1915.

Transferred to R.A.F., 1918; next year was granted permanent commission (Squadron Leader). Member of the Aeronautical Commission of Control in Germany; also on the Inter-Allied Commission of Control, Paris, 1920. Air Staff duties at No. 7 Group and No. 3 Group H.Q., in 1922; course at R.A.F. Staff College, 1924. At the end of 1925 he went to Iraq for Personnel Staff duties. Returning in 1927, he was appointed to command of R.A.F. Base, Gosport. He served again in Iraq, and then, in 1929, was posted to Air Ministry for Air Staff duties. In same year was Air Representative to League of Nations. Became A.O.C., R.A.F. Station, Halton, in December, 1934; commanded No. 24 (Training) Group, July, 1936-38. Apptd. A.O.C., H.Q., Far East, in 1938. Wing Commander, 1922; Group Captain, 1930; and Air Commodore, 1934 (awarded C.B.E.); promoted Air Vice-Marshal, July, 1937; C.B., 1939. In 1941 became A.O.C.-in-C., Technical Training Command, with acting rank of Air Marshal. K.C.B., June, 1942.

R.A.F. Leaders

BARRATT Air Marshal Sir Arthur Sheridan, K.C.B., C.M.G., M.C. *Air Officer Commanding in Chief, Army Cooperation Command.*

Born 1891 ; educated at Clifton and the Royal Military Academy, Woolwich. Joined R.A. in 1910 ; graduated from Central Flying School as pilot in 1914, going to France as Flying Officer with No. 3 Squadron on Army Coop. duties. Awarded M.C. in 1916 and four times mentioned in dispatches. Attached R.A.F. H.Q., Cologne, 1918–19. C.M.G., 1919. Later went to Air Ministry (Squadron Leader). In 1926 Commandant of School of Army Cooperation ; 1927, on staff of G.O.C., Shanghai, and went to No. 22 Group H.Q. After a period as Chief Instructor at R.A.F. Staff College, he commanded No. 1 Group in India. Director of Staff Duties at Air Ministry in 1934, two years later he became Commandant of Staff College. Made Air Vice-Marshal in 1936, was promoted Air Marshal in July, 1939. Selected as A.O.C., India, but in Sept., 1939, became Principal R.A.F. Liaison Officer with the French Army and Air Force. In 1940 he became A.O.C.-in-C., British Air Forces in France. After the evacuation he was made K.C.B., and later apptd. to Army Cooperation Command.

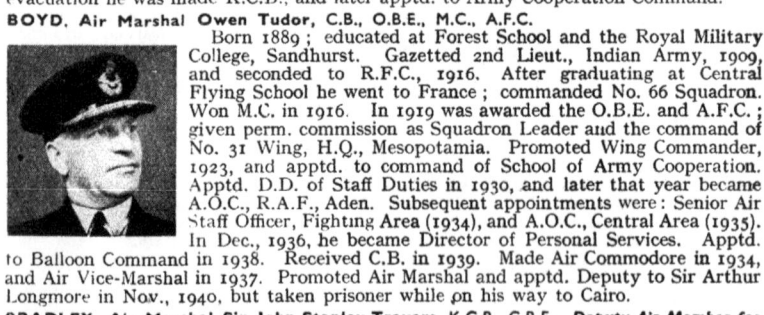

BOYD, Air Marshal Owen Tudor, C.B., O.B.E., M.C., A.F.C.

Born 1889 ; educated at Forest School and the Royal Military College, Sandhurst. Gazetted 2nd Lieut., Indian Army, 1909, and seconded to R.F.C., 1916. After graduating at Central Flying School he went to France ; commanded No. 66 Squadron. Won M.C. in 1916. In 1919 was awarded the O.B.E. and A.F.C. ; given perm. commission as Squadron Leader and the command of No. 31 Wing, H.Q., Mesopotamia. Promoted Wing Commander, 1923, and apptd. to command of School of Army Cooperation. Apptd. D.D. of Staff Duties in 1930, and later that year became A.O.C., R.A.F., Aden. Subsequent appointments were : Senior Air Staff Officer, Fighting Area (1934), and A.O.C., Central Area (1935). In Dec., 1936, he became Director of Personal Services. Apptd. to Balloon Command in 1938. Received C.B. in 1939. Made Air Commodore in 1934, and Air Vice-Marshal in 1937. Promoted Air Marshal and apptd. Deputy to Sir Arthur Longmore in Nov., 1940, but taken prisoner while on his way to Cairo.

BRADLEY Air Marshal Sir John Stanley Travers, K.C.B., C.B.E. *Deputy Air Member for Supply and Organization.*

Born 1888; educated privately. From University of London O.T.C. he was gazetted 2nd Lieut., 7th Batt. East Yorks Regt. and served during war of 1914–18 with Machine Gun Corps. In 1918 was apptd. Major in the R.A.F. and posted to Armament School, Uxbridge.

Granted perm. commission in 1919 (Squadron Leader) ; awarded O.B.E. and posted to H.Q., South-Eastern Area. In 1921–25 served in Middle East, Palestine and Iraq. In 1926 was promoted Wing Commander and posted to H.Q., Air Defence of Great Britain for Staff Duties. Posted to Station H.Q., Northolt, to command (1930) ; promoted Group Captain (1931). Posted to Air Ministry, 1934. Became Air Commodore and Director of Equipment, 1935. Promoted Air Vice-Marshal in 1938 and became A.O.C. Maintenance Command. Acting Air Marshal, Nov., 1940. C.B.E., 1941 K.C.B. 1942 Deputy Air Member for Supply and Organization, Oct. 1942.

COURTNEY, Air Chief Marshal Sir Christopher Lloyd, K.C.B., C.B.E., D.S.O. *Air Member for Supply and Organization.*

Born 1890 ; educated at Bradfield and in H.M.S. " Britannia." Sub-Lieut. in the R.N., 1909 (Lieut., 1911). Joined R.F.C. (Naval Wing) in 1913 as Flying Officer and became Flight Commander the same year. Served with No. 4 Sqdrn. of the R.N.A.S. between 1914 and 1917. Transferred to R.A.F. in April, 1918. At end of war was in command of 11th Brigade, Independent Force, France (Brig.-General). Awarded D.S.O. and C.B.E.

D.D. of Equipment, 1919 (Wing Commander). In India 1920–24, going to R.A.F. Staff College as instructor, remaining until 1929 (Group Captain). Returned to Air Ministry as D.D. of Operations & Intelligence. Went to Iraq in 1930 as Chief Staff Officer ; made C.B. in 1932. Director of Training in 1932 ; Director of Staff Duties in 1934 ; and Director of Operations & Deputy Chief of Air Staff in 1935. In 1937 he was given Iraq Command. Air Marshal in 1939 ; apptd. to Reserve Command ; created K.C.B. Air Member for Supply & Organization, 1940. Promoted temp. Air Chief Marshal, Jan. 1942.

R.A.F. Leaders

DOUGLAS, Air Chief Marshal Sir Sholto, K.C.B., M.C., D.F.C. *Air Officer Commanding in Chief, Middle East.*

Born 1893 ; educated at Tonbridge School and Oxford. Apptd. 2nd Lieut., R.F.A., in Aug., 1914, and posted as Observer Officer to No. 2 Squadron, R.F.C., in France in Jan., 1915. Became Flying Officer in July, and later commanded Nos. 43 and 84 Squadrons and No. 22 Wing H.Q., attaining rank of Lieut.-Colonel. Awarded M.C. & D.F.C., and three times mentioned in dispatches.

In 1920 was granted a perm. commission as Squadron Leader. Filled various staff and administrative appointments. Commanded the R.A.F. Station at North Weald in 1928, and subsequently served in Middle East. Became Director of Staff Duties at Air Ministry in 1936 ; apptd. Asst. Chief of Air Staff in 1938, and Deputy Chief in 1940. Promoted Wing Commander in 1925 ; Group Captain in 1932 ; Air Commodore in 1935 ; and Air Vice-Marshal in Jan., 1938. Air Marshal, 1940, and apptd. A.O.C., Fighter Command. Received C.B., 1940, and K.C.B. in 1941. Air Chief Marshal, July, 1942, apptd. A.O.C.-in-C. Middle East, Nov., 1942.

DRUMMOND, Air Marshal Roy Maxwell, C.B., D.S.O., O.B.E., M.C.

Born 1894 at Perth, W.A. ; educated at Scotch College, W.A., and Perth Technical College. Private, A.A. Medical Corps, Sept., 1914. 2nd Lieut., R.F.C., 1916, attd. Australian squadrons in Palestine. Flt. Cmdr. and Tmpy. Capt., 1917. Captain " A " R.A.F. 1918 ; permanent commission, 1919 ; M.C. 1917 ; D.S.O. March, 1918 (bar, July) ; mentioned dispatches, 1919.

Apptd. to H.Q., Middle East, for duty on aerial routes in May 1919 ; in following Dec. he assumed command of " H " Unit in the Sudan. For services in command of expedition against Garjak Nuers he received the O.B.E. (1921). Specially commended for a flight in a D.H.9, Cairo to Nasser, 1920. At School of Army Cooperation, Inland Area, 1921 ; Staff Course, R.A.F. Staff College, 1922 ; at Air Ministry for Staff duties, 1923. Promoted Squadron Leader. Attd. R.A.A.F. on special duty 1925-9. Wing Commander, 1931 ; in command of station H.Q., Tangmere. Returned to Air Ministry in 1933. In command at Northolt, 1936 ; Group Captain, 1937 ; went to Middle East as Senior Air S.O. at H.Q. Air Commodore in 1939 ; Acting Air Vice-Marshal, 1940. In June, 1941, he was apptd. Deputy A.O.C.-in-C., R.A.F., Middle East, with acting rank of Air Marshal. Created C.B., 1941.

GARROD, Air Marshal Alfred Guy Roland, C.B., O.B.E., M.C., D.F.C. *Air Member for Training.*

Born 1891 ; educated at Bradfield and University Coll., Oxford. Commissioned in 3rd Batt., Leics. Regt., Aug., 1914 ; seconded to R.F.C. as Flying Officer in 1915 ; served in France ; awarded M.C. in 1915 and D.F.C. in 1919 ; three times mentioned in dispatches.

In 1919 received perm. commission as Squadron Leader ; apptd. to H.Q., No. 29 Group, as Staff Officer ; posted to School of Army Cooperation, 1922 ; promoted Wing Commander, 1925. Apptd. to command of North Weald Station, 1927 ; in Iraq for Staff operational duties, 1931 ; promoted Group Captain, 1932, and received O.B.E. Apptd. D.D. of Organization at the Air Ministry, 1934. Promoted Air Commodore in 1936 and posted to H.Q., No. 23 Training Group, as tempy. A.O.C. Became A.O.C., Armament Group, in Feb., 1937 ; in March, 1938, was apptd. to Air Ministry for tempy. duty as Director of Equipment. Air Vice-Marshal, April 1, 1939 ; Acting Air Marshal in July, 1940, when he was apptd. Air Member for Training. Created C.B., 1941.

GOSSAGE, Air Marshal Sir Ernest Leslie, K.C.B., C.V.O., D.S.O., M.C. *Air Officer Commanding, Balloon Command.*

Born 1891 ; educated at Rugby and Trinity College, Cambridge. Commissioned in R.A., 1910 ; seconded to R.F.C., 1915. Served in France ; awarded M.C. in 1915, and D.S.O. in 1919.

Perm. commission as Squadron Leader, 1919. On directing staff of Staff College, Camberley, 1925. D.D. of Staff Duties at Air Ministry, 1928-30. Senior Air Staff Officer, H.Q., Air Defence of Great Britain, 1931-34. Air Commodore, 1932 ; Senior Air Staff Officer, Iraq, 1934. A.O.C., Aden, 1935. Air Vice-Marshal, 1936. A.O.C., No. 11 (Fighter) Group, 1936–Feb., 1940 ; Inspector-General of the R.A.F., and, later, Air Member for Personnel. Promoted tempy. Air Marshal in Sept., 1940, and apptd. to Balloon Command in Oct. Created C.B. and C.V.O., 1937 ; made K.C.B., 1941.

R.A.F. Leaders

HARRIS, Air Marshal Sir Arthur Travers, K.C.B., O.B.E., A.F.C. A.O.C.-in-C., Bomber Command.

Born 1892; educated at Gore Court, Sittingbourne, and All Hallows, Honiton. Joined 1st Rhodesian Regt. as bugler in Oct., 1914. Apptd. 2nd Lieut. on probation, R.F.C., in 1915, serving in France. Won promotion rapidly and in April, 1918, became Major, R.A.F. In the same year he was awarded the A.F.C.

He was granted a permanent commission as Squadron Leader in 1919 and served in succession in Iraq, the Middle East and at home. Promoted Wing Commander, 1927; Group Captain, 1933, he was advanced to Air Commodore and apptd. to command No. 4 (Bomber) Group in 1937. Visiting America next year as a member of the Air Ministry Commission, on his return in July he was apptd. to command H.Q. Palestine and Transjordan. Air Vice-Marshal, July, 1939; appointed to a Bomber Group, September, 1939; C.B., 1940. Air Marshal (Actg.), June, 1941, and seconded for special duty. Appointed A.O.C.-in-C., Bomber Command, Feb., 1942. K.C.B. June, 1942.

HILL, Air Marshal Roderic Maxwell, C.B., M.C., A.F.C.

Born 1894; educated at Bradfield and University College, London. Enlisted in Royal Fusiliers, Oct., 1914, and received commission in Nov. Joined R.F.C. in 1916, serving in France and at home for the remainder of the war. Awarded M.C. and A.F.C.

Obtained perm. commission as Major (Squadron Leader) in 1919; awarded bar to A.F.C. in 1922. Went to Iraq in 1924 to command No. 45 (Bomber) Squadron. Att. H.Q., Middle East, for Air Staff Duties, 1926. Returned to Gt. Britain, 1927, as instructor, R.A.F. Staff College. In 1931 apptd. chief instructor, Oxford University Air Sqdrn. Air A.D.C. to King, 1934–36. Promoted Group Captain, 1932; Air Commodore, 1936; went to H.Q., Palestine and Transjordan, to command. In 1938 he was apptd. Director of Technical Development; in Sept., 1940, he became Assistant to the Director-General of Research and Development. Air Vice-Marshal, 1939; Acting Air Marshal, 1940; Director-General of Research and Development. Created C.B., 1941.

LEIGH-MALLORY, Air Marshal Sir Trafford Leigh, K.C.B., D.S.O. A.O.C.-in-C., Fighter Command.

Born 1892; educated at Haileybury and Magdalene College, Cambridge. Served in European war, 1914–1918, received D.S.O., 1919, and was mentioned in dispatches. Granted permanent commission in R.A.F. as Squadron Leader, 1919; promoted Wing Commander, Jan., 1925. Was Commandant School of Army Cooperation, 1927–30; Instructor at Staff College, Camberley, 1930–31. Deputy-Director of Staff Duties at the Air Ministry, 1931–34. Promoted Group Captain, Jan., 1932. At Imperial Defence College, 1934. Commanded No. 2 Flying Training School, Digby, Lincoln, 1935. Air Commodore, Jan., 1936. Senior A.S.O., Iraq, 1936–37. Promoted Air Vice-Marshal, Nov., 1938. Air Marshal, July, 1942. Appointed Air Officer Commanding in Chief, Fighter Command, Nov., 1942. K.C.B., 1943.

LINNELL, Air Marshal Francis John, C.B., O.B.E.

Born 1892; educated All Saints, Bloxham. Entered R.N.R., Sept., 1914, as Warrant Telegraphist. Served in France and Belgium; Flight Sub-Lieutenant, R.N.A.S., May, 1915; Flight-Lieutenant, 1916; Flight-Commander, 1917. Served in Grand Fleet, 1915–19.

Permanent commission as Flight-Lieutenant in 1919. Served at H.Q., Coastal Command, 1920, and at Air Ministry Signals Division from 1921. Promoted Squadron Leader 1924, became first Chief Signal Officer A.D.G.B., Dec., 1925.

Commanded R.A.F. Base, Malta, 1931–32, and No. 99 (Bomber) Squadron and R.A.F. Station, Mildenhall. Appointed War Organization Branch, Air Ministry, 1935, becoming D.D.W.O., 1936. Group Captain, January, 1937, and Air Commodore, July, 1939. Posted Bomber Command H.Q. as Air Officer in Charge of Administration, Sept., 1939 (Acting Air Vice-Marshal). Air Vice-Marshal, Jan., 1941. Assistant Chief of Air Staff (T), Feb., 1941. In June, 1941, became Controller of Research and Development in the Ministry of Aircraft Production (Acting Air Marshal). Member of the Air Council and of the Aircraft Supply Council.

R.A.F. Leaders

PECK, Air Marshal Richard Hallam, C.B., O.B.E. 
Born 1893 ; educated at St. Paul's School and Brasenose College, Oxford. Gazetted 2nd Lieut., East Surrey Regt., 1914 ; seconded as Flying Officer to R.F.C. in 1916 ; served in France and at home. Promoted Temp. Lieut., 1916 ; Flt.-Cmdr. & Temp. Captain, 1916 ; Squadron Cmdr. & Temp. Major, 1917 ; Major, 1918. O.B.E., 1919. In 1919 he was granted permanent commission (Squadron Leader) and posted to School of Wireless Telephony. He proceeded to Group H.Q., Iraq, in 1921 (operations in Kurdistan ; mentioned in dispatches) ; returning to England in 1924, he was attached to Depot, Inland Area. Promoted Wing Commander in 1927, he was apptd. to Air Ministry (duty with Dept. of Chief of Air Staff). Posted to H.Q., Coastal Area, 1930 ; promoted Group Captain in 1932 and posted to No. 3 Flying Training School. He returned to Air Ministry in 1933, after service with No. 1 Air Defence Group H.Q. In 1936 he went to H.Q., India, for duty as Senior Staff Officer (promoted Air Commodore). He was appointed Director of Operations at the Air Ministry in March, 1939, and in the following February became Assistant Chief of Air Staff (Operations & Intelligence). Air Vice-Marshal, January, 1939; C.B., January, 1941 ; advanced to the acting rank of Air Marshal, July, 1941.

PEIRSE, Air Marshal Sir Richard Edmund Charles, K.C.B., D.S.O., A.F.C. *A.O.C.-in-C., India.* 
Born 1892 ; educated on H.M.S. "Conway" and at King's College. Served during war of 1914-18 with R.N.A.S., which he entered while a Sub-Lieut., R.N.V.R. ; awarded D.S.O. in 1915 for attacks on German submarine bases at Ostend and Zeebrugge. In 1919 he received the A.F.C. Until the end of 1936 he held many important posts in the R.A.F., including D.D. of Operations & Intelligence, and A.O.C. in Palestine and Transjordan. In Jan., 1937, he became Deputy Chief of the Air Staff ; he was made Acting Air Marshal and an additional Member of the Air Council in Nov., 1939. Promoted Vice-Chief of Air Staff in April, 1940, to Bomber Command Oct., 1940. K.C.B. 1940. Special appointment Feb. 1942 ; A.O.C.-in-C. India, March 1942.

TEDDER, Air Chief Marshal Sir Arthur William, G.C.B. 
Born 1890 ; educated at Whitgift School and Magdalene College, Cambridge. Entered Dorset Regt. as 2nd Lieut., 1913 (Captain, March, 1916). Seconded to R.F.C. in June, 1916. Served in France and Middle East and held command of several R.F.C. Units. Twice mentioned in dispatches.
Granted perm. commission in R.A.F. (Squadron Leader), 1919 ; with R.A.F. at Constantinople, 1922 ; assumed command of No. 2 Flying Training School in 1924. Posted to Directorate of Training, Air Ministry, in 1927 ; assumed command of Air Armament School, 1932. In April, 1934, he became Director of Training. Apptd. A.O.C., Far East Command, 1936. Promoted Wing Commander in 1924, Group Captain in 1931, Air Commodore in 1934, and Air Vice-Marshal in 1937. In 1938 he became Director-General of Research and Development ; and in 1940 Deputy Air Member for Development and Production (Min. of Aircraft Production). Received the C.B. in 1937. Promoted tempy. Air Marshal, 1941. Air Chief Marshal, 1942. Air Officer Commanding-in-Chief, Middle East, June, 1941-Nov., 1942. Vice-Chief of Air Staff, Nov., 1942. K.C.B., Jan., 1942. G.C.B., Nov., 1942.

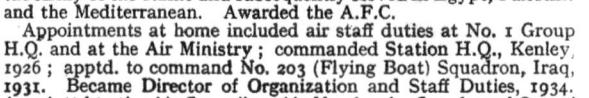

WELSH, Air Marshal Sir William Lawrie, K.C.B., D.S.C., A.F.C. 
Born 1891 ; joined R.N.A.S. from R.N.R. as Flight Sub-Lieut. in Nov., 1914. Served on aircraft carriers and in France. Transferred to R.A.F. in 1918, granted perm. commission (Squadron Leader) in 1919. For his services in France he received the D.S.C. and was mentioned in dispatches. Commanded a squadron with the Army of the Rhine and subsequently served in Egypt, Palestine and the Mediterranean. Awarded the A.F.C.
Appointments at home included air staff duties at No. 1 Group H.Q. and at the Air Ministry ; commanded Station H.Q., Kenley, 1926 ; apptd. to command No. 203 (Flying Boat) Squadron, Iraq, 1931. Became Director of Organization and Staff Duties, 1934. Appointed to the Air Council as Air Member for Supply and Organization in Sept., 1937, awarded C.B. Promoted Wing Commander, 1922 ; Group Captain, 1930 ; Air Commodore, 1934 ; and Air Vice-Marshal in 1937. Acting Air Marshal, May, 1940 ; A.O.C.-in-C., Technical Training Command, 1940-41. Awarded K.C.B., July, 1941. A.O.C.-in-C., Flying Training Command, July, 1941 ; A.O.C. of R.A.F. in N.W. Africa, Aug., 1942.

SECTION 1. K R.A.F. Leaders

WHITTINGHAM, Air Marshal Sir Harold Edward, K.B.E. *Director-General of Medical Services, R.A.F.*

Born 1887; educ. Christ's Hospital; Alan Glen's School, Glasgow; Edinburgh Univ. Professional qualifications include M.B.; Ch.B.; F.R.C.P.Edin.; F.R.F.P.S.Glas.; F.R.C.P.Lond. Commissioned in R.A.M.C. in 1916, Tempy. Lieut. Transferred to R.A.F. (Medical Branch) as Captain in 1918; 1919, permanent commission as Squadron Leader.

Carried out researches in Malta on sandfly fever, 1921–23. Commanded the R.A.F. Pathological Laboratory, Halton, and R.A.F. Central Medical Establishment; Director of Hygiene, Air Ministry, 1939. Wing Commander, 1923, Group Captain, 1932, and Air Commodore, 1936. Acting Air Vice-Marshal, 1940. Director-General of R.A.F. Medical Services in March, 1941, and Air Marshal. C.B.E., 1930; Honorary Physician to the King, 1938. K.B.E., July, 1941.

Late Appointments

DONALD, Air Marshal David Grahame, C.B., D.F.C., A.F.C. *A.O.C.-in-C., Maintenance Command.*

Born 1891; educated at Dulwich College and University College, Oxford. Served in R.N.A.S., 1914–18, joined R.A.F., 1918. He was awarded the D.F.C. and the A.F.C., 1919. Passed R.A.F. Staff College course 1923, and was an instructor in 1924. Commanded School of Naval Co-operation, 1929. Instructor R.A.F. Staff College, 1935, Chief Instructor Imperial Defence College, 1937. Appointed Director-General of Organization, 1940–41. Promoted Air Vice-Marshal, 1940. Awarded C.B., 1941. Deputy Air Member for Supply and Organization, 1941–42. Promoted Acting Air Marshal and appointed A.O.C.-in-C., Maintenance Command, Oct., 1942.

EVILL, Air Marshal Sir Douglas Claude Strathern, K.C.B., D.S.C., A.F.C.

Born 1892; educated at R.N. Colleges, Osborne and Dartmouth. Joined R.N.A.S. in 1914 and seconded to the R.A.F. in 1918. Received D.S.C. in 1916 and A.F.C. in 1919. Promoted Air Commodore 1936, he was appointed Senior Air Staff Officer, Bomber Command. He served as Senior Air Staff Officer with British Air Forces in France, and in 1940 became S.A.S.O., Fighter Command. Mentioned in despatches, Jan., 1941, and Jan., 1942. Received C.B., 1940. In Feb., 1942 he succeeded Air Marshal Harris as head of the R.A.F. delegation to Washington, and was granted acting rank of Air Marshal. Promoted Air Marshal (tempr.) May, 1942. K.C.B., 1943.

SLESSOR, Air Marshal John Cotesworth, C.B., D.S.O., M.C. *A.O.C.-in-C., Coastal Command.*

Born 1897; educated Haileybury. Served in R.F.C., 1915–18, awarded M.C. Permanent Comm. Flt.-Lt. in R.A.F., 1920. India, 1921–22. R.A.F. Staff College, 1924. Sdn. Ldr. 1925, Wing Commdr. 1932. Air Staff Air Ministry, 1928–30; Instructor Staff College, Camberley, 1931–34. India, 1935–37. A.O.C. No. 5 (Bomber) Group, and Group Captain, 1937; Director of Plans, Air Ministry, 1937–41. A.D.C. to the King, 1939. D.S.O., 1937; C.B., 1942. Air Commodore, 1939; Air Vice-Marshal, 1941. Promoted Air Marshal, Nov., 1942 and apptd. A.O.C.-in-C., Coastal Command.

SUTTON, Air Marshal Sir Bertine Entwisle, K.B.E., C.B., D.S.O., M.C. *Air Member for Personnel.*

Born 1886; educated Eton and University College, Oxford. Served in Westmorland and Cumberland Yeomanry, 1914–16; seconded to R.F.C. as Flying Officer Observer, 1916. Received D.S.O., 1917, and M.C., and was mentioned in despatches. O.B.E., 1919. Was Instructor at Imperial Defence College, 1929–32; took part in operations against Upper Mohmands, 1933. A.O.C. No. 1 Indian Group R.A.F., Peshawar, 1932–34. Senior A.S.O., R.A.F. India, 1934–36. Air Vice-Marshal 1937. A.O.C. Nos. 22 and 23 Groups, 1936–39, and 1939–40. Received C.B., 1939. Commandant R.A.F. Staff College, Nov., 1941. Air Marshal and K.B.E., 1942. Air Member for Personnel, Aug., 1942.

NOTE.—Air Marshals promoted Temp. or Acting Air Chief Marshals since the previous edition are entered under their original ranks.

The Women's Auxiliary Air Force
Its Purpose, Organization, and Service Conditions

How the W.A.A.F. came into being is here told, followed by tables of Groups, Trades and Rates of Pay, with a note on the commissioned ranks.

THE Women's Auxiliary Air Force, in which Her Majesty the Queen holds the rank of Commandant-in-Chief, was formed on June 28, 1939, by Royal Warrant. Miss K. J. Trefusis Forbes was appointed Director with the rank of Air Commandant.

Previously, the personnel of the Force had done duty in the Royal Air Force Companies of the Auxiliary Territorial Service, which was formed in July 1938. Experience showed, however, that there was considerable difference in the type of duty required from women working for the R.A.F. and for the army, and it was decided to make a complete severance between them. The khaki-clad pioneers of the R.A.F. Companies exchanged their uniform for one of Air Force blue.

The badges of rank of both officers and airwomen, as well as the style and colour of the uniform, conform with that of officers and airmen of the R.A.F. This was decided upon deliberately to show the close connexion of the W.A.A.F. with its parent fighting service. The uniform, which was submitted to, and approved by, the King, was first seen in public when a section of the W.A.A.F. took part in the National Defence Rally in Hyde Park in July 1939.

The W.A.A.F. is under the direct command of the R.A.F. Its object is to effect, when desirable, the substitution of women for Royal Air Force personnel in certain appointments and trades in the R.A.F. W.A.A.F. Flight Mechanics are able to fly in testing. The aim of the W.A.A.F. is, as far as possible, to enrol recruits who are qualified by their work in civil life. Training is, however, given in many trades.

At the outbreak of war there were only five different trades in which women could enrol in the W.A.A.F., but as airwomen continued to do their work efficiently and well, more and more trades became open to recruitment for women. Today there are over 60 of these different trades, which are enumerated here for information and guidance.

The Women's Auxiliary Air Force had a counterpart in the last war. The Women's Royal Air Force was formed on April 1, 1918, at the same time as the the R.A.F. came into existence as a separate fighting service.

Her Royal Highness the Duchess of Gloucester was gazetted an Air Commandant in the Women's Auxiliary Air Force on March 12, 1940.

Conditions of Service

With certain exceptions all trades are open for enrolment at the age of 17½. Those already skilled are enrolled in trades similar to their civilian occupations; those unskilled, in trades for which they are most suited. Pay varies from 1s. 4d. to 2s. 6d. a day (*see* table, p. 58). The upper age limit is 43, except where otherwise stated. Ex-service women of the last war may be accepted up to the age of 50.

All are required to undergo a medical

The W.A.A.F. uniform is smart and workmanlike from top to toe, as this photograph of a drum-and-fife band shows. Inset is an officer's cap with badge.

examination, and must attain the medical standard of fitness laid down. They are enrolled for the duration of the war, and will be entered in the rank of Aircraftwoman 2nd class. They will be eligible for promotion when qualified, as vacancies arise. Officers will normally be selected from the ranks. An airwoman is liable to serve in any part of the United Kingdom or overseas.

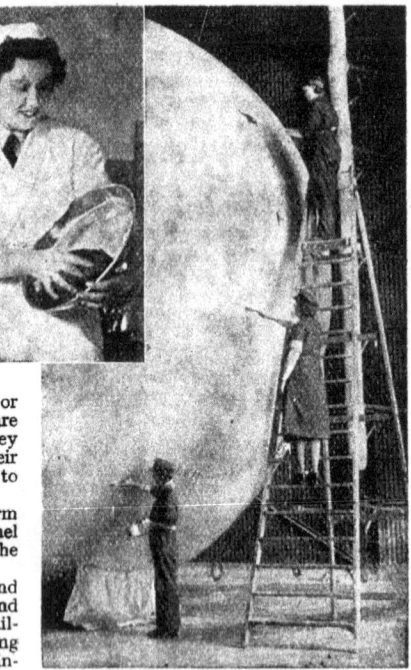

When a recruit is called up she is sent to a W.A.A.F. Depot, where she completes a fortnight's course of disciplinary training. Then, if qualified in her trade, she is posted to an R.A.F. Station or Headquarters. Untrained personnel are posted to a Training School where they receive a course of instruction for their trade. On completion they are posted to an R.A.F. Station or Headquarters.

The rates of pay (see table) conform roughly to two-thirds of R.A.F. personnel according to rank and trades (in the case of airwomen).

Airwomen receive free medical and dental treatment, free clothing, food and accommodation, as well as four free railway warrants per year when proceeding on leave—not to mention free entertainments, cinemas, sport, etc.

It is also possible under certain con-

There are over 60 trades in which airwomen of the W.A.A.F. can serve. These photographs show (above) a cook busy with her utensils, and (right) personnel servicing a barrage balloon.

ditions for airwomen to draw dependants' allowances.

An airwoman receives compensation for death or disability attributed to her service in the war.

W.A.A.F. Officers

Administrative. These officers are responsible to their R.A.F. Commanding Officer for the discipline and wellbeing of W.A.A.F. personnel.

Technical and Specialist. Code and cypher officers are included in this branch. They are responsible to their R.A.F. Commanding Officer for the safe custody of secret and confidential documents and for the interpretation of code and cypher messages.

Photographic officers are also included; they are responsible to their R.A.F. Commanding Officer for photographic interpretation of pictures taken over enemy territory.

In addition, there are openings for

Women mechanics in the W.A.A.F. do work of a varied nature. This instrument mechanic is testing an automatic pilot.

The W.A.A.F.

W.A.A.F. officers with specialized knowledge of the Signals Branch.

Catering. Includes W.A.A.F. unit catering officers (who replace R.A.F. messing officers), and hospital dietitians.

From time to time Air Ministry Selection Boards are held for the purpose of interviewing airwomen recommended by their Officers (R.A.F. and W.A.AF.) for appointment to officer rank.

Pay. The pay of a W.A.A.F. Officer is two-thirds that of the daily rate of an R.A.F. Officer (Equipment Branch) of equivalent rank.

TRADES IN THE W.A.A.F.

THE trades are divided into Groups for the purpose of pay. There are five of these Groups, and Group M, parallel to those of the R.A.F. (see page 12).

Except for skilled recruits in certain trades, airwomen undergoing trade training are placed in Group V. During the training period they are referred to as Aircrafthand u/t (under training), Equipment Assistant, etc. Once they have successfully completed their trade training they are placed in their appropriate trade Group and receive a rise in pay. *Unless otherwise stated, age limits are 17½–43.*

ACETYLENE WELDER (Group II).
Ex-Service, 50.
Candidates must be experienced acetylene welders in civil life.

ADMINISTRATIVE (Group IV).
Age limits 21–43.
Must have experience in organizing and dealing with people. Must have a high sense of leadership and responsibility.

AIRCRAFTHAND (Group V).
ACH General Duties.
These airwomen work in the kitchen, scrubbing and helping to keep cook-house clean and tidy ; they also help the cooks. Should be strong and accustomed to hard work

ARMAMENT ASSISTANT (Group V).
No special qualifications, although women with a mechanical bent are best suited. Stability an essential characteristic. Must be good at using their hands ; employed on general cleaning of guns, etc., and filling machine-gun belts

ARMOURER, GUNS (Group II).
Should be reasonably well educated, be intelligent and have some mechanical knowledge or bent. Work on machine-guns, cannon, small arms, turrets, camera guns and cine-camera guns, and care, handling of ammunition.

BALLOON OPERATOR (Group II).
Minimum height, 5 ft. 2 in. Must be robust and fond of outdoor life. Work on balloon sites.

BALLOON PARACHUTE HAND (Group V).
Average intelligence and deftness of fingers. Packing and inspection of balloons and parachutes

BATWOMAN (Group V).
Candidates from domestic service required. Hotel chambermaid experience an advantage. Personal servants to R.A.F. Officers Ex-S. 49

BOMB PLOTTER (Group V).
Women able to write quickly and legibly Employed on plotting results of practice runs at Air Gunnery and Bombing Schools

CHARGING BOARD OPERATOR (Group IV).
Training given to candidates on R.A.F. stations in the charging and maintenance of accumulators. Average intelligence ; robust physique.

CINE OPERATOR (Group V).
Average intelligence, no special technical knowledge, previous experience an advantage. Duties : Operation and daily maintenance of projectors. Repair and upkeep of films.

CLERK, EQUIPT. ACCOUNTING (Group IV).
Must have book-keeping or other accounting experience.

CLERK, GENERAL DUTIES (Group IV).
In addition to having previous clerical experience, candidates should be able to type not less than 20 words a minute. Fifty per cent of these clerks must be shorthand-typists.

CLERK, PAY ACCOUNTING (Group IV).
Must have book-keeping or other accounting experience.

CLERK, SPECIAL DUTIES (Group IV).
Age limits 17½–35.
Training is given. Must be able to assume responsibility under active war conditions and be mentally alert and accurate. Employed in tracking enemy aircraft as reported by R.O.C.

COOK (Group III).
Age limits 17½–50.
If experienced in cooking for large numbers, a candidate may enrol as a " skilled " cook after passing trade test. Without this experience may enrol as unskilled or u/t cook, for training.

DENTAL CLERK ORDERLY (Group M).
Candidates who have had experience as a receptionist to a dentist are eminently suitable.

DISPENSER (Group M).
Members of Pharmaceutical Society or certificate as assistant to an Apothecary (Society of Apothecaries) preferred. Responsible for dispensing and records of all medical supplies.

DROGUE PACKER AND REPAIRER (Group V).
Upholsterers, tailoresses, seamstresses and packers to machinists ; employed on general repairs and maintenance of tow targets.

ELECTRICIAN (Group II).
Bright and intelligent women required with slight working knowledge of electricity. Employed on electrical equipment, aeroplane wiring, starters, generators, motors, accumulators.

EQUIPMENT ASSISTANT (Group IV).
Recruits must have had experience of handling and accounting for stores of any kind.

FABRIC WORKER, FABRIC WORKER BALLOON *and* **FABRIC WORKER RIGGER (BALLOON) (Group III).**
Training is given. Candidates should have had experience as upholsterers, tailoresses, seamstresses or packers to machinists.

SECTION 1. L   The W.A.A.F.

FLIGHT MECHANIC, A (Group II).
Intelligent women with mechanical bent required. Work, maintenance and minor routine inspection of air-frames.

FLIGHT MECHANIC, E (Group II).
Requirements as A. Work is maintenance, inspection, starting, running up and testing of aeroplane engines.

HAIRDRESSER (Group III).
Previous experience in Cutting, Trimming, Washing and Setting hair required, but not in Waving. Prior to final acceptance, candidates are given practical trade test.

INSTRUMENT MECHANIC (Group II).
Recruit should be keen and deft-fingered. Experience of factory work or gramophone or wireless assembly shops desirable.

INSTRUMENT REPAIRER (Group II).
Intelligent women with a mechanical bent and liking for fine work, used to light mechanical tools. Work on all service instruments except wireless, electrical equipment and cameras.

LABORATORY ASSISTANT (Group M).
Certificate of the Pathological and Bacteriological Assistants Assn. desired. Employed on pathological, bacteriological and biochemical examinations as in a hospital laboratory.

MAINTENANCE ASSISTANT (Group V).
No special qualifications, but women with a mechanical bent are most suited. Candidates should have an interest in machinery.

MASSEUSE (Group M).
Members of the Chartered Society of Massage and Medical Gymnastics preferred. Those with experience may be accepted for training. Employed on massage and electrotherapy.

MESS STEWARD (Group V).
Duties include supervision of Mess Waitresses, general responsibility for upkeep of all Mess premises. This trade offers enormous scope to women of resource and imagination, particularly to women who like running a home efficiently or who have had experience in running a hotel.

METEOROLOGIST (Group II).
School Certificate standard, General School examination, or equivalent standard required. To make meteorological observations and plot synoptic charts.

MOTOR TRANSPORT DRIVER (Group V).
Candidates should be able to drive—this is not essential, however—as training will be given in servicing and handling service vehicles.

M.T. MECHANIC (Group II).
Knowledge of running repairs of vehicles and mechanical bent required. For maintenance, minor overhaul and repair by replacement of transport vehicles.

NURSING ORDERLY (Group M).
Age limits 23-43.
Candidates are required to do a course of training before being reclassified as "trained Nursing Orderlies. They gain experience in a W.A.A.F. Sick Quarters.

OPERATING ROOM ASSISTANT (Group M).
Candidates with reference from surgeon of hospital or from similar institute preferred. Employed in operating theatre and on operating table routine.

ORDERLY (Group V). *
Intelligent women not suitable for employment on rough and heavy work required. Employed as messengers and runners.

PARACHUTE PACKER (Group V).
Women of average intelligence, responsible, and with deft fingers required. Employed on routine inspection and maintenance of parachutes and harness folding and packing of canopy and rigging lines.

PARACHUTE REPAIRER (Group III).
Intelligent women clever with their fingers ; should have been upholsterers, tailoresses, seamstresses or packers to machinists.

PHOTOGRAPHER (Group II).
Commercial and practical photographic experience and in use of a standard camera desired, or a City and Guilds Cert. Prelim. trade test required. Work : all photographic processes (except heavy camera work), equipment maintenance and records.

RADIOGRAPHER (Group M).
Preference given to candidates with certificate of the Society of Radiographers. Those with experience may be accepted for training. Work in radiological photography and radiotherapy.

RADIO OPERATOR (Group IV).
Age limits 17½-35.
Must have special visual standards and. be able to assume responsibility in active war conditions.

RADIO TELEPHONY (Group IV).
High standard of intelligence, mental alertness, a clear speaking voice and freedom from shyness and nervousness essential. Should write with speed and legibility. Employed on operation and minor maintenance of R/T equipment at ground stations.

R.D.F. MECHANIC (Group I).
Age limits 17½-35.
School Certificate standard, including a study of mathematics and physics, necessary.

DAILY RATES OF PAY FOR AIRWOMEN BY GROUPS

Rank	Group I	Group II	Group III	Group IV	Group V	Group M
	s. d.	s. d.	s. d.	s. d.	s. d.	s. d.
A.C.W. 2nd cl.	2 6	2 4	2 0	2 0	2 2	1 4
A.C.W. 1st cl.	3 0	2 10	2 6	2 8	2 4	2 6
L.A.C.W.	3 8	3 4	2 10	3 0	2 8	2 10
Corporal	5 0	4 4	3 4	3 8	3 0	3 6
Sergeant	6 4	5 8	4 4	4 8	4 0	4 8
Flight Sergeant	7 8	6 8	5 4	5 8	5 2	6 4
Warrant Officer	9 4	8 4	7 8	7 8	7 8	9 0

A.C.W.=Aircraftwoman.   L.A.C.W.=Leading Aircraftwoman.
Group I (Radio and Wireless Mechanics) experimental at present.

War Pay at the rate of 8d. a day is issuable in addition to the rates of pay set out above. Increased rates for A.C.W. over 1 and 2 years' service, L.A.C.W. over 3 years, N.C.O.s over 3 and 4 years, and W.O.s over 5 years.

SERVICE POLICE (Group V).
Age limits 24-34.
Not be less than 5 ft. 4 in. in height and should have secondary education or the equivalent. Should possess common sense and be alert and easy conversationalists. Those who have served in large stores as shop walkers, first saleswomen or house detectives specially suitable. Required

W.A.A.F. RANKS and R.A.F. Equivalents

W.A.A.F.	R.A.F.
Air Commandant	Air Commodore
Group Officer	Group Captain
Wing Officer	Wing Commander
Squadron Officer	Squadron Leader
Flight Officer	Flight Lieutenant
Section Officer	Flying Officer
Assistant Section Officer	Pilot Officer

to maintain order and discipline outside Station Bounds. Wearing of civilian clothes sometimes necessary (3s. 6d. per week allowed as compensation for wear). On successful completion of training course promoted to Corporal.

SHOE REPAIRER (Group III). *
Experience of shoe repairing required. Work : to repair service boots and shoes. Should have knowledge of hand-sewing.

SPARKING PLUG TESTER (Group II).
Training is given. Candidates should be accurate, conscientious and deft-fingered. Experience of metal working is advantageous. Dismantling, cleaning, testing and re-assembling of sparking plugs.

TAILOR (Group III). *
Experienced tailoresses or dressmakers required. Work : to repair and alter uniforms.

TELEPHONE OPERATOR (Group V).
Training is given in this trade.

TELEPRINTER OPERATOR (Group IV).
Candidates should, if possible, be skilled teleprinter operators, but otherwise typists with a speed of not less than 30 words a minute. Training is given.

TRACER (Group IV). *
Mechanical. Experience of mechanical tracing required, should be neat script writers. Employed in tracing engineering drawings.

Map. Commercial artists with experience required : intelligent and painstaking.

WAITRESS (Group V). *
Women with experience in civil life desired.

WIRELESS MECHANIC (Group I).
Age limits 17½-35.
School Certificate standard of education, including mathematics and physics, necessary

WIRELESS OPERATOR (Group II).
Training is given. Candidates should be good at arithmetic, spelling and English and writing. Good sense of rhythm and touch for transmitting purposes are essential. Testing, inspection and operation of W/T sets.

W/T (SLIP READER) OPERATOR (Group II).
Candidates must be "touch typists." They will undergo course in Morse Code and "slip" reading, preparatory to training in the Automatic High Speed Telegraph Service.

WORKSHOP HAND (Group V). *
No special qualifications, although women with mechanical bent best suited. Employed on cleaning and degreasing plant, spray painting, valve-seat grinding, stripping small components, etc.

NOTE.—Training given in all trades except those marked *

PRINCESS MARY'S ROYAL AIR FORCE NURSING SERVICE

An important Branch of the R.A.F., which necessarily grows with it, is the Nursing Service, of which a brief account is given here.

THE Royal Air Force Nursing Service was formed in June 1918 to meet the needs of the Royal Air Force. A small establishment did duty at Station Sick Quarters, at the Training Camps and Convalescent Centres.

October 1918 and January 1919 saw the replacement of Army Nurses by Royal Air Force Nurses at Royal Air Force Hospitals.

On January 27, 1921, the Nursing Service was established under Royal Warrant as a permanent branch of the Royal Air Force.

The Nursing Service was honoured in June 1923 by His Most Gracious Majesty's consent, and that of H.R.H. the Princess Royal, with the designation of Princess Mary's Air Force Nursing Service.

On October 31, 1927, Her Royal Highness Princess Mary, Countess of Harewood, graciously consented to open a modern well-equipped hospital and Nursing Sisters' Quarters at Halton, named after herself. The Nursing Service is known by the abbreviation, P.M.N.S.

Today the number of members is ten times that of the R.A.F. Nursing Service of 1918. Members of this Nursing Service are recruited from civilian hospitals which have attached a first-class school for nurses. Members of the P.M.N.S. are now granted commissions of relative R.A.F. rank.

Candidates must be fully trained State-registered nurses. Many of these nurses are also well qualified in special branches of nursing, and are carefully selected for appointment to Princess Mary's Royal Air Force Nursing Service by members of the Nursing Service Advisory Board, of which the Director-General of Medical Services is the Chairman.

Hat worn by R.A.F. Nursing Service.

The Auxiliary Air Force

This branch of the Service bears the same relationship to the Royal Air Force as the Territorials to the Regular Army. Wearers of the " A " badge have equal pride in their share of triumphs won in battle.

BROUGHT into being by the Auxiliary Air Force and Air Force Reserve Act (1924), the first four Squadrons of the A.A.F. were formed in the following year.

The Auxiliary Air Force consists of Flying and Balloon Squadrons, and at the outbreak of war in September, 1939, there were in existence twenty of the former and forty-four of the latter.

Air gunner of the City of Edinburgh (No. 603) Bomber A.A.F. Squadron all set for a practice pre-war flight. *Fox*

Squadrons are recruited by the County Territorial Army and Air Force Associations. Members are drawn from the district in which the Headquarters are situated, and in peacetime training is carried out after working hours on weekdays and during week-ends. Once a year the Squadrons move into camp for a fortnight of intensive training.

During Annual Camp and other occasions involving full-time service, personnel receive R.A.F. rates of pay. For voluntary attendances after working hours and at week-ends an hourly rate of training allowance is paid as well as an allowance to cover the actual cost of travelling to the Headquarters or Aerodrome. In addition, bounties are payable annually in November to personnel who have attained a certain standard of efficiency and also attended the full period of camp during the previous twelve months. Flying pay is also provided for members of air crews who have become proficient at their various duties.

In peacetime officers are required to serve for a minimum period of five years on the active list, to be followed by a similar period on the A.A.F. Reserve. Extensions of service on the active list are granted in certain clearly defined circumstances. Airmen are required to engage for an original period of four years, after which they may apply for an extension of service on the active list or for transfer to the Reserve.

The uniform of the A.A.F. is identical with that of the R.A.F. with the exception that the " A " badge is worn by officers on the collar of the jacket and on the shoulder straps of the greatcoat. Airmen wear the " A " badge on the sleeve of the jacket and greatcoat immediately below the eagle badge.

On the outbreak of war all recruiting for the Auxiliary Air Force was closed down in accordance with a pre-arranged plan so that in wartime there should be a single channel of entry into the R.A.F. and the A.A.F.

Flying Squadrons

These comprise the following County and other Squadrons :

500 (Cty. of Kent)	608 (North Riding)
501 (Cty. of Gloucester)	609 (West Riding)
502 (Ulster)	610 (Cty. of Chester)
504 (Cty. of Nottingham)	611 (West Lancashire)
600 (City of London)	612 (Cty. of Aberdeen)
601 (Cty. of London)	613 (City of Manchester)
602 (City of Glasgow)	
603 (City of Edinburgh)	614 (Cty. of Glamorgan)
604 (Cty. of Middlesex)	
605 (Cty. of Warwick)	615 (Cty. of Surrey)
607 (Cty. of Durham)	616 (South Yorkshire)

In peacetime as well as in war, the Squadrons are allocated to operational Groups. They are equipped with the latest types of Fighter, General Reconnaissance or Army Cooperation Aircraft in accordance with the rôles allotted to them. In peacetime each Squadron is provided with a Training Flight which enables newly joined pilots and crews to assimilate the Squadron spirit during their period of training and also provides flying facilities for those who have been transferred to the Reserve.

Auxiliary Air Force

Pilots of a Hurricane of No. 601 (County of London) A.A.F. Squadron, which has destroyed more than 100 enemy machines. Note squadron badge on tail. Ten of the squadron's pilots have won the D.F.C.

In 1938 an Auxiliary Officer was appointed to the Air Ministry as Director of the Auxiliary Air Force to advise the Air Council on matters appertaining to this Branch of the Service.

The outbreak of war in September, 1939, found the A.A.F. Flying Squadrons ready and eager to put to the test the results of the intensive training which had been carried out following the Munich crisis. The distinction of being the first to shoot down a German bomber on to British soil was earned by a pilot of the Auxiliary Air Force on October 16, 1939. It has also been established that the famous German pilot, Major Helmuth Weick, who is credited with no fewer than fifty-six "confirmed" victories, fell to the guns of an Auxiliary Spitfire pilot off the Isle of Wight on November 28, 1940. The long list of awards gained by A.A.F. personnel during the first eighteen months of the war testifies to the fighting spirit of the Squadrons and the quality of their training in pre-war days.

The incidence of promotion, casualties and transfers to training units have to a large extent changed the character of A.A.F. Squadrons, but the districts from which they were recruited in peacetime continue to take a very close interest in their achievements. It is not surprising that the auxiliary officers and airmen who gave up so many of their leisure hours and so many week-ends before the war in preparing to defend their country regard their "A" badges with justifiable pride.

Balloon Squadrons

There can be very few branches of any of the Services to compare with the Balloon Barrage for rapidity of growth.

In spite of the fact that the first Auxiliary Balloon Squadron was formed as recently as in May, 1938, there were in existence on the outbreak of war in September, 1939, no fewer than forty-four squadrons. As in the case of the flying squadrons, the County Territorial Army and Air Force Associations have been responsible for recruiting, and men came forward in peacetime with commendable keenness to man the balloons. The upper age limit was fixed at fifty years and the original squadrons contained a high proportion of ex-servicemen.

Since the outbreak of war recruiting for the Auxiliary Air Force has stopped and the vast expansion of the Balloon Barrage has been on an R.A.F. basis. The pre-war volunteers can, however, still be picked out by their "A" badges.

Officers and men of the Balloon Command have to be able to perform their varied duties under the most trying conditions. Not only on land do they serve, and if ever there was a handy man it must be the trained member of a balloon crew stationed on a barge moored in an exposed estuary (*see also* pp. 105–106).

Work of the Royal Observer Corps

Not officially part of the R.A.F., but a civilian corps transferred to the Air Ministry on the outbreak of war, the Royal Observer Corps performs services on which the success of interception of enemy aircraft by the R.A.F. largely depends. Its important duties are here made clear.

DURING the War of 1914–1918 it became apparent that the movements of all hostile aircraft flying over this country must be continuously tracked and reported, for two reasons:

(1) To enable Fighter Aircraft to be sent to the correct position to make an interception.
(2) To enable Air Raid warnings to be issued to places in advance of the direction in which the raiders are proceeding.

The simplest method of achieving this result is by the creation of a ground Observation system consisting of Observer Posts, manned by personnel living in the vicinity and trained in observing duties and the recognition of aircraft.

Speed of reporting is essential and every Observer Post has a permanent telephone connexion to its appropriate Centre.

Normally, a number of Posts covering an area of a medium-sized county are connected to a Centre; a Centre and its Posts is called an Observer Group. Posts are connected in bunches of three, so that any two Posts can overhear reports from the third. This reporting network covers the whole of the county where enemy aircraft may be expected to fly.

Post Crews are supplied with gridded maps, binoculars, and an instrument to assist in getting corrected heights of aircraft.

At each Observer Centre there is a gridded map around which are seated the plotters, who receive plots from the Post Crews. By placing counters on the grid squares reported by Post Crews, tracks of aircraft are obtained.

Tellers overlooking the table "tell" these tracks to the Royal Air Force.

Every aircraft, friend or enemy, is tracked whilst flying across country up to the capacity of the organization.

Personnel. Members are recruited for Observer Centres and Posts from the town or village in which the Centre or Post is situated. They are recruited from all classes of the community and are carefully selected.

They are trained in plotting, height finding, and recognition. Continuous watch is maintained day and night.

The majority of members are those enrolled as special constables prior to the war, who performed their duties without pay. On the outbreak of war they were transferred to the Air Ministry and receive 1s. 3d. an hour whilst on duty to cover travelling and subsistence expenses and loss of wages. There are two classes:

Class A.—48 hours duty a week and receive £3 plus any general cost of living bonus.
Class B.—Duty up to 24 hours a week, in addition to civil occupation.

Organization. There is a Head Observer in charge of each Post and an Observer Group Officer with two assistants in charge of the Posts in a Group. There is a Controller with one assistant in charge of each Observer Centre.

Several Observer Groups normally form an Area, and are controlled by an Area Commandant and two Deputies.

The Commandant of the R.O.C. is responsible to the C.-in-C. Fighter Command for operational work and to the Air Ministry for administration and equipment.

The Royal Observer Corps is ancillary (not auxiliary) to the R.A.F. Officers wear uniform of R.A.F. blue with black braid on the cuff and a special cap badge. Other members wear a one-piece pattern uniform.

Men at an R.O.C. post with telephone and height corrector. (Inset, R.O.C. badge.)

SECTION 1. O

The Air Training Corps
New Opportunities for Air-Minded Boys

A new field for boys who are ambitious to take their part in the achievements of the finest Air Force in the world is the A.T.C., which offers opportunities of a more elastic nature than direct apprenticeship.

A NEW opportunity for boys who are ambitious to take their part in the achievements of the finest Air Force in the world is the A.T.C. In the words of Sir Archibald Sinclair, the A.T.C. is a "broad highway from the Elementary Schools, from the Public Schools and from the Universities into the Royal Air Force."

The Air Training Corps, which came into being in February, 1941, quickly reached a strength of well over 150,000 boys. Its aim is to provide a wide field of selection from which the R.A.F. can draw in the future for air crews and technical staff. All boys of 16 and upwards who are physically fit and intend eventually to join the R.A.F. or Fleet Air Arm are eligible for membership of the Corps, which provides them with instruction designed to make them more efficient recruits when the time comes for them to join the Service.

The emphasis is on equality of opportunity. The Corps consists of three kinds of unit:

(i) University Air Squadrons at some twenty universities and university colleges throughout the United Kingdom (*see* University Short Course, p. 65).

(ii) School units, organized by the school authorities.

(iii) Local units, raised under the leadership of civic authorities and administered by representative local committees. Education authorities and youth organizations have given their co-operation.

Boys in school and local units attend parades two or three times a week. Instruction is given through the voluntary services of officers of the "T" Branch

Cap Badge, A.T.C.

Button, A.T.C.

Instruction given to lads of the Air Training Corps is thorough and practical, providing a groundwork for later and more advanced coaching. Here youngsters are getting first-hand knowledge about the fusing of bombs.
Photo, British Official : Crown Copyright

Of absorbing interest, it is clear, was this lesson on different types of aircraft, explained to the A.T.C. cadets with the help of realistic models.

of the R.A.F.V.R., aided by a very large number of civilian instructors. One of the main objects of the Corps is to provide such educational assistance as will enable boys to reach the high standards required for air-crew candidates.

The course of instruction consists first of drill, physical training, mathematics, Morse code and general lectures. In the second stage there is more specialization in two main categories, according to the duties for which the candidate is most suited:

(1) *Air crew*—mathematics, navigation and Morse, aircraft identification, and administration.

(2) *Technical*—courses for wireless operators and mechanics (E), Mechanics (A), instrument repairers, electricians and M.T. mechanics.

The cadet uniform, which is in Air Force blue material with chromium buttons bearing the A.T.C. crest, is issued free. The Field Service cap is worn. Officers wear A.T.C. distinguishing badges on their R.A.F.V.R. officers' uniform.

The units are given a grant of £1 per annum for each "efficient," and 10s. for each "proficient" cadet. Certificates of proficiency are awarded on the results of oral and written examinations. Thus, at the school or local squadron, the cadet after a period of six months' service can take the first Proficiency Certificate, divided into technical or air-crew subjects. Provision is made for a more advanced Certificate after a year or more in the Corps. The possession of these Certificates will earn a proportionate reduction in the usual period of training inside the Service.

Affiliation to R.A.F.

Most of the squadrons are affiliated to R.A.F. stations in the vicinity. Regular visits to the stations provide an ever-growing acquaintance with the way in which the R.A.F. works, both by the material knowledge gained from lectures, and by the opportunity, within the limits imposed by wartime restrictions, of being taken on flights in Service aircraft. From this association, which includes regular visits by R.A.F. personnel to A.T.C. units, a link is formed which enables the "younger brother" when he enters the Service to extract the utmost advantage from his training in the shortest time. Officers of the A.T.C. attend spare-time lectures at near-by stations and are attached to R.A.F. stations for short continuous periods of instruction.

The scope of opportunity provided for all types of boys by the A.T.C. is completed by the University Short Courses. Young men of 17.6 to 18.8 years of age who are regarded as potential officers for air-crew duties and who have suitable educational qualifications may be nominated for a six months' course at a university at Air Ministry expense (*see page 65*).

The Commandant is Air Commodore J. A. Chamier, C.B., C.M.G., D.S.O., O.B.E. The Director of the A.T.C. is Mr. W. W. Wakefield, M.P. The Headquarters of the Corps is: **Montrose, Gordon Avenue, Stanmore.**

Crest and motto of the A.T.C.

The University Short Course
Air Ministry's Scheme for Pilots and Observers

This new opening for young men selected for possible commissions in the R.A.F. general duties (flying) branch offers great attractions to boys who between the ages of 17½ years and 18 years 8 months would normally be going up to a University.

THESE Courses are for boys who wish to become pilots or observers in the R.A.F.; and, although for obvious reasons no definite promise can be given, it is expected that they will all be approved for commissions at the end of their flying training. For pilots and observers who are going to hold commissioned rank the R.A.F. wants the very best. Nowhere is quality more important than in the air; and the R.A.F. will never willingly lower its present standards of quality, mental and physical.

The University Short Course is a deliberate attempt to select the best material the country has to offer and then give to it the best training the war conditions allow. The method is nomination by headmasters of candidates, from among their present boys or old boys, who will be between 17.6 and 18.8 months before the Course opens (usually in April and October). R.A.F. Boards select from these candidates those whom they believe most likely to benefit from the Course and to make the best officers. In making this selection, they are guided solely by the merit of the boy. The underlying principle of the Air Ministry's policy is simply this, that six months at a University makes a boy a better recruit, for R.A.F. purposes, than he would otherwise be.

Life at the University

THE greater breadth of outlook, the greater maturity, the increased "poise," the very fact of having been for even six months in the environment of a University, all these are believed to be worth having in the young pilot. The R.A.F. is already a corps of volunteers, of picked men; the purpose of these Courses is to improve the quality still further.

The boy goes to the University for six months. He will not be sent up until he is 17.9, and if he is still at school he is recommended to stay there till he goes to the University. He may express a preference for a particular University and for a particular course of study. He goes up as an ordinary member of a College or a hostel (not segregated, for that would destroy an important part of the purpose of the scheme), a matriculated member of the University, subject to its normal laws and partaking in its normal privileges and activities. The Air Ministry pays for his board and lodging, for all his tuition, for his membership of the usual College athletic clubs, for any medical attention he may need. The only expenses which fall on him or his parents are in respect of pocket money.

University Air Squadron

WHILE he is there he is required to join the University Air Squadron, where he completes the training programme of the Initial Training Wing. That is one-half of his existence, the Service part, and for that he will normally wear uniform. But in the mornings he is a civilian. He attends University lectures, given by the academic staff of the University, on subjects related to, but not officially part of, the University Air Squadron training. He must take a course in Mathematics, Mechanics, and Physics, and also one of the optional groups, Engineering or Navigation, including Meteorology. He need not have been a mathematician or a scientist at school; all he needs is the equivalent of a "credit" in Elementary Mathematics in the School Certificate. And the Universities have agree that, whenever it is possible, these courses will be allowed to count towards a degree after the war.

On completion of the six months' course candidates who secure a certificate of proficiency for their work with the University Air Squadron and satisfy the Joint University Recruiting Board of their diligence and progress in their other studies, and are recommended by the Board as in all respects suitable to receive commissions, will proceed to a Receiving Centre for kitting and then either to an elementary flying training school or to an observer school (omitting the course at the Initial Training Wing) and, provided they complete every stage of their training as pilots or observers satisfactorily, will receive, on completion, commissions in the R.A.F.V.R. Full details can be obtained from the Air Ministry, D.P.E.T., Adastral House, Kingsway, W.C.2.

While nobody would assert that a University in wartime is the same institution as it is in peacetime, this scheme gives the young man a remarkable opportunity of making the best of both worlds, and, it is hoped, of himself. He need lose nothing, in time, by comparison with the volunteer who goes into the R.A.F. through the normal channels, and he can hardly fail to be a better man at the end of his six months of University residence.

Air Forces of the Dominions
With a Note on the Empire Air Training Scheme

It was obvious that when the call to arms came the Empire would rally in the air as on land and sea. Here are brief statements of what is being done by each Dominion in the struggle for victory in the air.

OFFICERS and other ranks from all the Dominions earned great distinction in the air during the war of 1914 - 18. Then the only Dominion air forces were the Australian Flying Corps (which had three squadrons in France and one in Palestine) and the South African Aviation Corps, which was formed for, and operated throughout the campaign in South-West Africa. Apart from these, air personnel from the Dominions, including many Australians and South Africans, served in the Royal Flying Corps or the Royal Naval Air Service.

After the war of 1914-18 air forces came into being in all the Dominions, manned by officers and men who had proved their worth in the war.

During the years preceding the present war officers from the Air Forces of the Dominions attended courses at the Royal Air Force Staff College and at the Imperial Defence College, and there were temporary exchanges of personnel between the R.A.F. and the Air Forces of the Dominions. Thus at the outbreak of the present war there were not only the ties of friendship between officers of the various Air Forces of the British Commonwealth but also mutual understanding and the ability to cooperate closely.

The Air Forces of all the Dominions have been in action against the enemy : the Royal Canadian Air Force and the Royal New Zealand Air Force in the United Kingdom, the Royal Australian Air Force in the United Kingdom and in the Middle East, and the South African Air Force in East Africa. Rhodesian squadrons of the Royal Air Force have shared in the fighting.

In all these operations there has been a repetition of the gallantry, skill and determination so notable in the last war, and the work of the technical and maintenance personnel has been of an equally high standard. Much is therefore expected from the many squadrons of the Dominions' Air Forces which are to be formed.

Pupil pilots of the Royal Australian Air Force are instructed on Wirraway and Wackett aircraft such as these seen at the Commonwealth Factory aerodrome.

Dominion Air Forces

Royal Australian Air Force

IN the 1914–1918 war Australia was the only Dominion to establish its own Air Force (the Australian Flying Corps A.I.F.). As early as 1911, following on decisions made at Imperial Conferences in London, the Australian Government had decided to make provision for the establishment of military aeronautics in the Commonwealth Forces. A Central Flying School had been established at Point Cook, in Victoria and such progress in air training had been made that early in 1915 it was possible to send a small air unit (a half Flight) of the Australian Flying Corps to serve with the British Forces in Mesopotamia. This unit was the forerunner of the Royal Australian Air Force. By the time of the Armistice the Force overseas consisted of one Squadron in Palestine, three in France, and a Training Wing in the United Kingdom. The British Government provided Australia with a gift of approximately one million pounds' worth of Air Force equipment, and so made possible the peacetime Air Force in Australia. This eventually became the Royal Australian Air Force, the organization, training and general make-up of which have always closely followed those of the Royal Air Force. The uniform resembles that of the R.A.F., but is dark blue, and officers carry miniature wings on the sleeve above the rank rings.

Considerable expansion has taken place in the Home Defence Force, the operational Squadrons of which are now gradually being re-equipped with the most modern types of aircraft.

As regards activities overseas, the R.A.A.F. was very early in the picture—a complete General Reconnaissance Sunderland Squadron of its permanent Air Force being placed at the disposal of the R.A.F. in the Coastal Command by December, 1939. This Squadron has been in continuous operation to date and has achieved notable successes. In addition, there are a number of other Squadrons of the permanent Air Force on active service in the Middle East and in the Far East.

Australia is taking a very considerable share in the Empire Air Training Scheme. In addition to the air crews who are dispatched via Canada to complete, in Canadian Schools, their Service air training, there is a much greater flow of trained air crews whose entire air training is completed in Australia. There is a subsidiary flow of air crews who have completed only their Initial Training in Australia but who

Clad in cold-weather kit, personnel of the Royal Canadian Air Force refuelling a plane at Trenton Air Base, Ontario.

complete their entire air training in Southern Rhodesian Schools.

Under the Empire Air Training Agreement the British Government has agreed to organize the Royal Australian Air Force air crews sent abroad into R.A.A.F. Squadrons. Australia on her part has also assumed responsibility for providing the complete ground personnel to man these E.A.T.S. Squadrons. Already a number of these Squadrons is on active service in the United Kingdom, the Middle East and the Far East, and the balance are formed or forming.

In August 1941, Air Marshal R. Williams, C.B., C.B.E., D.S.O., was appointed A.O.C. R.A.A.F. Overseas Headquarters, which when formed will absorb the present Air Liaison office organization in London.

Royal Canadian Air Force

ROYAL CANADIAN AIR FORCE personnel in large numbers are now actively engaged against Germany both as members of R.C.A.F. squadrons and as attached to squadrons of the Royal Air Force. Most of them are products of the British Commonwealth Air Training Plan, which may well be considered the Dominion's major effort in this war. The squadrons are manned principally by graduates of the Air Training Plan and commanded by officers of the permanent R.C.A.F. One fighter squadron served throughout the Battle of Britain and tour of the officers received D.F.C.s. At that time the squadron was designated No. 1 Fighter Squadron R.C.A.F., and was a composite unit of the Auxiliary Active Air Force and the Permanent Active Air Force. Prior to this an "All Canadian" squadron of the R.A.F. had won great honour over Dunkirk.

The first R.C.A.F. squadron to arrive in England was an Army Cooperation unit slated for service with the Canadian Army. A second Army Cooperation squadron and No. 1 Fighter squadron arrived with the second Canadian Division in June, 1940. The fighter squadron completed training and became operational in the middle of August, 1940. With little activity being undertaken by the Army, the second Army Cooperation squadron was disbanded and reorganized in December, 1940, as No. 2 Fighter Squadron, and has been actively engaged in operations since that time.

Until August of 1941 most of the permanent force officers of the R.C.A.F. were retained in Canada to provide trained personnel for instructional duties and as administrators of the Air Training Plan. However, with more instructors being made available from graduates of the Air Training Plan, experienced permanent R.C.A.F. officers are being posted to take command of the R.C.A.F. squadrons overseas.

At the outbreak of war the strength of the Royal Canadian Air Force was 410 officers and 3,390 airmen. Two years later it was more than ten times as large.

The R.C.A.F. also maintains a Home War Establishment which is responsible for the defence of the Dominion. Squadrons of the Home War Establishment, which are manned largely by Permanent Force personnel, have been participating in the Battle of the Atlantic since the day war was declared. From bases along the East coast they daily patrol the sea lanes, acting as convoy escort.

The administrative structure of the R.C.A.F. is patterned after that of the Royal Air Force. The governing body is the Air Council, composed of the Minister of National Defence for Air; the Deputy Minister; Chief of the Air Staff; Deputy Chief of Air Staff; Air Member for Personnel; Air Member for Training; Air Member Air Staff; Air Member for Supply; and the Air Member for Aeronautical Engineering.

Air Vice-Marshal L. S. Breadner, D.S.C., is the Chief of the Air Staff and the Hon. C. G. Power, M.C., the Minister of National Defence for Air. The uniform worn is identical with that of the R.A.F.

Royal New Zealand Air Force

THOUGH there were New Zealanders in the R.A.F. during the 1914-18 war, there was no New Zealand Air Force.

Three fighter pilots of the South African Air Force discussing tactics over a map in the Northern Frontier region of Kenya. The S.A.A.F. wears uniform of a "veldt" colour, resembling khaki.
British Official Photograph

which did not come into existence until 1923, although it was three years before this that Col. Bettington had been sent out from England with 33 old wartime machines to be fashioned into a nucleus of a future force. In 1934 the prefix "Royal" was added, and in 1937 the R.N.Z.A.F. was constituted a separate service.

At the outbreak of war in 1939 the Air Force was not large, the Regulars numbering 91 officers and 665 men and the Territorials 79 and 325. The equipment included Tiger Moths, Vickers Vincents and Vildebeeste, Fairey Gordons and Airspeed Oxfords. Vickers Wellingtons were on order, and personnel had been sent to take delivery, but they were retained here and formed into a squadron in the R.A.F. The Chief of the Air Staff is Air Commodore H. W. L. Saunders.

In the last war there were New Zealand names which were distinguished for their flying, and Lieut. Brandon will be remembered for his encounters with the Zeppelins L15 and L33. In this war no one will forget the name of "Cobber" Kain, who, before his untimely death, was the victor in many fights on the Western Front in 1940.

South African Air Force

SOUTH AFRICA was early into the world of flight, and it was only two years after the first demonstration of flying near Cape Town by Paterson and Driver in 1911 that a flying school for officers was formed near Kimberley. On the outbreak of the 1914 war these officers proceeded to England, joined the R.F.C. and went to France in No. 2 Squadron. They returned to England and the South African Aviation Corps was formed. This, equipped with

'PER ARDUA AD ASTRA'

The motto of the R.A.F. has been the subject of discussion, for it has no satisfactory equivalent in English. Its origin has now been established. In 1912 Gen. Sir Frederick Sykes, who was then raising and commanding the Royal Flying Corps (Military Wing), asked for suggestions for a motto and received from two officers of the Royal Engineers the combination of various Latin quotations which, then adopted, quickly became world-famous.

About the same time the pilot's badge, the "wings," was designed by Sir Frederick Sykes and Gen. David Henderson and sanctioned by the King.

"Ad astra per ardua" is the motto of the Drummond family of Midhope, Co. Perth. A well-known phrase of Virgil's is "Sic itur ad astra," while the motto of Birmingham University is "Per ardua ad alta." The meaning of the R.A.F. motto is indicated by the rough translation "Through difficulties (heights, steeps) to the stars (success or immortal fame)."

---

aircraft supplied by the R.F.C. and R.N.A.S., went to South-West Africa, where it operated until the end of the campaign, about July, 1915.

Later the personnel returned to England, forming No. 26 Squadron R.F.C., and as such went to East Africa. The best-remembered name is Beauchamp-Proctor, who was decorated with the V.C., D.S.O., M.C., and D.F.C.

After the war van Ryneveld and Brand made an adventurous flight out to The Cape, starting in a Vickers Vimy and finishing, after two crashes, in a DH 9. The former is now Lieut.-General Sir Pierre van Ryneveld, chief of staff of the Union Defence Forces. The South African Air Force was formed in 1920 and is part of the Army, and its ranks are those of the Army.

At the outbreak of this war the Junkers 86s and 52s of South African Airways were taken over by the S.A.A.F. and, ironically enough, were used effectively against the nation which made them. It was Junkers 86s which intercepted the "*Watussi*" off Cape Town and so caused the German crew to scuttle her. But since then this Dominion Air Force has had many victories in Italian East Africa in conjunction with the Royal Air Force.

The Indian Air Force

THE Indian Air Force was formed in 1932, the first cadets being trained at Cranwell. Its composition, with the exception of some of its technical staff, is entirely Indian. Its first squadron was fully equipped in 1938-39, and in 1940 a second was formed. Further regular squadrons were being formed with a considerable reserve of trained pilots and mechanics under an expansion scheme put in force directly war began. A Volunteer Air Force reserve was formed for defence duties, mainly coastal.

The duties of the I.A.F. are to combine with the R.A.F. in operations on the N.W. Frontier and to assist the field Army and the Navy in the event of invasion. It is administered and maintained by the Government of India, Defence Department, and is distinct from the R.A.F. squadrons of the Indian establishment.

As part of a long-term plan a considerable expansion of the regular I.A.F. was put in hand in May, 1940, apart from the increase in auxiliary forces. The great problem was the provision of skilled mechanics, but this was being overcome.

Two Harvard training aircraft in flight over an R.C.A.F. station in Canada, where pilots come for the final stages under the Empire Air Training Scheme (see p. 70).

THE EMPIRE AIR TRAINING SCHEME

The Empire Air Training Scheme was an obvious result of two things, the importance of the air arm in modern warfare, and the desire of the Dominions to stand with the United Kingdom in resisting all attempts to tear down Democracy. And it had the desirable characteristic of doing the training out of reach of bombing. It was got under way with great speed, the agreement between the three self-governing Dominions—Canada, Australia and New Zealand—and the United Kingdom being signed three months after the declaration of war. Put briefly, the agreement provided for the training of airmen from these Dominions and the United Kingdom at stations to be established in New Zealand, Australia and Canada, but principally the last, owing to its great size and comparative proximity to England.

All recruits are enlisted into the ranks for ground training. Then pilots have a course at an Elementary Flying Training School, followed by intermediate and advanced training at a Service Flying Training School. Air observers do courses of reconnaissance and photography, then bombing and gunnery, followed by advanced navigation. The radio operator-air gunners have a course of radio and then gunnery training. Rates of pay are at Royal Air Force rates as soon as the trainees embark for the United Kingdom; previous to this they are at the rate applicable in each Dominion.

Ground crew at a Royal Canadian Air Force training station are lifting a light dual control 'plane to have its wings and tail unit attached, ready for flying.

R.A.F. TRUMPET CALLS

The Trumpet, not the bugle, is employed in the Royal Air Force for sounding salutes and calls. The principal ones are: Royal Salute, Air Salute, Reveille, Retreat, First Post, Tattoo, Last Post, Lights Out.

Reveille. From the French *réveiller*—to awaken. Indicates the opening of the day

Retreat. Is given by Drum or Trumpet, and is followed by the evening parade, roll call and lowering of the Ensign.

First Post, Tattoo Sounding. Marks the posting of sentries for the night and the beginning of Tattoo.

Tattoo. Tattoo is properly a period of time between First and Last Posts, and was introduced by William of Orange as a signal for the ale-houses to close and the final muster to be made, as the men retired to their billets. The word is derived from the Dutch "tap," meaning "ale-house," and "toe," meaning to shut.

Last Post, Tattoo Sounding. Showed the close of the day and men were not marked as absentees until this call sounded.

Lights Out. The call for all lights and fires to be extinguished. It indicates that troops have returned for the night. No call other than the "Alarm" may be sounded between "Lights Out" and "Reveille."

Equipment. The original draft of the Scheme provided that Canada and Australia were to manufacture several of the aircraft types needed for training and the United Kingdom was to send out to them Fairey Battles and Avro Ansons for the advanced flying. Though this has been adhered to as far as possible, shortage of aircraft in England has caused the Dominions to rely more upon their own factories. So Australia is making Tiger Moths (about two per day) and Wirraways (one per day) for the Scheme. The engines for these, the Gipsy and the Pratt and Whitney Wasp, are also being made in Australia.

Canada is doing an even greater volume of aircraft manufacture, and the Fleet M-62 and the Tiger Moth are being made for elementary work and the Noorduyn Aviation Company is making Harvards and Norsemen for use at the Service Flying Schools. Ansons are also being made, and it is possible that a new kind of fuselage made of plastic-bonded plywood may be developed for this type to make more use of local materials. New Zealand as yet makes only Tiger Moths, her other requirements being sent out for assembly there.

The Royal Air Force Benevolent Fund
Its Work for the Service and its Needs

Here in outline is an account of the magnificent work done for members of the Flying Service and their dependants by the Fund, together with notes on the special trusts and funds administered by it

This Fund, which has done so much to relieve need among all ranks of the R.A.F. and their dependants, was founded by Lord Trenchard as long ago as 1919 and was registered under the War Charities Act in 1920. Under its charter its object is the relief of distress, and not only present but past members of the Royal Air Force, with their dependants, are eligible for its assistance. In 1939 the scope of the Fund was widened to permit of help being given to commissioned and enlisted personnel also of the Auxiliary Air Force, the R.A.F. Reserve, and the W.A.A.F. where distress is attributable to R.A.F. service.

The Fund is therefore prepared to assist those disabled by flying, and the dependants of those killed; other casualties and their dependants; and sufferers on account of sickness and general distress. Its scope, as will be obvious, is very wide. The general policy is controlled by the Council (of which until his death in 1941 the Chairman was Viscount Wakefield of Hythe, G.C.V.O., C.B.E., a most generous benefactor and untiring worker) and put into effect through the Grants, the Vanbrugh Castle School, and the Finance Committees. Late in 1940 Viscount Nuffield made a donation of £250,000 to be used for general purposes.

Only Two Limitations

There are no hard and fast rules as to cases which may be helped or the amount of financial assistance which may be given. In fact, the only limitations are those prescribed by the dictates of common sense and by the amount of money available.

Within these limits the aim of the Fund is to provide relief equally and adequately, to enable dependants to carry on in some semblance of the life to which they are accustomed, and to help children into the careers that their fathers might reasonably have expected them to follow. The Fund, as a Service Fund, must take into account not only the human side but service given.

Casualty cases are normally more lasting, and, if adequate relief is to be given, must be more expensive than those of temporary distress through sickness or unemployment.

The Vanbrugh Castle School

This was presented to the Fund in 1920 by Mr. Alexander Duckham to provide the sons of deceased airmen with a home, education, and eventually a start in life. It is situated at Blackheath and is maintained by a General Fund at an average cost of £2,500 per annum. The ages of admission are 5 to 10 years, and it is hoped that those received will choose the Royal Air Force as a career. With the opening of the "Wakefield Wing" in May, 1939, it became possible to admit a further 25 boys, making a total of 67 then in residence, of whom 32 were attending the Roan Secondary School, Blackheath. The new wing was formed by the purchase and modernization (by the generosity of the late Lord Wakefield) of a large residence adjoining the School.

From the opening of the School in 1921 56 boys had completed their education by the end of 1939, and of these 27 passed into the Aircraft Apprentices Training Establishments at Halton and Cranwell. During 1939 four boys completed their education, two of them passing into Halton.

Rooks Hill House

In 1939 Mr. Alexander Duckham presented to the Fund this fine mansion near Sevenoaks, together with some 200 acres of land surrounding it. The house stands on high ground (some 800 feet up) and Mr. Duckham expressed the intention that it should be used as a home for the children of Officer and Sergeant Pilots killed flying. The donor settled the sum of £1,000 per annum towards the upkeep and maintenance of Rooks Hill House. As a preliminary step he accepted about twenty young children between the ages of 2 and 8 years as his guests, and provided for their care and maintenance under his Lady-in-Charge and personal staff.

Lawrence of Arabia Educational Fund

That gallant officer who preferred to be known as Aircraftman T. E. Shaw devoted the proceeds of his book "The Revolt in the Desert" to the establishment of an educational fund for the benefit of the children of Officers of the Royal Air

R.A.F Benevolent Fund

'Per Ardua ad Astra.' Royal Air Force War Memorial, on Victoria Embankment, London. It was unveiled on July 16, 1923.

Force past and present, preference being given to children of Officers who had met their death or had been invalided while serving in the R.A.F. on active service or whilst on duty. The sum of £15,000 was thus invested for the object stated. In deference to the donor's wishes his identity was kept a secret, and only after his untimely death in May, 1935, was the Fund (previously entitled the Anonymous Education Fund) renamed so as to record both the identity and the modesty of " Lawrence of Arabia." The income at the end of 1939 was £514 per annum, and in the period since the Educational Fund came into being, in 1929, a total of £6,056 was expended, including £388 in 1939 At the beginning of 1940 twelve children were receiving assistance from it.

Salting Benefaction

In 1920 the late Mrs. M. E. Salting presented to the Trustees of the Benevolent Fund some property around Ascot, the sale of which realized just over £8,000. It was Mrs. Salting's desire that the income from the benefaction should be devoted to the education of Officers' children, and a total of £5,707 had been thus expended by the end of 1939, including £396 in the latter year. Twelve children are receiving assistance.

Struben Memorial Trust

Created in 1922 by Major A. M. A. Struben, O.B.E., late R.A.F., in memory of his son, the late Flying Officer Henry Marinus Struben, No. 25 Squadron, R.A.F., who was killed on June 24, 1921, while flying on duty. Major Struben's object was to foster the squadron spirit and to promote happiness and courage in the execution of duty through a feeling of family security. Accordingly the income is devoted, under certain conditions, to the education of children of disabled or deceased Officers of No. 25 Squadron, preference being given to children of Officers whose normal duty included flying. During the year 1939 the sum of £31 10s. was expended on the only case at that time eligible.

Viscount Wakefield Benefaction

In December, 1936, the late Lord Wakefield presented a cheque for £10,000 to be used at the discretion of the Council for the educational and other purposes of the Benevolent Fund, and especially for

Vanbrugh Castle School, Blackheath, where sons of deceased R.A.F. men are given a home, education and a start in their chosen career.

R.A.F. Benevolent Fund

the training of young Officers or Airmen who have left the Service, or for the education after leaving school of the dependants of R.A.F. personnel. Those who receive grants from this Fund for higher education are known as Wakefield Students. From the year 1937 (when the Benefaction was inaugurated) until the end of 1939 £756 was expended, including £294 on six cases in 1939.

Observer Corps Fund

Created after the outbreak of the present war by the Commandant of the Royal Observer Corps to provide assistance in necessitous cases to Serving Members where distress is caused by service with the Royal Observer Corps.

Future of the Fund

Since its formation the Fund has dealt with over 15,000 cases, including, of course, commitments arising from the war of 1914-18. With the outbreak of the present war it had to face an additional heavy demand, growing in magnitude and imposing an unpredictable strain upon its resources. The Council appeal for the generous and wholehearted support of the Service and of the public to meet the call.

It is the experience of the Fund that assistance made necessary by casualties, especially where education is involved, is a cumulative responsibility which will increase with the years, as it becomes necessary to provide for the education of children of Officers and Airmen killed or disabled in the present war. Then, too, it must be borne in mind that the Royal Air Force is growing to tremendous proportions, so that it is inevitable that demands upon the Benevolent Fund in years to come will be great. The debt of the nation and the Empire to its Royal Air Force is beyond computation and impossible to repay, but it is within the power of everyone to contribute to the R.A.F. Benevolent Fund, which cares for those broken in the conflict and for their dependants.

Viscount Wakefield, who died early in 1941, was a generous benefactor of the R.A.F. Benevolent Fund and was for long its Chairman.

The Royal Air Force Benevolent Fund

Patron: H.M. The King

Trustees: The Rt. Hon. the Viscount Weir of Eastwood, P.C., G.C.B.; Marshal of the R.A.F., The Viscount Trenchard of Wolfeton, G.C.B., G.C.V.O., D.S.O., D.C.L., LL.D.; The Rt. Hon. the Lord Quickswood of Clothall, P.C.

The Council

The Rt. Hon. Lord Riverdale, G.B.E., LL.D., J.P. (*Chairman*).
Dame Helen Gwynne-Vaughan, G.B.E., LL.D., D.Sc., F.L.S. (*Deputy Chairman*).
Air Commodore B. C. H. Drew, C.M.G., C.V.O., C.B.E. (*Hon. Treasurer*).
Air Marshal Sir John T. Babington, K.C.B., C.B.E., D.S.O., M.C.
Air Marshal P. Babington, C.B., M.C., A.F.C
Mrs. L. M. K. Pratt Barlow, O.B.E.
Air Commodore J. W. Cordingley, C.B.E.
Air Marshal D. G. Donald, C.B., D.F.C., A.F.C.
Air Marshal Sir Sholto Douglas, K.C.B., M.C., D.F.C.
The Rev. M. H. Edwards, O.B.E., B.A., K.H.C. (Chaplain-in-Chief, R.A.F.).
Air Vice-Marshal Sir Philip W. Game, G.C.V.O., G.B.E., K.C.B., K.C.M.G., D.S.O.
Air Marshal Sir Arthur T. Harris, K.C.B., O.B.E., A.F.C.
Mrs. F. Vesey Holt.
Air Chief Marshal Sir Philip B. Joubert de la Ferte, K.C.B., C.M.G., D.S.O.
Air Vice-Marshal Sir Charles A. H. Longcroft, K.C.B., C.M.G., D.S.O., A.F.C.
Air Vice-Marshal N. D. K. MacEwen, C.B., C.M.G., D.S.O.
Air Chief Marshal Sir John M. Steel, G.C.B., K.B.E., C.M.G.
Air Marshal Sir Bertine E. Sutton, K.B.E., C.B., D.S.O., O.B.E., M.C.
Air Commandant K. J. Trefusis Forbes, C.B.E.
Secretary: Squadron Leader V. S. Erskine-Lindop, R.A.F. (retd.).
Hon. Secretary Appeals Committee: Mr. Bertram T. Rumble.

ABBREVIATIONS OF TITLES AND TERMS
EMPLOYED BY THE R.A.F.

A.A.F. Auxiliary Air Force.
A.A.F.G.L. Auxiliary Air Force General List.
A.A.F.R.O. Auxiliary Air Force Reserve of Officers.
Air Cdre. Air Commodore.
AC Aircraftman (followed by 1 or 2 to denote class).
A.C.A.S. Assistant Chief of the Air Staff.
Ach Aircrafthand.
A.C.M. Air Chief Marshal.
A.Ct. Air Commandant (W.A.A.F.).
A.M. Air Marshal.
A.M.P. Air Member for Personnel.
A.M.S.O. Air Member for Supply and Organization.
A.M.T. Air Member for Training.
A.O.C. Air Officer Commanding.
A.O.C.-in-C. Air Officer Commanding-in-Chief.
A.P/O. Acting Pilot Officer.
A.S.I. Air Speed Indicator.
A.S.O. Assistant Section Officer (with W.A.A.F.).
A/SRS. Air Sea Rescue Service.
A.T. Anti-tank.
A.T.C. Air Training Corps.
A.V.M. Air Vice Marshal.

(B.) Balloon Branch Officer.
B.P.S.O. Base Personnel Staff Officer.

C.A.S. Chief of Air Staff.
Ch. Chaplain.
Cpl. Corporal.
C.T.T.B. Central Trade Test Board.

(D.) Dental Branch Officer.
D.A.F.L. Director of Allied Air Cooperation and Foreign Liaison.
D.B. Ops. Director of Bomber Operations.
D.C.A.S. Deputy Chief of the Air Staff.
D.E.S. Director of Educational Services.
D.F. Ops. Director of Fighter Operations.
D.G.A.S. Director-General of Aircraft Safety.
D.G.C.A. Director-General of Civil Aviation.
D.G.D. Director of Ground Defence.
D.G.E. Director-General of Equipment.
D.G.M.S. Director-General of R.A.F. Medical Services.
D.G.O. Director-General of Organization.
D.G.S. Director-General of Signals.
D.G.W. Director-General of Works.
D.M.C. Director of Military Cooperation.
D.M.O. Director of the Meteorological Office.
D.O.N.C. Director of Operations (Naval Cooperation).
D. of A. Director of Accounts.
D. of C. (A.M.) Director of Contracts (Air Ministry).
D. of I. (O.) Director of Intelligence (Operations).
D. of I. (S.) Director of Intelligence (Security).
D. of M. Director of Manning.
D. of O. Director of Organization.
D. of Plans. Director of Plans.
D. of R. Director of Radio.
D. of S. Director of Signals.
D. of Tels. Director of Telecommunication.
D.O.O. Director of Operations (Overseas).
D.O.R. Director of Operational Requirements.
D. of P. Director of Postings.
D.P.E.T. Director of Pre-Entry Training.
D.P.R. Director of Public Relations.
D.P.S. Director of Personal Services.
D.S.M. Director of Servicing and Maintenance.
D.T.F. Director of Flying Training.
D.T.O. Director of Operational Training.
D.T.T. Director of Technical Training.
D.U.S. Deputy Under-Secretary of State.
D.W.A.A.F. Director of the Women's Auxiliary Air Force.
D.W.O. Director of War Organization.

(E.) Equipment Branch Officer.
E.F.T.S. Elementary Flying Training School.
E.O. Education Officer.

F.A. Financial Adviser.
F/Lt. Flight Lieutenant.
Fl.O Flight Officer (W.A.A.F.)
F/O. Flying Officer.
F/Sgt. Flight Sergeant.

(G.) Air Gunner-Officer.
G/C. Group Captain.
G.O.C. (-in-C.) General Officer Commanding (-in-Chief).

(I.) Intelligence Officer.
(I.A.F.) Indian Air Force Officer.
I. of R. Inspector of Recruiting.
I.T.W. Initial Training Wing.

J.A.G. Judge Advocate-General of the Forces.

(L.) Legal Branch Officer.
LAC Leading Aircraftman.
L. of C. Line of Communication.
L./T. Line Telegraphy.

(M.) Medical Branch Officer.

(Mc.) Marine Craft Officer.
M.D.S. Main Dressing Station.
(Met.) Meteorological.
M.L.O. Military Landing Officer.
M.R.A.F. Marshal of the Royal Air Force.

(N.) Navigation Instructor Officer.
N.T.O. Naval Transport Officer.

(O.) Observer Officer.
O.T.U. Operational Training Unit.

P.A.S. Principal Assistant Secretary.
P. Det. Port Detachment.
(Ph.) Photographic Officer.
(P.M.) Provost Marshal Duties Officer.
P.M.R.A.F.N.S. Princess Mary's R.A.F. Nursing Service.
P/O. Pilot Officer.
P.R.O. Public Relations Officer.
(P.T.) Physical Training Officer.
P.U.S. Permanent Under-Secretary of State.

Q.F. Quick Firing.
Q.M.G Quartermaster-General
Qr.M. Quartermaster.

R.A.A.F. Royal Australian Air Force.
R.A.F.O. Reserve of Air Force Officers.
R.A.F.V.R. Royal Air Force Volunteer Reserve.
R.C.A.F. Royal Canadian Air Force.
R.N.Z.A.F. Royal New Zealand Air Force.

S.A.S.O. Senior Air Staff Officer.
S.F.T.S. Service Flying Training Squadron.
Sgt. Sergeant.
S.I.O. Senior Intelligence Officer.
S/Ldr. Squadron Leader.
S.O. Section Officer (W.A.A.F.)
S. of S. Secretary of State.
Sq.O. Squadron Officer (W.A.A.F.).
S.P. Service Police.
(Sp.) Special Duties.

(T) (a) Armament Officer.
(T) (e) Engineer Officer.
(T) (s) Signals Officer.

V.C.A.S. Vice-Chief of the Air Staff.

W.A.A.F. Women's Auxiliary Air Force.
W.A.A.F. (Fl.O.). Women's Auxiliary Air Force, Flight Officer.
Wg.Cr. Wing-Commander.
Wg.O. Wing Officer (W.A.A.F.).
W.O. Warrant Officer.

Elements of Flying

A. Training and Practice in Flying

The general training of the air crew is discussed in Section I. E (pages 20-29). Here is an outline of the technical training of the pilot himself from dual control to aerobatics. The air fighting aspect is covered in Section 4. A (pages 141-147).

CAREFULLY planned and very comprehensive training is the basis of Royal Air Force flying practice. Indeed, it is acknowledged that training in the British service reaches a higher degree of efficiency than in any other air service in the world. The method is based on long experience and on the specialized work of a few officers who have shown a genius for understanding the problems of flying technique and devising methods of teaching it.

If the subdivisions are left aside for the time being, it may be said that the flying experience of a Royal Air Force pilot will normally fall into five periods. First, initial training; second, elementary training; third, advanced training; fourth, operational training, and, fifth, operational experience. As the pilot progresses from group to group he handles aircraft of steadily increasing performance.

To begin with, the initial training is purely ground training. Then comes elementary training done with low-powered aeroplanes, some of which were developed from the light aeroplane class. These machines are small and handy and they are constructed so that they are capable of all aerobatics. The consequence is they provide in miniature the whole flying regime (with the exception of retractable undercarriage and variable pitch propeller) and enable pupils to be thoroughly well grounded before they tackle the faster and more powerful aircraft.

Elementary training and advanced training both use a system which had its origins in the Gosport school of Colonel Smith-Barry, but this system has been greatly developed in recent years, and in the advanced section it includes means of coping with the great complexity of modern machines.

Dual Control and Solo Flying. Dual control is the first step in the actual learning to fly, though it is worth recalling that the earliest pilots learned in an altogether different way. They began by making short hops over the ground, gradually extending their length and finally taking off without having previously handled an aeroplane in the air.

Today the dual control methods enable the whole handling of the machine to be studied by the pupil without risk, for the pilot instructor is always at hand to correct faults and to get the pupil out of difficulties.

Dual control, as fitted to modern elementary training aircraft, is complete in all respects. Here again an advance is to be noted, for the earlier dual control machines had no instruments in the pupil's compartment.

The time taken to the first solo varies with the pupil, but in the Royal Air Force the method is to avoid any attempts at rushing people through this part of their training. While the flying training goes on there runs parallel with it ground training, which helps the pupil to understand all the principles of navigation and which gives him a grounding in the construction of the aircraft.

Initial trainers are both biplanes and monoplanes. From them the pupil passes to the advanced trainers, which are still dual control machines but have much higher powered engines and are capable of greater performances. They also have the retractable undercarriages, which are a feature of most operational types and which the pupil has to learn to use early in his career.

Landing and taking off are the real problems before the pupil. The handling of an aircraft in the air may be allowed to come slowly afterwards. There is, of course, a wide gap between flying an aeroplane and flying it really well.

Drill of Vital Actions. It is when the pupil comes on to these more advanced machines that he learns the importance of the system of memorizing the flying procedure which is used in the service. This method is called the drill of vital actions and it is best understood by citing an example. A catchword is used for example,

SECTION 2. A — Flying Training and Practice

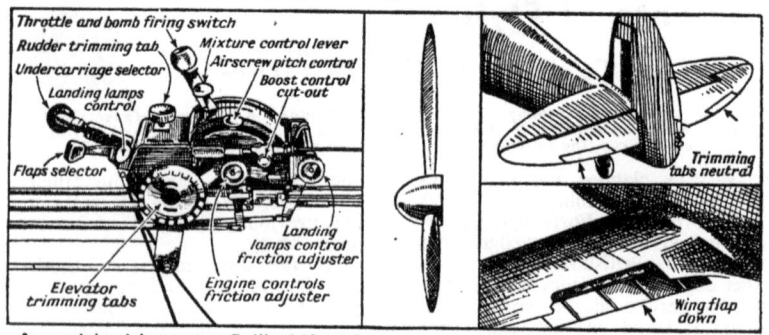

Labels on diagram:
- Throttle and bomb firing switch
- Rudder trimming tab
- Undercarriage selector
- Landing lamps control
- Mixture control lever
- Airscrew pitch control
- Boost control cut-out
- Flaps selector
- Landing lamps control friction adjuster
- Elevator trimming tabs
- Engine controls friction adjuster
- Trimming tabs neutral
- Wing flap down

As explained in text, a Drill of Vital Actions is taught the pupil so that he neglects none of the vital controls. These diagrams illustrate the drills "T.M.P." and "Flaps"

"T.M.P." and "Flaps." This refers to the following things:

- T = Trimming tabs. These the pupil must remember to set neutral before taking off.
- M = Mixture controls. These, which control the strength of the mixture to the engines, must be set for rich before taking off.
- P = Pitch of airscrew. Before taking off this must be set in the fine position.
- Flaps = Wing flaps, which have to be correctly set according to the instructions before taking off. This usually means that they must be up, or, at any rate, only depressed a small part of their travel.

This is a general catchword which would cover a great many machines, but the drill of vital actions has to be varied for particular types.

Before taking off the pilot is instructed always to do the drill of vital actions. He has to do this just before he begins the taking-off run. He is instructed then to make quite sure that no other aircraft is approaching the landing ground, and that there is nothing on the line of take-off. He then releases the wheel brakes and begins the taking-off run, which has to be made directly into wind during these instructional flights. Later the pilot learns to take-off across wind, and to land across wind. After he has taken off there is another drill of vital actions, also memorized by a catchword. The object of the catchword is to ensure that the pilot does not neglect any of the controls and is to guarantee, as far as possible, against lapses of memory.

Many accidents in the past were due to lapses of memory, which can occur about the simplest and most obvious things. But the drill of vital actions, if it is gone through conscientiously, enables a pilot to make sure that he has taken all the correct measures.

While the flying training goes on the pupil is taught to meet emergencies, and the question of what he should do if the engine fails when taking off, of the dangers of attempting to turn if the engine fails when the machine is taking off, and similar problems are treated. Instrument flying is also gradually taught.

When the pupil goes over to high-speed aeroplanes he is made familiar with the big acceleration forces which may be generated in quick turns. These are usually spoken of as multiples of "g," or, in other words, multiples of the forces of gravity. The pupil is taught that high speed makes map reading more difficult, though navigation becomes easier owing to the proportionate reduction of drift resulting from the wind.

Chiefly, too, the effects of good streamlining and the flying qualities of aircraft are taught, and the pupil has to be ready for the very flat glide when undercarriage is retracted and flaps are up, and for the very rapid increase of speed in a dive. There are many other special things which he has to learn before he is competent to fly the higher performance types, and these instructions go with appropriate instructions as to how the engine must be treated. Aerobatics as such come later in the schedule, but spinning has to be thoroughly mastered at an early stage, because this is a form of manoeuvre with which all pilots must

Flying Training and Practice SECTION 2. A

be able to deal almost from the beginning of their flying career. Intentional spins are made with the initial training machines, and the pupil is taught the method of extricating the aircraft from spinning by centralizing the controls. Recovery is made by giving full opposite rudder and by easing the control stick forward. The pilot is then able to pull out of the dive which follows.

Aerobatics in Training. Aerobatics are an essential part of the training of an operational pilot, for, they are the finest form of training for handling aircraft.

Spinning, illustrated here, and extrication from a spin are taught at the outset of flying training.

Aerobatics are generally regarded as all manoeuvres other than turning, gentle diving and side-slip landing. Side-slipping itself, when done apart from landing, is probably best classified as an aerobatic. Training in aerobatics is not begun until the pupil is thoroughly competent in ordinary flying. They start usually with the loop and stall turn, and the pupil is instructed from the start that he must practise aerobatics only when he has a considerable margin of height. For if he makes any mistake, he will need the height in order to recover and to resume normal flight.

Some aerobatics are extremely difficult to do well, but a pilot who has mastered the approach and landing from all types of aircraft usually finds little trouble with aerobatics provided he spends enough time at practising them.

While all this practical flying is going on the pupil gathers information and instruction on navigation, on what to do in emergencies, on meteorology, and he begins to learn something about night flying. Forced landings are studied nowadays scientifically, and a complete and simple system is provided to help the pilot on such occasions. The precautions to be taken when flying high, and the methods of using oxygen are taught, and the pilot is also given full instruction for the use of his parachute.

Service Flying. So far the Royal Air Force pilot has gone through a course which resembles closely that of a Civil pilot. But he moves forward from there to the special matters of Service flying, and to certain things in which they differ completely from Civil flying. It is now that the tactical side of war flying comes into view, and all the problems of inter-communication in flight, methods of attack, and formation flying have to be considered. In addition, flying in bad visibility has to be specially studied, and some information and instruction about flying in tropical countries must be given.

Formation Flying. This subject is dealt with in Section 4. B.

Flying Instruction Routine. An attempt will now be made to summarize the routine of flying instruction as it is given in the Royal Air Force. First of all the pupil is grounded in the theory of flight and in those things in which preliminary verbal

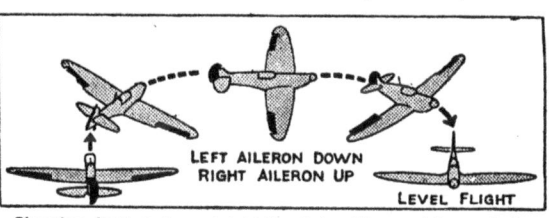

Showing how a turn (right-hand in this case) is made by use of rudder and aileron control in conjunction.

Section 2. A — Flying Training and Practice

instruction is necessary before he handles an aircraft in the air.

Straight and level flying is taught as the first step in the actual air work. It comes immediately after the pupil has been familiarized with the effects of the separate controls. After straight and level flying a study of stalling is usually given because this affects all aircraft movements. Then come climbing, gliding and turning.

Stalling occurs when the aeroplane is flying at such an angle (more loosely speaking, so slowly) that its wings fail to give it support. The aeroplane then stalls, the nose drops and it goes into a dive. It then gathers speed and the wings get a grip again.

Before the pupil can go solo he must be completely competent in the two most difficult things to the novice, taking off and landing. Landing is taught by frequent practice. The method of the instructional circuit, which has been developed over a period of years in Civil and Service training, is used, and there is no better method of training and probably never will be. With the aid of the dual controls the pupil learns how to approach the aerodrome on an appropriate glide with the engine closed down and how to hold it off until it sets down in a correct landing.

Tricycle undercarriage aircraft are coming into the Royal Air Force in increasing numbers and these require some modification in taking off and landing technique, but at present this technique is taught at a later stage. Cross wind take-offs and landings are taught, and there is the practice of forced landings, the pupil being instructed in how to select appropriate surfaces from the air. Night flying begins with a study of the uses of lights and instruments and especially of cockpit lighting.

Retractable Undercarriages. Modern machines are all fitted with retractable undercarriages and with variable pitch airscrews, and it is noteworthy that directly an aeroplane of this type has left the ground the pilot immediately retracts the undercarriage.

This is usually done by an engine-driven pump, which actuates the hydraulic gear that actually lifts the wheels, and Royal Air Force pilots when they are seen taking off from an aerodrome to go into action invariably raise the undercarriages of their machines the instant the machines are air-borne.

This is a sound measure for two reasons. First of all, it enables the aircraft to accelerate quickly, for directly the drag of the undercarriage is removed the speed goes up rapidly. In the second place, it is a wise precaution against a forced landing.

Modern engines are very trustworthy, but if one happened to fail when the aircraft was taking off the pilot would be more likely to effect a landing without injury to himself if he did it with the undercarriage retracted.

With the undercarriage down an aeroplane that is landing is readily turned over if it strikes an obstacle. And if it does turn over it is likely to do serious damage to itself and probably to its pilot. If, on the other hand, the aeroplane is forced-landed with the undercarriage retracted it will be damaged and the airscrew blades will almost certainly be bent, but the total damage to the machine is likely to be much less than when the other method is used, and the chance are that the pilot will be unhurt. That is why the Royal Air Force encourages retraction of the undercarriage the moment the aircraft is air-borne.

High Flying. This is another of the special classes of work which has been greatly developed in recent months, and pilots have to familiarize themselves with manoeuvring at height.

The best aeroplanes lose their powers of manoeuvre when they are flying near their ceilings at very great heights. The air there, being thinner than near the ground, fails to support them as firmly and the machine cannot be turned about rapidly without the

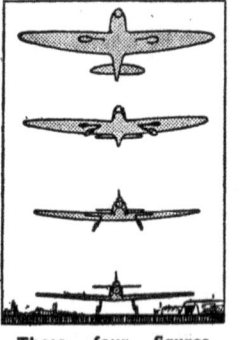

These four figures show how the retractable legs are taken up on leaving the ground.

Flying Training and Practice — SECTION 2. A

risk of its losing height or even going into a spin. Modern Service pilots have to handle their machines at great heights. They use oxygen and are protected against the cold by cockpit heating and by appropriate clothing.

Controls. The major instruments are the control column, which works the elevator and ailerons;. the rudder bar; and the engine throttle, which con-

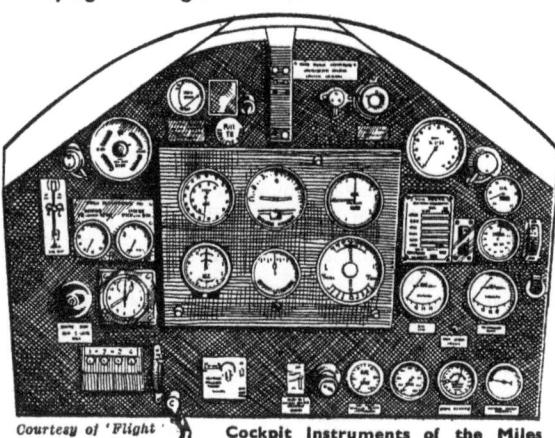

Courtesy of 'Flight'

Cockpit Instruments of the Miles Master Trainer

1, Flaps Indicator; 2, Airspeed Indicator Correction Card; 3, Speaking Tube; 4, Reflector Sight Lamp; 5, Reflector Sight Dimmer Switch; 6, 10, Cockpit Lamps Dimmer Switches; 7, Undercarriage Indicator; 8, Instrument Flying Hood Release; 9, Revolution Indicator; 11, Signalling Switchbox; 12, Main Magneto and Undercarriage Indicator Switches; 13, Oxygen Regulator; 14, Air-speed Indicator; 15, Artificial Horizon; 16, Rate of Climb Indicator; 17, Oil Thermometer; 18, Oil Gauge; 19, Boost Gauge; 20, Fuel Gauge; 21, Cockpit Lamp; 22, Landing Lamps Switch; 23, Time of Flight Clock; 24, Altimeter Switch; 25, Directional Gyroscope; 26, Turn and Bank Indicator; 27, 28, Fuel Contents Indicators; 29, Fire Extinguisher Switch (under Flap); 30, Bomb Selector Switches; 31, Radiator Flap Indicator; 32, Bomb Jettison Switch; 33, Oil Cock; 34, Starting Magneto Switch; 35, Engine Priming Pump; 36, Pneumatic Pressure Gauge; 37, Radiator Temperature Gauge; 38, Fuel Contents Indicator Switch; 39, Brake Triple Pressure Gauge; 40, Hydraulic System Pressure Gauge; 41, Control Box; 42, Radiator Flap Control; 43, P.6 Compass.

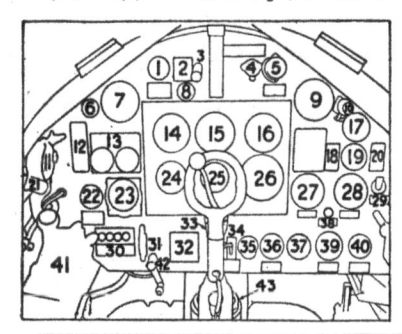

trols the engine speed. The throttle must be considered in relation to the constant speed airscrew control; the standard fitting is a throttle lever near the left hand of the pilot, fully open in the forward position and closed in the back position.

The elevator controls the aircraft in pitch, or, in other words, causes it to point up or down. The ailerons control it laterally, or cause it to tip to one side or the other. And the rudder controls it in yaw, or makes it skid round to right or to left. If the rudder is used alone the machine tends to skid

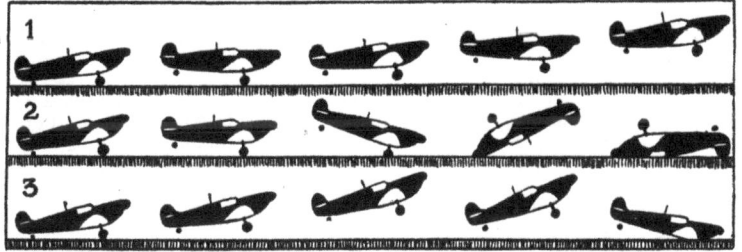

Good take-off is shown in (1). If the tail is held too high (2), the aircraft may turn over. If tail is too low at take-off (3), the 'plane will fail to rise.

Flying Training and Practice

round, and for a proper turn the ailerons must also be used to apply bank when the rudder is used.

The characteristic aeroplane turn is therefore a mixture of rudder and ailerons, and is not only a yawing of the machine but also a banking of the machine.

Almost all aeroplane manoeuvres are done by combined movements of stick and rudder bar, and there are very few that can be done by the movement of one control alone.

Taking Off and Landing. Taking off, for example, demands that the aircraft be first of all put into flying position by raising the tail, and then here again the rudder and ailerons must be used all the time if the path of the aeroplane is to be properly adjusted, and the elevator alone is not enough to make the landing.

Instruments. The instruments with which a modern aircraft is fitted and which its pilot must know how to use appear to be so numerous as to be almost incomprehensible. But, in fact, they are so grouped that a pilot can accustom himself to them fairly rapidly. There are the master instruments which give such things as the air speed of the machine, the engine revolutions, the height, and the course, and these are generally kept together with certain of

In making a proper landing the aircraft, having turned into the wind, is flattened out and sinks down on its undercarriage and tail wheel.

PLANE TURNS INTO WIND
GLIDING IN
FLYING LEVEL
3 - POINT LANDING

Below, a faulty landing is shown; the tail was dropped too soon.

that it runs across the aerodrome gathering speed, and then is lifted from the ground. It might seem that this entire process could be done with the elevator, and it is true that the tail is lifted in the first part of the run by pushing the stick forward and depressing the elevator. It is also true that the machine is coaxed off the ground when it has gathered sufficient speed by easing the stick back and so raising the elevator and causing the machine to climb.

But all these elevator movements must be accompanied by rudder and aileron movements or the machine will get out of its true path.

Similarly, when a landing is being made the elevator is the master control, and it causes the aeroplane to flatten out and to hold off from the landing ground until it sinks down on to its **undercarriage and tail wheel.** But the blind flying instruments which aid in the control of the machine within cloud or fog. The remaining instruments give information about such things as oil temperatures, fuel quantities, and so on, and are therefore instruments to which the pilot refers from time to time but which do not occupy his whole attention.

Flying has become more and more complicated as time goes on and the consequence is that the training of a pilot has become more complex. Especially is this true of the **Service** pilot, whose responsibilities have increased tenfold. The Royal Air Force methods of training are unequalled in giving each man who passes through the proper courses a full understanding of his work and in practising him in the handling of his machine so that he may obtain the best results in action.

BRITISH & AMERICAN AIRCRAFT IN R.A.F. SERVICE

SUPERMARINE SPITFIRE

One of the finest fighters of all time, the Spitfire dates back to 1936. In latest form armament comprises two cannon and four machine-guns in the wings. Fuselage is of monocoque construction and this, with the single-spar wings, has a stressed-skin flush-riveted covering. Engine, a Rolls-Royce Merlin 61 with two-speed, two-stage supercharger maintaining induction pressure up to 40,000 ft. To absorb the increased power of the newest engine a four-bladed air-screw is fitted.

HAWKER HURRICANE

The latest Hawker Hurricane is armed either with twelve machine-guns or four cannon, all mounted in wings. Also used as a light bomber, with four 20-mm. cannon. Considered to be most formidable and versatile single-seater fighter yet in service; has been used in many low-level attacks on ships and land targets in offensive sweeps. Original Hurricanes first went into service with squadrons early in 1938. Span, 40 ft. Length, 31 ft. 5 in. Height, 13 ft. 3 in. Engine, Rolls-Royce Merlin.

82

BOULTON PAUL DEFIANT

Two-seater fighter. Armament, four machine-guns in power-operated turret behind pilot's cockpit. Highly successful, especially as a night fighter. Wings, fuselage, and tail, metal - covered and flush - riveted. Engine, Rolls-Royce twelve-cylinder Merlin II, 1,030 h.p. at 3,000 r.p.m. In plan wing shape similar to that of Hurricane.

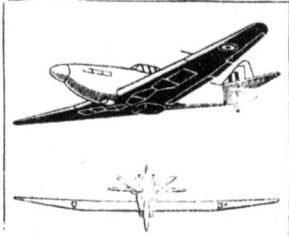

BRISTOL BEAUFIGHTER

Used both as a night fighter and on day duties. Two Bristol Hercules 1,400 h.p. sleeve-valve engines. 1,500 miles range; speed exceeding 300 m.p.h. Six Browning m.g. in wings and four 20 m.m. Hispano-Suiza type cannon in nose. On Bristol lines. Span, 57 ft. 10 in. Length, 41 ft.

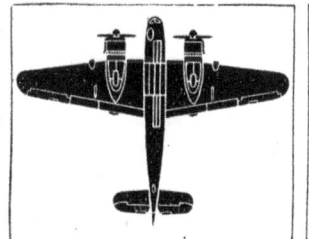

BRISTOL BEAUFORT

A torpedo-bomber in service since early 1940. With Coastal Command, has taken heavy toll of enemy shipping in torpedo attacks. Note similarity to Bristol Beaufighter. Engines, Bristol Taurus II radials, 1,065 h.p. each. The wings stressed-skin design, covered light alloy. Span, 57 ft. 10 in. Length, 44 ft. 2 in.

LOCKHEED LIGHTNING

American. Striking feature is the twin tail boom arrangement; booms are extensions of the engine mountings built into the wings. Engines, 1,090 h.p. liquid-cooled Allisons; pilot in streamlined nacelle amidships. Armament: 4 or more machine-guns and cannon, all arranged in nose. All-metal construction; tail unit has twin rudders and fins. Span, 52 ft. Length, 37 ft. 10 in.

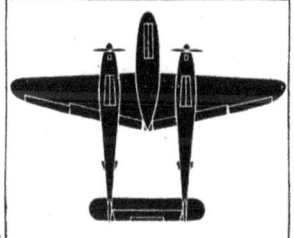

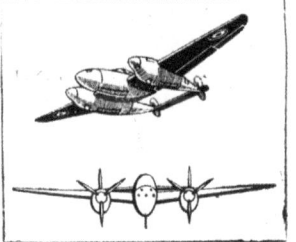

84

DOUGLAS HAVOC
High mid-wing twin-engined American monoplane. A night fighter; also engaged in low-level attacks on enemy aerodromes. A modified version of Boston bomber. Two Double-Row Cyclone radial engines, 1,600 b.p. Retractable tricycle undercarriage. Carries crew of three. Span, 61 ft. 4 in. Length, 47 ft. 7 in. Speed 325 m.p.h.; range 1,200 miles.

BREWSTER BUFFALO
American single-seater highly manoeuvrable fighter notable for rotund fuselage into which undercarriage retracts. Air-cooled radial Wright Cyclone engine, 1,200 h.p.; speed, 330 m.p.h. Six machine-guns, two on engine cowling. Recognized by position of wings in relation to fuselage, and barrel-like shape. Metal construction and stressed-metal covering. Span, 35 ft. Length, 26 ft.

REPUBLIC THUNDERBOLT

Low-wing monoplane fighter, fastest and biggest U.S.A. machine of the type, weighing six tons and having a top speed in excess of 400 m.p.h. The engine is a Pratt & Whitney Double Wasp, of 2,000 h.p., with 18 cylinders. Diagrams show the characteristic deep oval cowling to engine, the small tips and curved trailing edge of wings. Span, 41 ft.; length, 32 ft. 8 in.; height, 13 ft

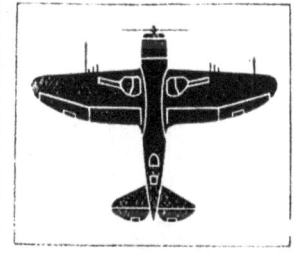

CURTISS KITTYHAWK

Monoplane single-seater fighter; later development of Curtiss Tomahawk, the American aircraft which is giving excellent service in the war in the Middle East. Kittyhawk has boosted 12-cylinder Allison engine, which develops 1,325 h.p. Recognized when flying by distinctive wing shape. Leading edge is untapered and the trailing edge is of swept-forward pattern.

LOCKHEED VENTURA

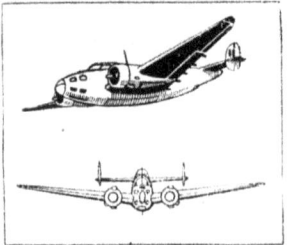

Twin-engined reconnaissance bomber, a development of the Lockheed Hudson so largely used by Coastal Command. Though larger, similar in outward appearance; important difference is that under end of tail is swept up. Two Pratt & Whitney Double Wasp radial air-cooled engines, 2,000 h.p. Speed about 275 m.p.h. Length 49 ft. 10 in.; span 65 ft. 6 in.; height 11 ft. 10 in.

VULTEE VENGEANCE

An American dive-bomber in service with the R.A.F. A two-seater, with a Wright Cyclone engine of 1,600 h.p. The long cockpit cover and distinctive wing plan are shown in the diagrams; the tail fin is tall. Diving brakes on outer wing panels. Length, 36 ft.; span, 48 ft.; height, 12 ft. 10 in. Dihedral confined to outer wing panels. It carries bombs internally.

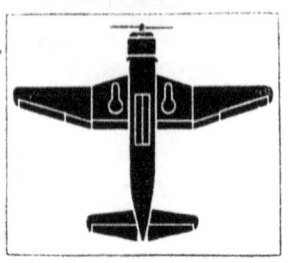

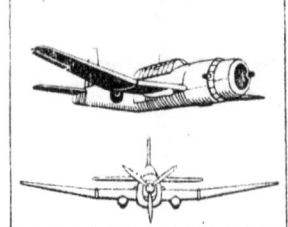

N. AMERICAN MUSTANG

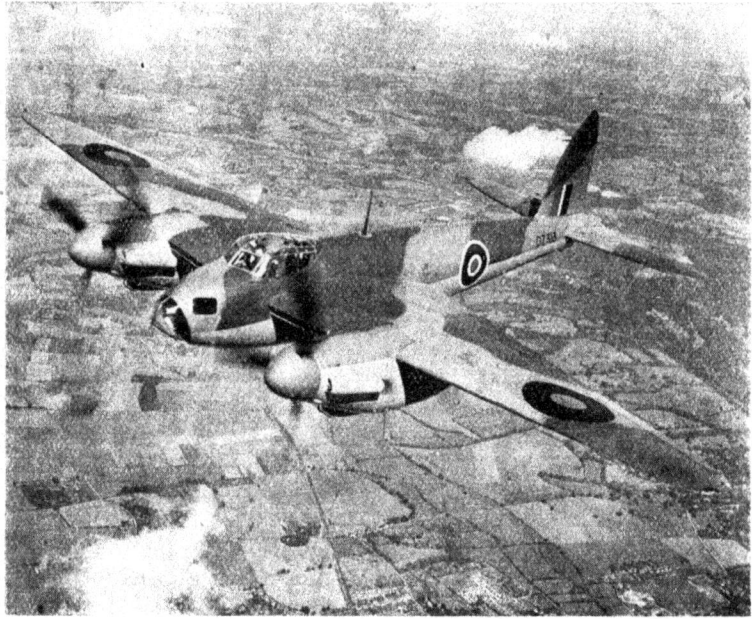

In service with Army Cooperation Squadrons of R.A.F. for use in low-flying attacks against ground targets. One liquid-cooled Allison engine of 1,150 h.p.; fastest machine in Army Cooperation Command type. Armed with two machine-guns in each wing and two more synchronized to fire through airscrew. Length, 31 ft. 3 in.; span, 37 ft. 3 in.; height, 8 ft. 8 in.

DE HAVILLAND MOSQUITO

A remarkable reconnaissance bomber which has made some outstanding long-range operations against enemy-occupied Europe. Of wooden construction, powered with two Rolls-Royce engines; three-bladed airscrew. Armament may consist of four cannon and four machine-guns. Length 40 ft. 9 in.; span, 54 ft. 2 in.

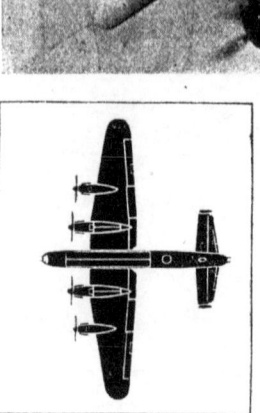

AVRO LANCASTER

Described as the world's finest four-engined bomber, and is the fastest British machine in this class. Power plant is four Rolls-Royce Merlin engines, each of 1,260 h.p. The gross weight is 60,000 lb.; length, 69 ft.; span, 102 ft.; height, 20 ft. 4 in. Top speed is about 300 m.p.h., and the range is about 3,000 miles. The armament is 10 rifle-calibre machine-guns in four turrets—two each in nose, dorsal and ventral turrets, and four in tail.

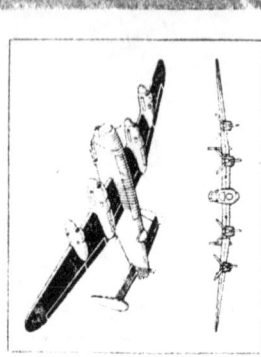

AVRO MANCHESTER HEAVY BOMBER

The Manchester is unusual because, although classed as a heavy bomber, it is driven by only two engines—Rolls Royce Vultures (liquid-cooled, 24-cylinders) with a power output of about 1,845 h.p. It is an all-metal mid-wing monoplane, and the long oval fuselage is well shown by the diagrams. Two machine-guns in nose, two in the dorsal turret, and four in rear of fuselage. Span, 90 ft. 1 in.; length, 70 ft.; height, 19 ft. 6 in. Bomb-aimer's compartment in nose has sloping glass panel. The Lancaster was developed from this aircraft.

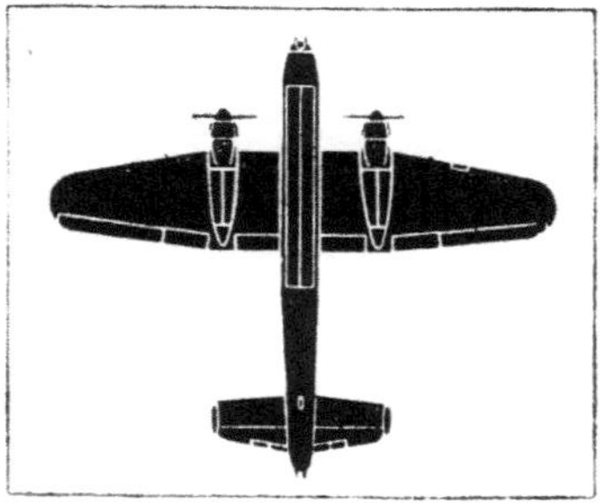

SHORT STIRLING

This great four-engined bomber came into service in March, 1941, and has since been engaged in day and night attacks on targets in Germany and Italy. A product of the firm of Short Brothers, Ltd., it is worthily upholding the reputation of this pioneer company. The machine is a mid-wing monoplane, powered with Bristol Hercules engines of 1,400 h.p. Owing to its heavy armament and the fact that its great size and weight do not impair its manoeuvrability, the Stirling is capable of tackling enemy fighter aircraft so that an escort is not always necessary. The excessively long nose, single fin, and rudder arranged well forward of the tail turret are main points of recognition. Above, in flight.

HANDLEY PAGE HALIFAX

Manufactured by one of Britain's pioneer aircraft firms, the Halifax is playing a major part in long-range bombing attacks on the enemy. It is a fast, extremely powerful mid-wing monoplane with a wing span of 99 ft. Power is derived from four Rolls-Royce Merlin engines. One of the special qualities of the Halifax is its ability to take off from ordinary aerodromes under heavy over-load conditions. The general performance is enhanced by the inclusion of slotted flaps in the wings. The Halifax is very heavily armed, with guns arranged in turrets in nose and tail.

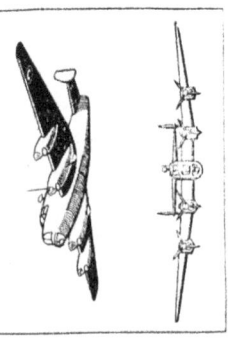

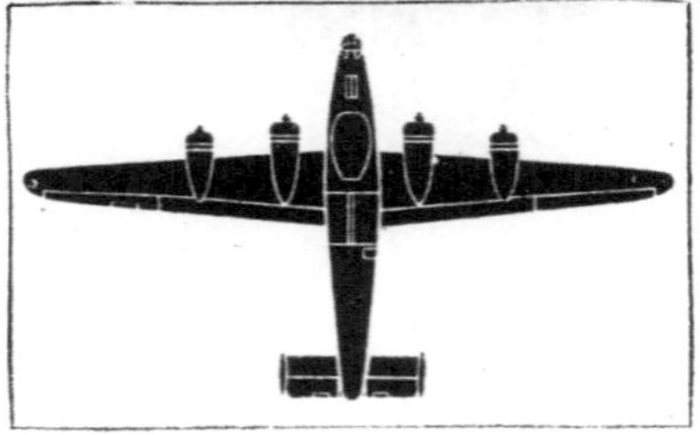

CONSOLIDATED LIBERATOR

A high-wing four-engined monoplane bomber, one of several heavy types supplied to Britain by the United States. The engines are 1,200 h.p. Pratt and Whitney radials. Gun turrets are installed in the nose and tail and there are also gun positions in the fuselage. Points of recognition are the long tapering wings, the twin fins and rudders arranged on the tail, and the retractable tricycle undercarriage. The wing span is 110 ft. Length, 63 ft. Height, 19 ft.

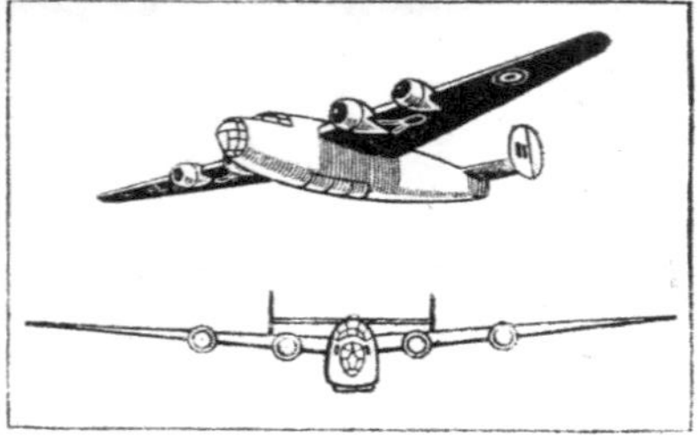

BOEING FLYING FORTRESS

An American aeroplane which has taken part in outstanding daylight raids carried out at great height. Specially designed for operations in the substratosphere, the four 1,200 h.p. Wright Cyclone engines being fitted with exhaust-driven superchargers. Carries a crew of seven, and is outstanding in the heavy-bomber class. The tapered wings and engine mountings projecting well ahead of the leading edge are distinguishing features. Span, 103 ft. 9 in. Length, 67 ft. 10 in.

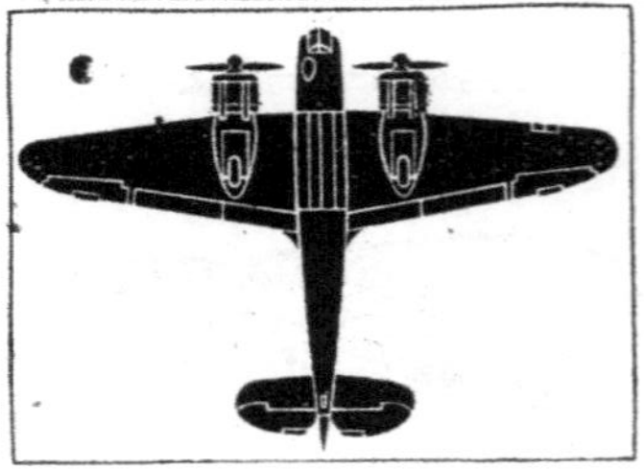

BRISTOL BLENHEIM, Mk. IV

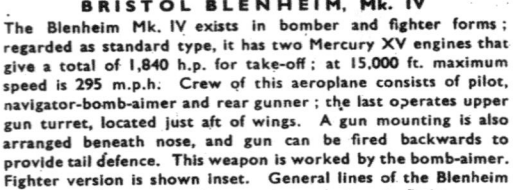

The Blenheim Mk. IV exists in bomber and fighter forms; regarded as standard type, it has two Mercury XV engines that give a total of 1,840 h.p. for take-off; at 15,000 ft. maximum speed is 295 m.p.h. Crew of this aeroplane consists of pilot, navigator-bomb-aimer and rear gunner; the last operates upper gun turret, located just aft of wings. A gun mounting is also arranged beneath nose, and gun can be fired backwards to provide tail defence. This weapon is worked by the bomb-aimer. Fighter version is shown inset. General lines of the Blenheim are shown, with, insets, a second view in flight.

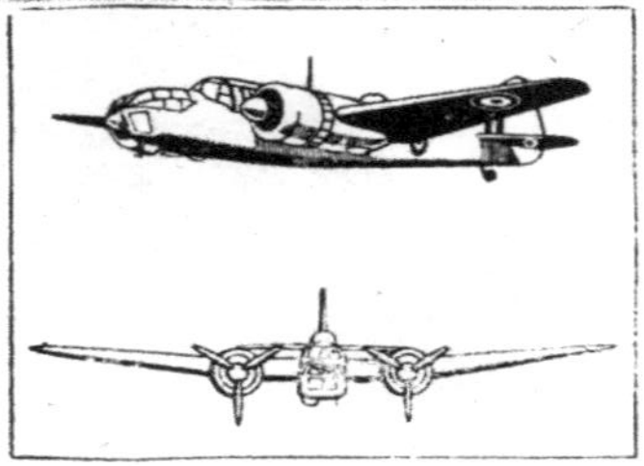

CONSOLIDATED CATALINA

This flying-boat is one of several types of aircraft now in service with the Coastal Command. Manufactured by the Consolidated Aircraft Corporation, of San Diego, California, it has earned a great reputation as a reconnaissance machine with an immense range (some 4,000 miles). Catalinas played a notable part in the tracking of the 'Bismarck.' It has a metal-stressed skin and also fabric covering in the control surfaces. It is powered with two 1,200 h.p. Twin Wasp engines. Note floats folding up on to wings.

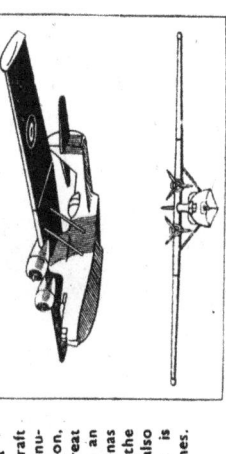

SHORT SUNDERLAND

Sunderlands are engaged in convoy work, submarine patrol and other duties far out over Atlantic and North Sea. Have achieved many rescues of men of Merchant Navy after attack by U-boats. Mess rooms and a galley in the hull. Four 1,000 h.p. Bristol Pegasus engines.

SARO LERWICK

In service with the Coastal Command. Fastest aircraft of its type in operation. Special features are the great depth of hull, and the thin section and sharp taper of the wings. Bristol Hercules sleeve-valve engines. Three power-operated gun turrets.

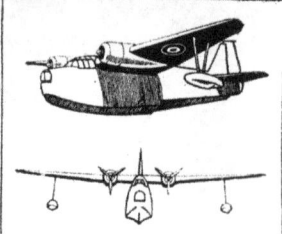

SECTION 2.

Aircraft Employed by the R.A.F.
Principal Types of British and American Machines Now in Use

Conditions of security prevent this review of aircraft used by the R.A.F. from being complete or even up-to-date, but it does present an account of the main types in service which has considerable reference value and great interest.

THE success of the Royal Air Force in this war may justly be attributed to four principal causes: (1) the fighting spirit of British and Empire manhood, (2) the excellent system of training, (3) the skill of our aircraft designers and constructors, and (4) the policy laid down by certain nameless worthies at the Air Ministry. Those unknown tacticians laid it down that, desirable as high speed is, it is not the only or even the most important quality in an Air Force aeroplane. A certain amount of speed, they decided, must be sacrificed to fighting ability. It was not enough for a fighter to be able to overtake its opponent if it was not more than probably able to shoot it down. A certain degree of manoeuvrability would have to be sacrificed in order to get greater speed—that was inevitable when the low-wing monoplane superseded the more agile biplane—but once combat was joined the British fighter must possess overwhelming fire power.

Fighters. Consequently the day-fighters of the R.A.F. were each given eight machine-guns of .303 calibre, mounted in the wings where the rate of fire would not be slowed down by an interrupter gear, as is the case when guns fire through the arc of the airscrew. The shell-firing "cannon" was held in reserve, to be introduced (as it has been) when the deadly fire of the eight Brownings forced the enemy to introduce armour into his

Above, Curtiss Tomahawk single-seat fighter, speed 360 m.p.h. at 16,000 feet (U.S.A.).

Left, Armstrong-Whitworth Whitley bomber, showing the deadly gun turrets.

Consolidated 28/5A Amphibian (U.S.A.). Floats shown retracted.

E

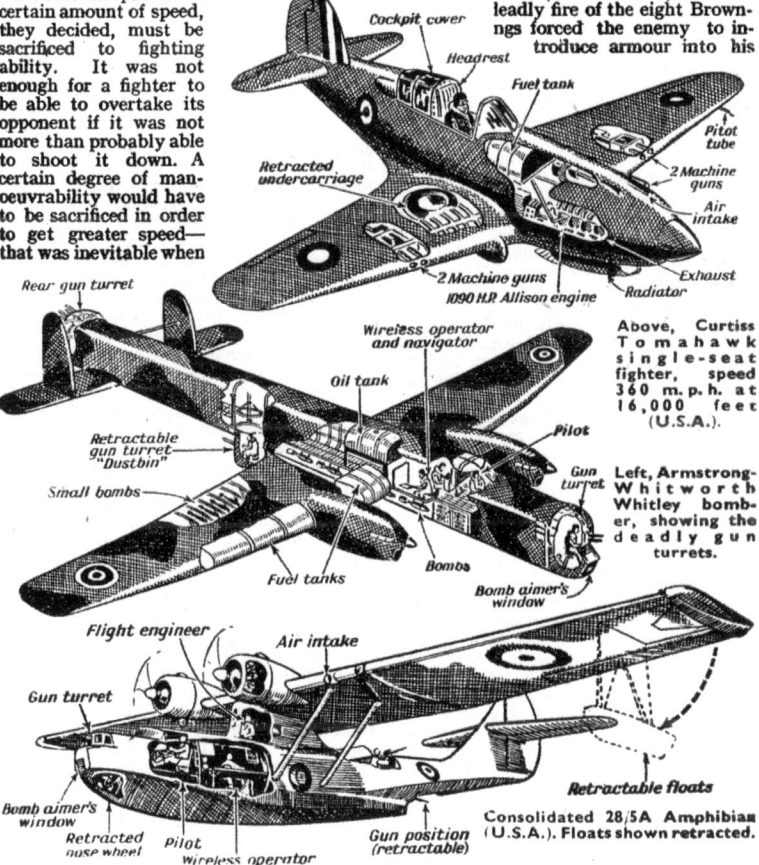

Aircraft of the R.A.F.

machines—and thereby reduce the load of bombs or petrol which they could carry. Despite this heavy armament the Hurricane and the Spitfire have top speeds well over 300 m.p.h., while the latter was the fastest fighter in service with any Air Force in the world. A recent development in fighters is the two-seater class which does not depend on forward fire but has a turret behind the pilot (*e.g.* Defiant night-fighter).

Apart from playing their major role—*e.g.* combating enemy aircraft in the air, the newer R.A.F. fighters with their armament of four 20 mm. cannon are now being employed on an increasing scale for low-level attacks on a variety of targets. They have proved highly effective when enemy aerodromes, gun emplacements, coastal shipping, railway and road transport and ground forces have been assaulted in offensive sweeps.

Heavy bombers and Flying Boats. A similar decision was taken in the case of heavy bombers and flying boats. The civil war in Spain seemed to confirm the theory that bombers could not hold their combat against fighters, and therefore must find safety in speed rather than in fire power. The Germans thereupon (in 1935) put into production the Heinkel 111 K, at the time faster than existing British fighters, but having only three machine-guns which the gunners had to swing, depress or elevate. This Heinkel could neither fight a Spitfire or Hurricane, nor escape from it unless a cloud was near.

The Air Ministry boldly decided to give British bombers a powerful armament, by providing gun turrets operated by the power of the engines and making no demands on the strength of the gunners. These turrets involved a large cross-section in the fuselage, and that, as well as the drag of the turrets, meant a slower speed. These turrets can mount one, two or four guns. Consequently, our Wellingtons, Whitleys, and Sunderlands have often shot down fighters which attacked them. The medium-sized Blenheim and the reconnaissance Hudson also have a turret.

Reconnaissance Machines. For reconnaissance several classes of aircraft are used. For short, tactical reconnaissance for the Army the standard type is the Lysander, a two-seater high-wing monoplane. The main requirements are a good view below and a wide range of speed. The pilot is also the observer, while the back seat is occupied by an air gunner. For longer or strategical reconnaissance, medium bombers such as the Blenheim have been used.

For reconnaissance over the sea both flying boats and landplanes are used. The former have the longer range, but the latter somewhat higher speed. The Sunderland flying boat and the Hudson landplane are the two most prominent types used by the Coastal Command. The Beaufort has done much good work as a torpedo-bomber, as well as general reconnaissance. The Botha is a general reconnaissance landplane

Training Craft. The first types to which the pilot pupil will be introduced will naturally be the training machines. The Tiger Moth is an elementary trainer, and when the pupil is expert in that, he will receive advanced training in either single-engined or twin-engined types. The Master is an advanced single-engined trainer, and the Oxford Airspeed, a twin-engined type.

Design Tendencies. After more than two years of war the trend of aircraft design is breaking fresh ground. For fighters and bombers the call is for more and more height; this entails greater power from engines, new forms of airscrew, de-icing devices, and special cabins for pilots and crew. Increase in horse-power is being secured by multiplicity of cylinders, by new superchargers and by fresh grades of fuel. This rise in power output has compelled designers to make changes in airscrew design, and the normal three-blade airscrew is being replaced by four- and six-blade airscrews, the latter of the contra-rotating type which provides a satisfactory means of overcoming the effect of engine "torque" and improving take-off. Important developments are being made in the design of superchargers which are not gear-driven in the orthodox manner but are worked by means of the residual gases in the engine exhaust.

Notable progress is being achieved in the heavy bomber class. The Short Stirling and the Handley Page Halifax are two outstanding examples of British design in which speed, range and bomb-carrying capacity are unexcelled.

As the war continues the influx of American aircraft of all types into service with the R.A.F. continually expands. At home the Douglas Havoc is used as a night-fighter and many German bombers have been destroyed by it. Squadrons in the Bomber Command are now equipped with the American Flying Fortress, introduced as a sub-stratosphere bomber.

In long-range patrol work over the Atlantic the twin-engined Catalina flying-boat shares honours with the Lockheed Hudson, an American veteran of the war in the air. In the Middle East American-built aircraft have proved their worth repeatedly. The Glenn-Martin Maryland bomber figured prominently in the Taranto episode, and has been engaged in countless raids on Italian objectives. The Curtiss Tomahawk fighter continues to grapple with the Italian air force with marked success, and is also in use in many squadrons stationed in Britain.

R.A.F. AIRCRAFT IN SERVICE

Makers	Machine	Engines	Armament	Top Speed
\multicolumn{5}{c}{*Fighters*}				
Gloster	Gladiator	1 Bristol Mercury (840 h.p.)	6 machine-guns	255
Supermarine	Spitfire	1 R.R. Merlin (1,030 h.p.)	8 machine-guns	367
"	Spitfire V	1 R.R. Merlin	2 cannon 4 m.g.	—
"	Spitfire IX	1 R.R. Merlin 61	4 m.g., 2 cannon	—
Hawker	Hurricane I	1 R.R. Merlin III (1,030 h.p.)	8 machine-guns	335
"	Hurricane IIB	1 R.R. Merlin xx (1,260 h.p.)	10–12 m.g.	—
"	Hurricane IIC	" " "	4 20-mm. cannon	—
"	Typhoon	1 Napier Sabre (2,350 h.p.)	—	—
Boulton Paul	Defiant	1 R.R. Merlin (1,030 h.p.)	4 m.g. in turret	—
Westland	Whirlwind	2 R.R Peregrine (885 h.p.)	4 20-mm. cannon	350
Bristol	Beaufighter I	2 Hercules (1,400 h.p.)	4 20-mm. cannon + 6 m.g.	over
"	Beaufighter II	2 R.R. Merlin		330
\multicolumn{5}{c}{*Bombers*}				
Armstrong	Whitley	2 Merlin(1,030 h.p.) or 2 P.&W. Wasp (1,200 h.p.)	2 gun turrets	245
Vickers	Wellington	2 B'tol Peg. XVIII (1,000 h.p.)	6 m.g., 2 turrets	265
"	Wellington II	2 R.R. Merlin x (1,370 h.p.)	" "	—
Handley-Page	Hampden	2 Pegasus XVIII (1,000 h.p.)	" "	265
"	Hereford	2 Napier Dagger VIII (1,000 h.p.)	" "	—
Bristol	Blenheim I	2 B'tol Mercury (840 h.p.)	1 gun, 1 turret	285
"	Blenheim IV	2 Mercury xv (920 h.p.)	" " "	295
Short	Stirling	4 Hercules (1,600 h.p.) or 4 Wright Cyclone (1,600 h.p.)	8 m.g. in 3 turrets	300
Avro	Manchester	2 R.R. Vulture (1,845 h.p.)	" " "	—
"	Lancaster	4 R.R. Merlin xx (1,175 h.p.)	10 m.g. in 4 tur.	300
Handley Page	Halifax	4 R.R. Merlin xx (1,175 h.p.)	8 m.g. in 3 tur.	300
De Havilland	Mosquito	2 R.R.	? 4 cannon, 4 m.g.	—
\multicolumn{5}{c}{*Army Cooperation*}				
Westland	Lysander	1 Perseus XII (905 h.p.)	3 m.g.	230
\multicolumn{5}{c}{*General Reconnaissance Landplanes*}				
Avro	Anson	2 Cheetah IX (350 h.p.)	1 forward m.g.; fuselage turret	188
Bristol	Beaufort	2 Bristol Taurus II (1,065 h.p.)	4 m.g.; fus. tur.	—
\multicolumn{5}{c}{*Flying Boats*}				
Short	Sunderland	4 Pegasus XXII (1,010 h.p.)	2 turrets; fus. guns	210
Saro	Lerwick	2 Hercules II (1,375 h.p.)	3 turrets	—
\multicolumn{5}{c}{*Trainers*}				
Phillips&Powis	Master	1 R.R. Kestrel xxx (585 h.p.)	—	250
" "	Master II	1 Mercury	—	250+
" "	Magister	1 D.H. Gipsy (130 h.p.)	—	142
" "	Martinet I	1 Mercury xx or xxx (820 h.p.)	—	—
Blackburn	Botha	2 Bristol Perseus (900 h.p.)	—	—
Airspeed	Oxford	2 Cheetah x (375 h.p.)	—	197
De Havilland	Tiger Moth	1 Gipsy Major (130 h.p.)	—	109
\multicolumn{5}{c}{*Target Towing and A.A. Training Aircraft*}				
Hawker	Henley (target)	1 R.R. Merlin	—	272
De Havilland	Queen Bee (wireless controlled, A.A.)	1 Gipsy (130 h.p.)	—	109
Airspeed	Queen Wasp (wireless controlled, A.A.)	1 Armstrong-Siddeley Cheetah (375 h.p.)	—	—
\multicolumn{5}{c}{*Communications*}				
De Havilland	D.H. 86B	4 D.H. Gipsy Six (200 h.p.)	—	166
" "	D.H. 90	2 D.H. Gipsy Major (130 h.p.)	—	145
" "	D.H. 89A	2 D.H. Gipsy Six (200 h.p.)	—	157
Handley-Page	Harrow	2 Pegasus (925 h.p.)	—	200
Percival	Proctor	1 D.H. Gipsy Six (200 h.p.)	—	170
"	Q.6	2 D.H. Gipsy Six (200 h.p.)	—	195
Phillips&Powis	Mentor	1 D.H. Gipsy Six (200 h.p.)	—	170

R.A.F. AIRCRAFT IN SERVICE

Makers	Machine	Engines	Armament	Top Speed
Troop Transports				
Bristol	Bombay	2 Pegasus (1,010 h.p.)	Nose & tail turrets	192
De Havilland	Flamingo & Hertfordshire	2 Perseus (930 h.p.)	—	239

U.S.A. Machines Used in Association with R.A.F.

Makers	Machine	Engines	Armament	Top Speed
Fighters				
Curtiss	Mohawk	1 Pratt & Whitney Twin-Wasp (1,100 h.p.)	6 machine-guns	323
,,	Tomahawk*	1 Allison (1,090 h.p.)	2 cannon ; 4 m.g.	328
,,	Kittyhawk I	1 Allison (1,325 h.p.)	8 machine-guns	380
,,	Kittyhawk II	1 R.R. Merlin (Packard) (1,280 h.p.)	Heavy	400
Bell	Airacobra	1 Allison (1,150 h.p.)	1 20-mm. cannon ; 6 m.g.	375
Brewster	Buffalo	1 Wright Cyclone (1,200 h.p.)	—	330
Lockheed	Lightning	2 Allison engines (1,150 h.p.)	—	365
N. American	Mitchell	2 Cyclone (1,600 h.p.)	? 5 m.g.	308
Vultee	Vanguard	1 P. & W. (1,600 h.p.)	—	—
Republic	Thunderbolt	1 Wasp (2,000 h.p.)	Heavy	?400
* Also Army Cooperation.				
Army Cooperation				
N. American	Mustang	1 Allison (1,150 h.p.)	6 m.g.	400+
Vultee	Vigilant	1 Wasp (1,600 h.p.)	—	—
Bombers				
Boeing	Fortress II	4 W. Cyclone (1,200 h.p.)	13 m.g.	300+
Consolidated	Liberator II	4 P. & W. Twin-Wasp (1,200 h.p.)	—	300
Curtiss	Cleveland*	1 W. Cyclone (1,000 h.p.)	—	240
Douglas	Boston I†	2 Twin-Wasp (1,050 h.p.)	—	315
,,	Boston (Havoc II)†	2 Cyclone (1,600 h.p.)	7 m.g. (U.S.)	350
,,	Dauntless	1 Wright Cyclone (950 h.p.)	—	275
Martin	Maryland	2 Twin-Wasp (1,050 h.p.)	—	316
,,	Marauder	2 P. & W. (1,850 h.p.)	—	346
,,	Baltimore	2 Cyclone (1,600 h.p.)	7 m.g. with 1 tur.	350
V. Sikorsky	Chesapeake*	1 Twin-Wasp Junior (825 h.p.)	—	257
Vultee	Vengeance*	1 Wright Cyclone (1,600 h.p.)	—	—
Brewster	Bermuda I*	1 Wright Cyclone (1,700 h.p.)	—	—
* These are dive-bombers. † Also employed as night-fighter and known as the Havoc.				
General Reconnaissance Landplanes				
Lockheed	Hudson V	2 W. Cyclone (1,200 h.p.)	6 m.g.	284
Lockheed-Vega	Ventura	2 Double-Wasp (2,000 h.p.)	1 turret	275
Flying Boat				
Consolidated	Catalina	2 Twin-Wasp (1,200 h.p.)	—	190
Trainer				
N. American	Harvard	P. & W. Wasp (550 h.p.)	—	210

U.S.A. Aero Engines Used by the R.A.F.

Makers	Name	Type	Cyl.	Swept vol. (litres)	Bore and Stroke (in.)	Weight lb.	H.P. (max.)
Liquid-cooled V							
Allison	—	V-1710-C15	12	28·02	5·5 × 6	1,340	1,150
Air-cooled Radial							
Pratt & Whitney	Wasp	R-1340	9	22·03	5·75 × 5·75	864	550
,, ,,	Twin-Wasp	R-1830-SC3-G	14	29·97	5·50 × 5·50	1,420	1,050
,, ,,	Double-Wasp	R-2800	18	45·9	5·75 × 6	2,245	2,000
Wright	Cyclone	R-1820-G5	9	28·5	6·125 × 6·875	1,210	1,000
,,	D'ble-row Cyclone	GR-2600-A5B	14	42·6	6·125 × 6·312	1,950	1,600

A Note on 'Plane Flight and Structure
Theory of the Aeroplane Simply Explained

Without the basis of a clear grasp of the elementary principles of flight it is not possible to build up a sound mental structure of advanced theory. Here in a few words the reader is told why and how an aeroplane flies.

THE public in general long ago ceased to wonder at the fact that an aeroplane flies through the air although it is heavier than air, but comparatively few people understand the reason. Perhaps the theory may be grasped most easily by thinking of a boy's kite—for a kite is an aircraft. No boy takes out his kite unless there is a wind; flight is impossible unless the air meets the aircraft with some violence. It does not matter whether moving air encounters a stationary aircraft or a moving aircraft meets stationary air. The force with which an aeroplane meets the air is called "thrust," and the resistance of the air is called "drag."

The boy's kite has a tail which tilts the nose up and makes it certain that the whole kite will meet the air at an angle. The wings of an aeroplane are also set at an angle to the path of its flight, and this is called the "angle of incidence." Put very simply, this angle drives the air underneath and so forces the kite or wing upwards. The aeroplane wing, however, is not a flat plane, as many kites are.

Why a Wing Rises

Looked at from the end (or, in engineering language, in section) it is curved, and the curve is called the "camber." There are hundreds of designs for the section of a wing, and they are called "aerofoils." Generally speaking, a thick aerofoil gives greater lift, while a thin one makes for higher speed. There is usually more camber on the upper surface of a wing than on the lower. The effect of this is to produce an area of reduced pressure in the air above the wing, which may be described as having a sort of sucking effect and so drawing the wing upwards. There is an area of increased pressure below the wing, and this also creates a tendency for the wing to rise.

Actually about two-thirds of the lift is due to the camber on top of the wing and one-third to the pressure below it. Advanced students of aeronautics learn about the vortices created in the air by the passage of an aeroplane through it, but the above description puts the theory of flight in its simplest form.

An aeroplane needs stability sideways, in direction, and fore and aft. The fore and aft (or longitudinal) stability is provided

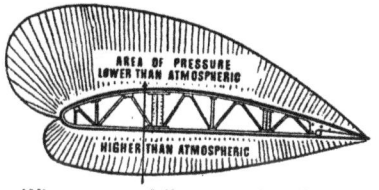

When an aerofoil at an angle is forced through the air, high pressure develops beneath and a region of low pressure above, producing a lift; the arrow in this diagram shows the centre of pressure

Slope of wings upwards is dihedral angle: it gives lateral stability.

by the tailplane. Its size, shape, and angle of incidence must be nicely calculated so that it supports the fuselage (or body) of the aeroplane in the correct position. It is a fault if a machine flies "nose-heavy" or "tail-heavy."

Directional stability is provided by the fin, an upright member at the rear of the fuselage, to which the rudder is attached, and which checks any tendency to yaw from right to left or vice versa.

Lateral stability is provided by the "dihedral angle." In many aeroplanes the wings when viewed from in front slope slightly upwards from the centre to the tips, and this slope is called the dihedral angle. If the machine inclines over to the left, the "horizontal equivalent" of the port wing is increased and that of the starboard wing diminished. In simpler words, the port wing stretches out farther and the starboard wing not so far. As a result, the pressure under the port wing is increased and that

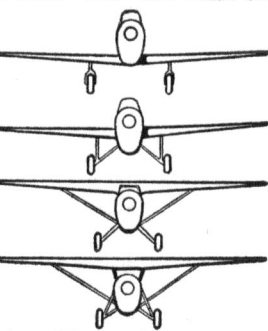

Four different wing positions for monoplanes: top, low-wing; second, mid-wing; third, high-wing; fourth, parasol.

SECTION 2. C **Aeroplane Structure** 102

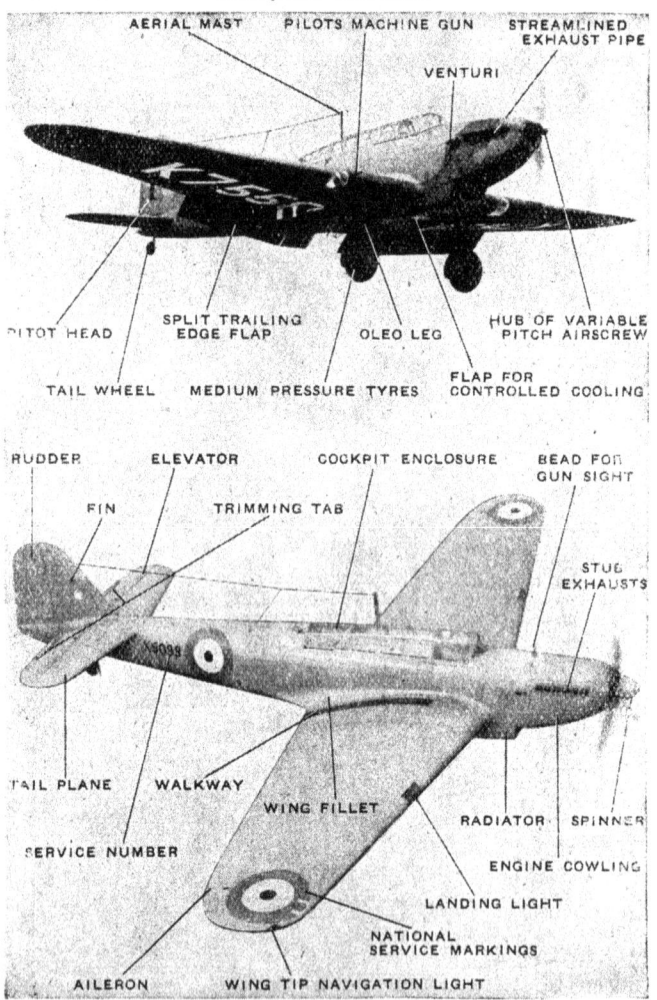

Constructional details and parts of typical low-wing cantilever monoplanes. Top is a Fairey Battle and lower one a Fairey P.4/34. The wing is attached to the bottom of the fuselage, and is strong enough not to need struts or wires.

wing is forced upwards again, while the right wing naturally tends to drop.

To make the aeroplane do what he wants, the pilot has three sets of controls. These are the *rudder*, the *elevator*, and the *ailerons*. The rudder needs no explanation. Cables or rods connect it to a bar on which the pilot's feet rest, and when he pushes the left foot forward the aeroplane turns to the left. Elevator and ailerons are both connected to the control column (the "joystick"), which the pilot grasps with one hand. If he pulls it back, the elevator rises, catches the wind, and the tail is forced down, thus making the machine climb. Pushing the column forward makes it dive.

Movement of the column to one side

Aeroplane Structure

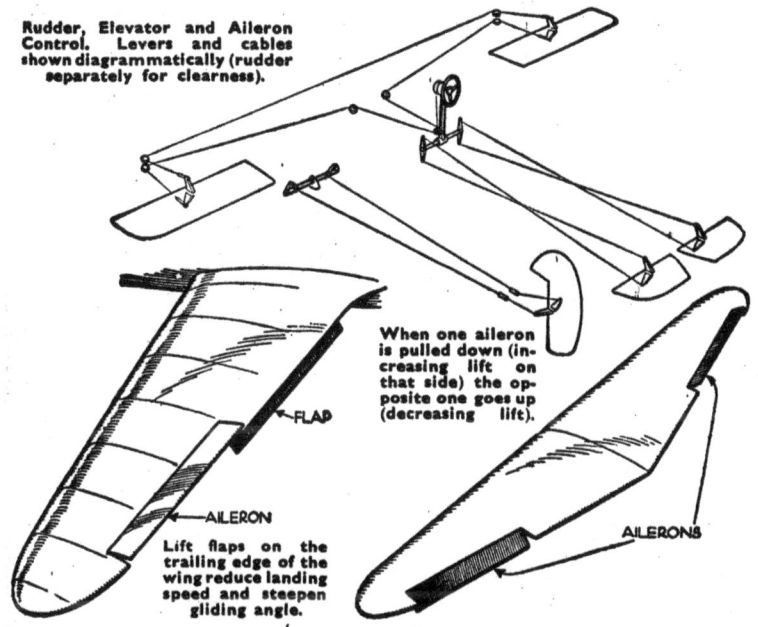

Rudder, Elevator and Aileron Control. Levers and cables shown diagrammatically (rudder separately for clearness).

When one aileron is pulled down (increasing lift on that side) the opposite one goes up (decreasing lift).

FLAP

AILERON

Lift flaps on the trailing edge of the wing reduce landing speed and steepen gliding angle.

AILERONS

or the other works the ailerons. These are movable flaps in the rear part of each wing, which move in opposition to each other. Pushing the column over to the left raises the port side aileron and depresses the starboard one. The wind catches them and forces the port wing tip down and the starboard one up. This operation is called "banking," and is used in conjunction with the rudder when turning. If a pilot tried to turn without banking, his machine would have a tendency to skid—just as a bicycle would overturn if the rider turned the handle bars without leaning inwards.

Monoplane and Biplane

Everyone is now familiar with the terms monoplane and biplane. The monoplane is more efficient, especially if its wings are cantilever and have no external bracing struts or wires. Monoplanes are described as "high-wing," "mid-wing," and "low-wing," according to the position at which the wings are attached to the fuselage. Low-wing monoplanes are popular now, largely because in that class of machine it is easier to arrange for the wheels and undercarriage to retract.

Framework and Covering

The framework of an aeroplane may be of metal or of wood, and the outside covering may be metal, doped fabric, or sometimes wood. When a metal covering is used (and the same applies to wings covered with plywood) the covering must add to the strength of the whole aeroplane and thus permit the interior framework to be much lighter than it is in the case of a machine with fabric covering. Such a metal cover is known as a "stressed skin." The methods of designing the interior framework are too numerous to be described here.

The different classes of aircraft are tabulated below.

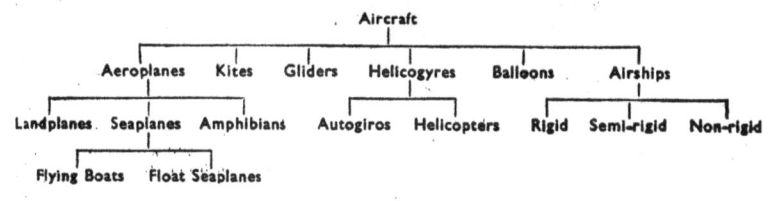

```
                          Aircraft
   ┌──────┬──────┬──────┬──────────┬──────┬──────┐
Aeroplanes  Kites  Gliders  Helicogyres  Balloons  Airships
   │                          │              │
┌──┴──┐                  ┌────┴────┐    ┌────┼────┐
Landplanes Seaplanes Amphibians  Autogiros Helicopters  Rigid Semi-rigid Non-rigid
        │
   ┌────┴────┐
Flying Boats  Float Seaplanes
```

HAWKER HURRICANE

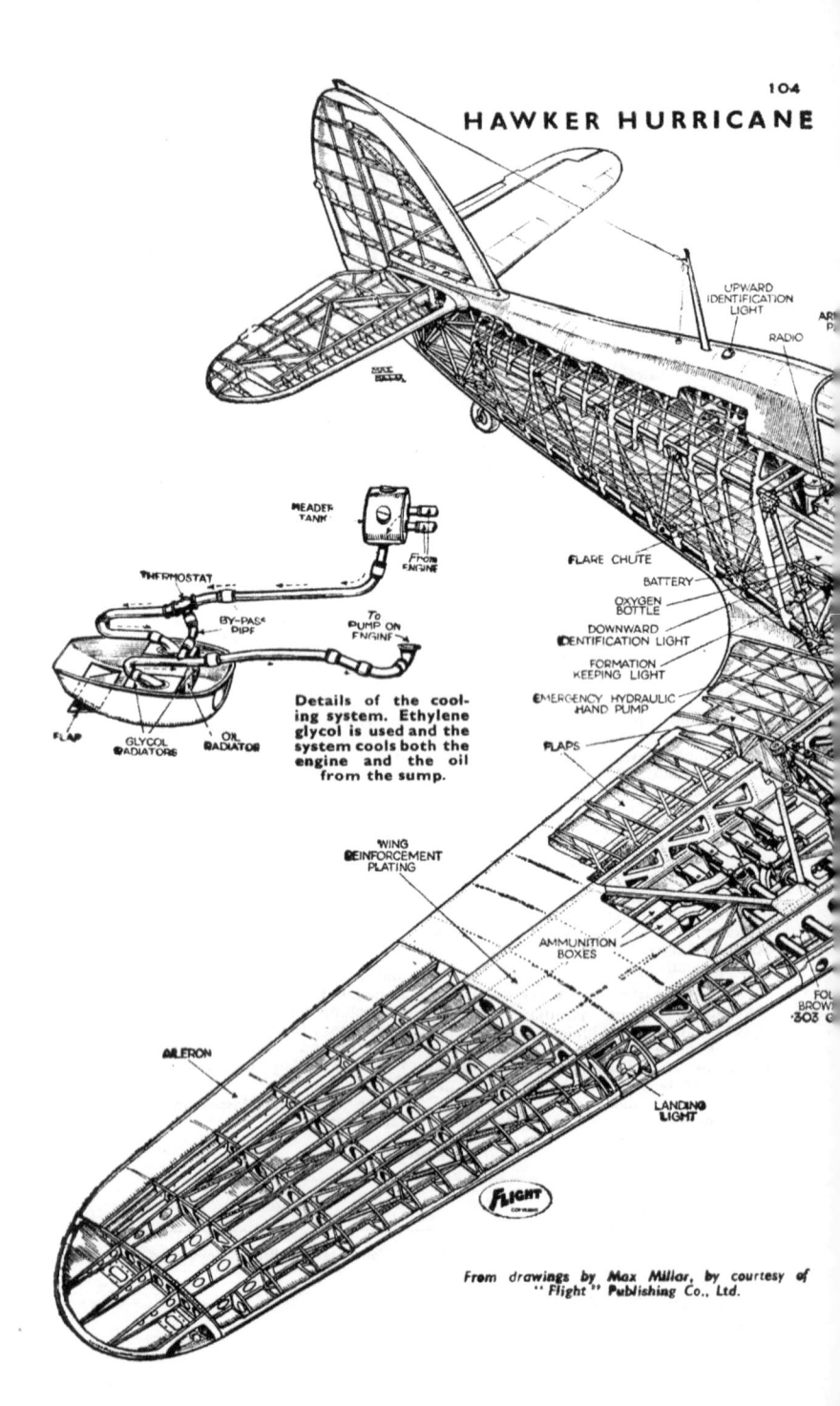

Details of the cooling system. Ethylene glycol is used and the system cools both the engine and the oil from the sump.

From drawings by Max Millar, by courtesy of "Flight" Publishing Co., Ltd.

IN PART-SECTION DIAGRAM

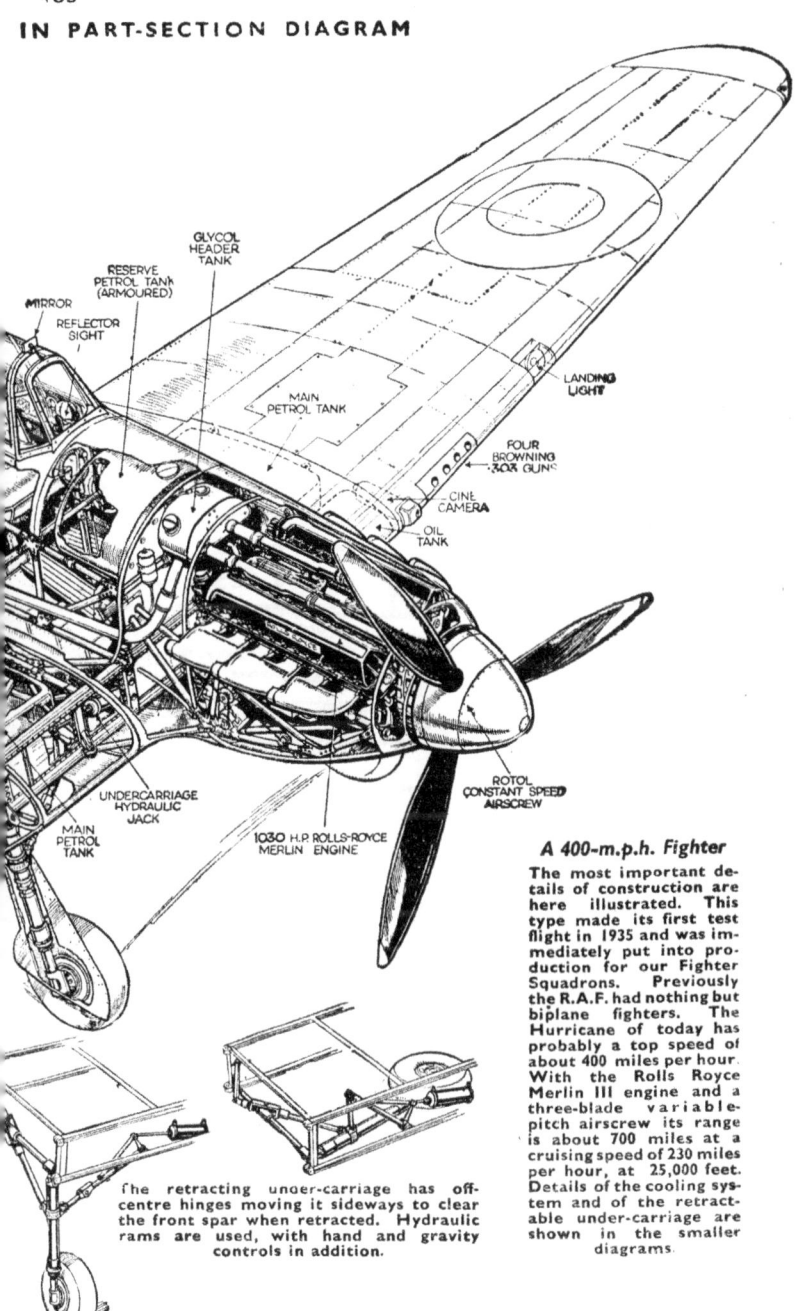

Labels on diagram:
MIRROR
REFLECTOR SIGHT
RESERVE PETROL TANK (ARMOURED)
GLYCOL HEADER TANK
MAIN PETROL TANK
LANDING LIGHT
FOUR BROWNING .303 GUNS
CINE CAMERA
OIL TANK
UNDERCARRIAGE HYDRAULIC JACK
MAIN PETROL TANK
1030 H.P. ROLLS-ROYCE MERLIN ENGINE
ROTOL CONSTANT SPEED AIRSCREW

The retracting under-carriage has off-centre hinges moving it sideways to clear the front spar when retracted. Hydraulic rams are used, with hand and gravity controls in addition.

A 400-m.p.h. Fighter

The most important details of construction are here illustrated. This type made its first test flight in 1935 and was immediately put into production for our Fighter Squadrons. Previously the R.A.F. had nothing but biplane fighters. The Hurricane of today has probably a top speed of about 400 miles per hour. With the Rolls Royce Merlin III engine and a three-blade variable-pitch airscrew its range is about 700 miles at a cruising speed of 230 miles per hour, at 25,000 feet. Details of the cooling system and of the retractable under-carriage are shown in the smaller diagrams.

The Internal Combustion Engine
A Simple Explanation of Petrol Engine Theory

Here the principles of the engines employed in modern aircraft are made clear. Both the original poppet valve and the later sleeve-valve engines are considered. In the next page actual engines used by the R.A.F. are described and listed.

THE steam engine is an *external* combustion engine, for its fuel is burnt under the boiler which generates steam; steam is the working fluid which acts in the cylinders and by its pressure and its expansion forces out the pistons which turn the wheels. In internal combustion engines—for example, the gas engine, petrol engine or oil engine—the fuel is burnt inside the cylinders, and the fuel-gas itself is the working fluid by whose sudden expansion when exploded the pistons are pushed out.

The Four-Stroke Cycle. The steam engine delivers power at every stroke, whereas the internal combustion engine (I.C.E.) has one power stroke in every four (four-stroke cycle) or one in every two (two-stroke cycle). Aircraft petrol engines employ the four-stroke cycle, which is illustrated in the accompanying diagrams. When the propeller is swung, or the engine is set going by a starter, the rotation of the shaft causes some of the pistons (not all of them will be in the " first-stroke " position at the time) to act as pumps as they are drawn outwards; they suck in the mixture of air and petrol vapour from the induction pipe that connects the carburettor to the cylinders, and so fill the cylinders with this explosive mixture. (*See* the top diagram, which shows the piston moving outwards on the first or *Suction* stroke. Note that the inlet valve A is open and the exhaust valve E is shut.)

As the shaft continues to turn, the pistons come back again, on the *Compression* stroke; since both valves are shut there is no outlet for the mixture and it is compressed—becoming very hot. At or just before the end of the compression stroke a spark jumps the gap of the sparking plug, whose end projects into the cylinder, and ignites the mixture, which explodes and expands enormously, pushing out the piston on the third (*Power*) stroke.

Now the engine will continue to run. The pistons come back again and, the exhaust valve only being now open, push out the burnt gases on the *Exhaust* stroke. Continuing with a fresh cycle, the exhaust valve shuts, the inlet valve opens, and the pistons move out on another suction stroke; so the sequence continues.

The valves are opened and shut at the proper time by cams driven by the engine; the electric spark is produced by a generator (magneto) also driven by the engine. The supply of petrol vapour mixed with air is regulated by a throttle valve which allows more or less air to enter the induction pipe, and the air entrains with it petrol vapour from the carburettor jet.

We have described the sequence in only one cylinder, but the same thing takes place in all; in order to equalize the action it is arranged that when some cylinders are on first stroke others are on other strokes, but in every one the same complete cycle is carried out. In the Rolls-Royce Merlin engine fitted to many R.A.F. aircraft there are twelve cylinders, the bore (or internal diameter) being 5.4 inches and the length of piston stroke being 6 inches.

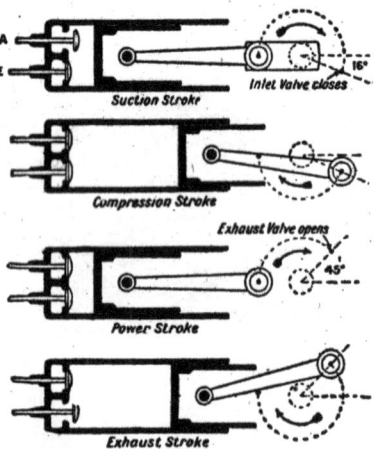

Internal Combustion Engine: one cylinder shown. Top diagram illustrates suction stroke, with mixture being drawn in through open inlet valve (A); during compression stroke and power stroke both valves are shut; during exhaust stroke the exhaust valve (E) is open. Arrows show direction of motion; dotted circular lines indicate the duration of the phase.

Sleeve-Valve Engines. The valves mentioned above are " mushroom " or poppet valves, kept closed by strong springs until lifted at the proper time by cams. But there is another system in use, in which the inlet and exhaust " ports " are opened and shut by a sliding sleeve—or by two such sleeves one within the other—situated within the cylinder and moved up and down automatically. The piston works inside the innermost sleeve. As the sleeves slide up and down, certain openings in them come opposite ports in the cylinder walls connected with the inlet and the exhaust passages, and allow mixture to enter or burnt gases to escape, according to the particular stroke of the cycle. The sleeves at the same time shut the valve not required to be open. There are certain advantages in the use of sleeve valves, and they are employed in some Bristol aircraft engines. See the following article.

STANDARD BRITISH AERO ENGINES

SUPERIORITY in the air is dependent upon many factors, and especially upon the power and reliability of engines. It is fortunate for this country that for more than a decade British aero-engine designers have made such progress in the production of power units of widely differing types that the aircraft now in service with the Royal Air Force are unequalled by those of any other country in the world.

The engines which now power our fighters, bombers, reconnaissance machines and our long-range flying-boats fall into three distinct categories. These are the liquid-cooled upright Vee, the air-cooled radial and the air-cooled H type. Most famous of all engines is the Rolls-Royce Merlin, which, in differing form, is fitted to the Supermarine Spitfire, the Hawker Hurricane, the Boulton Paul Defiant, the Vickers-Armstrong Wellington Mk. II, the Armstrong-Whitworth Whitley Mk. IV, and the Fairey Fulmar. The Merlin is a twelve-cylinder supercharged motor with the cylinders arranged in two banks of six at 60 degrees. It is produced in four types. There are the Merlin Mk. II, the Mk. III and the Mk. IV. These three are basically the same, but differ in certain details which are incorporated to meet specific requirements. Each develops 1,030 h.p. and is supercharged. There is also the Mk. X Merlin, a specially boosted engine which develops 1,145 h.p.

Great power with light weight and compactness are amongst the outstanding characteristics of the Merlin engine. With its supercharger and many auxiliaries this 1,030-h.p. motor weighs only 1,335 lb., and is only 69 inches long and 41 inches in height.

Sharing honours with the Rolls-Royce engines are various types of Bristol air-cooled radial engines which are manufactured by one of the oldest aircraft concerns in the country, the Bristol Aeroplane

The Bristol Hercules Mk. IV is an air-cooled radial engine with sleeve valves. Its 14 cylinders are in two rows.

Company. Simplicity, a high power-weight ratio, ease of maintenance and great reliability are the salient qualities of all Bristol types, which power nineteen different aircraft now in service with the R.A.F. Bristol engines are of two distinct types—those incorporating the normal poppet-valve system and those fitted with sleeve valves. All are supercharged. The Bristol Company is the originator of the air-cooled sleeve-valve aero engine, which has the advantages of ease of manufacture and maintenance, and low fuel consumption. The poppet-valve types are known as the Mercury and Pegasus; the Hercules, Taurus and the Perseus are the sleeve-valve motors.

The most powerful of the Bristol sleeve-valve type, the Mk. II Hercules, develops 1,375 h.p. at 4,000 feet; the Mk. IV Hercules yields 1,220 h.p. at 5,500 feet. Hercules engines are fitted to the Saro Lerwick flying-boat which is used by the Coastal Command. A front view of the Mk. IV is given above.

The Mercury is a nine-cylinder engine of 840 h.p. The famous Blenheim bomber

The Rolls-Royce Merlin engine (liquid-cooled Vee type) is the power unit in our Hurricanes and Spitfires.

British Aero Engines

	Make	Name	Type	Cyl.	Swept Volume	Bore and Stroke in.	Weight lb.	H.P. (Max.)
LIQUID-COOLED VEE TYPE	Rolls-Royce ,, ,, ,,	Merlin ,, ,, ,,	II–IV X XX 61	12 ,, ,, ,,	27 litres ,, ,, ,, ,, ,, ,, ,,	5·4 × 6 ,, ,, ,, ,, ,, ,,	1,335 1,394 1,450 1,600	1,030 1,145 1,260 ?
LIQUID X TYPE	Rolls-Royce	Vulture	X	24	42·5 ,,	5 × 5·5		1,845
AIR-COOLED RADIAL TYPE	Bristol ,, ,, ,, ,, ,, ,, ,,	Hercules ,, Mercury ,, Pegasus ,, Taurus Perseus ,, ,, and	II IV VIII XV XVIII XXII II X XII XIIc XIVc	14 ,, 9 ,, ,, ,, 14 9 ,, ,,	38·7 ,, ,, ,, 24·9 ,, ,, ,, 28·7 ,, ,, ,, 25·4 ,, 24·9 ,, ,, ,, ,, ,,	5·75 × 6·5 ,, ,, ,, ,, ,, ,, 5·75 × 7·5 ,, ,, 5 × 5·625 5·7 × 6·5 ,, ,, ,, ,,	1,680 ,, 1,010 ,, 1,030 ,, 1,300 1,085 1,090	1,375 1,220 840 920 1,000 1,100 1,065 880 905 890
AIR-COOLED H TYPE	Napier ,,	Dagger Rapier	VIII VI	24 16	16·85 ,, 8·80 ,,	3·812 × 3·75 3·5 × 3·5	1,390 707	1,000 395

For American engines see p. 100

and the Gloster Gladiator fighter are Mercury-engined. Pegasus engines are used in the Short Sunderland flying-boat, the Vickers Wellington Mk. Ia bomber, the Bristol Bombay troop-carrier, the Handley Page Hampden bomber, and the Vickers Wellesley.

The Taurus, which has fourteen cylinders and develops 1,065 h.p., is employed

This view of the Bristol Taurus (air-cooled radial with sleeve valves) should be compared with that of the Hercules in page 107.

in the Bristol Beaufort and the Fairey Albacore torpedoplanes. The engine is illustrated above, and this view of a radial should be compared with that of the Hercules in page 107. Perseus nine-cylinder 890-h.p. engine is used on the Blackburn Roc, the Blackburn Skua, the Westland Lysander and the D.H. Hertfordshire troop transport machine.

The H-type engine is represented by the Napier Dagger and the Napier Rapier. The former has 24 cylinders arranged in four banks of six, H fashion on a common crankcase. The motor is air-cooled, supercharged, and when delivering its full power of 1,000 h.p., runs at 4,200 r.p.m., which is unusually fast for an aeroplane engine of such size. The Dagger is fitted to the twin-engined Handley Page Hereford. The Rapier is an unsupercharged engine of comparatively small size. It has sixteen air-cooled cylinders arranged in four banks of four. It develops 395 h.p. and is used in the Fairey Seafox light reconnaissance seaplane.

These three types of engine — the liquid-cooled Vee, the air-cooled radial, and the air-cooled H-type — though differing widely in basic and detail design, have common qualities in being completely dependable and unexcelled by anything so far produced by the enemy. As time passes they will be replaced by newer types of even higher horse-power and greater efficiency.

The Napier Dagger engine is an example of the H-type arrangement, two blocks of six cylinders being vertical and two blocks inverted.

Maps & Map Reading
Practical Notes for the Airman

The following notes on air map work include the different types of maps in use and the importance of skilled knowledge in map reading. A note on the work of the Map Officer is given.

WITHOUT maps an aircraft cannot find its way to its destination and, what is perhaps worse, cannot find its way home again. A map is, in fact, a vital necessity to an aircraft and it differs from the one hundred and one other such necessities in this one particular. Whereas a sparking plug will fire equally well over England or over Italy and an airscrew will turn equally freely in either hemisphere, a map will only fulfil its object in just one area, and that is the area which it represents. Hence the importance of seeing that every aircraft has the right map at the right time in the right place.

Now the right map does not only mean a map of the right area, it also implies the right type of map. There are many different types of maps designed for different purposes. There are maps on a "small scale," that is, maps which show a relatively large area of country on each sheet, and maps on a "large scale," which show only a small area of country, but which show that area in much greater detail. There are maps for navigation which are used in the same way as a chart on a ship at sea, by drawing lines and plotting the course and position of the aircraft on it. These, of course, can be used equally well by night or by day.

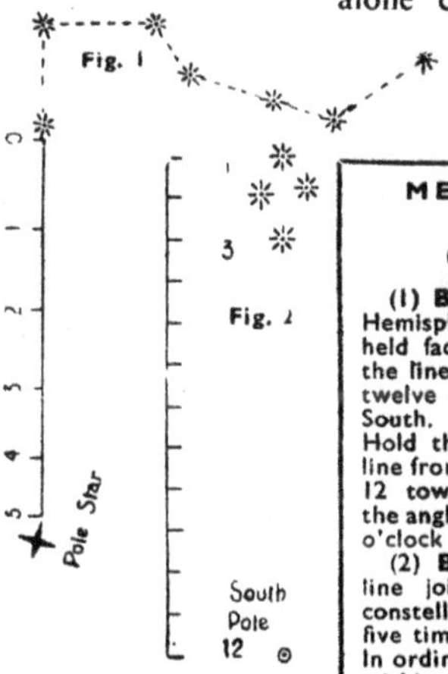

Then there are maps which are used for visual recognition of the country, so that an observer can compare the ground beneath him with the representation of it which he holds in his hand. There are also maps which show with special emphasis any particular object to which the aircraft is to devote its attention, perhaps the Beer Hall at Munich, or a marshalling yard at Hamm.

All these maps are specially designed to fulfil the object in view and they differ very much from the type of map to which one is accustomed when hiking or motoring. In an aircraft the country must be recognized from a height of several thousand feet, on the ground from a height of about 5½ feet, and, of course, the view obtained and hence the design of the map concerned is necessarily entirely different in each case.

Skill at "reading a map," as it is called, must be acquired, and practice alone can make perfect. The map maker goes part of the way by designing and drawing the map so that it is as easy to read as possible, but the

Fig. 1

Fig. 2

Pole Star

South Pole
12

METHODS OF FINDING TRUE NORTH
Other than by a Compass

(1) **By a Watch.**—(a) In the Northern Hemisphere. If the hour hand of a watch held face upwards be pointed at the sun, the line bisecting the angle between it and twelve o'clock will point roughly to the South. (b) In the Southern Hemisphere. Hold the watch face upwards. Point the line from the centre of the dial to the figure 12 towards the sun. The line bisecting the angle between the hour hand and twelve o'clock will point roughly to the North.

(2) **By the Pole Star.**—In Fig. 1 the line joining two stars indicated in the constellation of the Great Bear, if produced five times its length, ends at the Pole Star. In ordinary latitudes the Pole Star is always within 2° of the True North, and may be taken as the pivot round which all the other stars appear to revolve.

(3) **By the Southern Cross.**—Consider the Southern Cross as a kite (see Fig. 2). Prolong the greater axis three times in the direction of the tail and the point reached will be approximately the South Pole. If a piece of paper marked off along its edge by twelve lines at equal intervals apart be held so that the first and third scale lines coincide with the head and tail stars of the kite, the twelfth scale line will mark the approximate position of the South Pole. There is no bright star in the Southern Cross.

user must also do his share. Reading a map is indeed like learning a foreign language, only much less difficult, for the map maker has provided a "dictionary" in the margin of each sheet in the form of a table of conventional signs by which the features of the ground are depicted.

The map maker, the printer, the storage organization, the supply service, all have their task in equipping the R.A.F., but the work must be supplemented by the user of the map, who must learn to read the language that it speaks.

The Map Officer and Clerk

The R.A.F. can go anywhere, within the range of the aircraft concerned, at the shortest possible notice, and the maps for such movements must be instantly available. A Squadron might well operate over Norway, over Berlin and over Northern Italy within the same week.

The responsibilities of those who look after maps for the R.A.F. are best summed up in the words of the order which defines the duties of the station map officer . . . , " to ensure that all those who need maps or charts can obtain them without delay, whilst maintaining the strictest economy in their use." The most perfect map in the world is useless if it arrives 5 minutes too late. To avoid this, careful organisation is necessary, both as regards demanding and supplying maps: it is true that requirements must often be filled "at panic speed," but there is also much truth in the adage "nothing is urgent—someone has lacked foresight."

The maintenance of maps on operational stations is largely undertaken by W.A.A.F. personnel, who are encouraged to volunteer for the newly created trade of "Clerks G.D. Maps." A real welcome, careful training and an important and responsible job await any who have some knowledge of maps and who have, or feel they may acquire, that enthusiasm for the subject which becomes a characteristic of all those who have to deal with maps.

Memory Sketching

Sketching at the time of a reconnaissance may not always be possible. A memory sketch may then form a useful complement to a report. Notes on direction, distances, and the shape of the ground should be made, but, if this is not practicable, details should be memorized in the following order: the stream lines or drainage system; hill features; roads, railways, woods, etc.

Navigation of Service Aircraft

SECTION 2. F

Following upon the article on Map Reading comes naturally the application of map work to the art of navigating the skies. Special reference is made to the work of the navigator-bomb-aimer.

NAVIGATION is the art of getting from one point on the earth's surface to another; it is, of course, a sailor's art, which airmen have adopted and made their own.

The basis of all navigation, both at sea and in the air, is dead reckoning—the method used by the navigator to determine his position at any given moment by calculating the track and ground speed made good since his last position. If the weather is fine the airman can fix his position by map reading, that is, by looking at the ground and identifying landmarks seen there with those marked on the map.

The airman does not spend all his time alternately referring to the map and to the ground; he makes his calculations in advance and looks for landmarks where his calculations suggest they would be. When the landmark is recognized, then the airman is said to have obtained a "visual fix"; the word "fix" merely means the position of the aircraft. The maps used by air navigators are much like ordinary motoring maps except that they contain rather less detail. Few villages are marked, but, instead, anything likely to be noticed from the air, such as roads, railways, and rivers, are very clearly defined. Hills and mountains are also marked very clearly, and this is because in an aircraft the altimeter does not give the height of the aircraft above the ground at any given point, but the height above the place at which the aircraft left the ground or above sea level, according to how it has been set.

Aircraft of the Coastal Command in particular sometimes use Admiralty charts because they work over the sea; the navigator may have to know about rocks, tides, currents, the depth of water, and so forth.

It is largely to prevent enemy aircraft from getting a visual fix or drifts (*see* definitions in p. 119) that we have to have the black-out, and it is by no means only to prevent the enemy from dropping bombs on lighted buildings.

If the weather is bad and clouds hide the ground the navigator cannot obtain a visual fix, but there are other kinds of fix. He may obtain a "radio fix" by getting in touch with two wireless stations. Both stations take a bearing of the aircraft at the same time, and the master station plots two bearings on a map and gives the navigator his position.

Or again, if the aircraft is over cloud and with clear sky above, the navigator may use the stars and get an "astro"

Aircraft Navigation

fix. The navigator takes "sights" of two stars, and calculating his position is a simple matter. This is an adaptation of a method used by sailors, and the chief instrument is still the sextant.

And he must also have his compass, a smaller edition of a ship's compass and built to stand rougher treatment; the compass, for example, must not be disturbed if the aircraft should turn upside down. There are also methods of aiding the navigator during the last few miles before landing; thus the radio beam is used in bad weather to bring the aircraft in.

To enable him to get from one position to the next the navigator must work out his course and ground speed in relation to the speed and direction of the wind. It is a common notion that an aircraft flies straight, but far more often it moves sideways, being subject to drift. The aircraft is like a boat crossing a swift stream; the man at the wheel will aim at a point on the opposite bank above the actual position at which he intends to land.

Similarly an aircraft coping with a cross wind cannot go straight for its objective, but must fly into the wind. Thus the direction in which the aircraft is heading is known as the "course," while the direction in which it is actually going is known as the "track." It is only when the wind is dead behind or dead against the aircraft that track and course are one and the same. The speed of the aircraft over the ground is, however, affected by these conditions.

When a flight is planned the first thing which the navigator wants from the meteorologists is the speed and direction of the wind at different heights, since from this he calculates his course and his speed over the ground. Unfortunately there is no instrument in the aircraft which

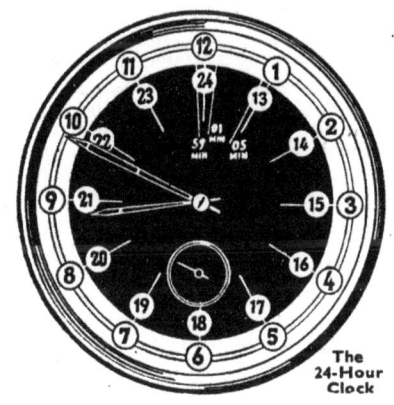

Navigator of a Short Sunderland flying-boat plotting his course at the chart table in his tiny cabin. *Flight*

automatically registers the speed and direction of the wind, but the navigator can calculate this from drift measurements, etc. When over the sea these can be obtained by dropping a sea marker.

It must always be remembered that an aircraft can never stand still. If the aircraft is lost there is no way of anchoring while the navigator thinks things out. He must be calculating the whole time, and another difficulty is that while he is actually reckoning his position the aircraft may have moved four or five miles, and these miles must also be taken into account. The fighter, which travels short distances, is usually assisted by ground control. In the bomber the navigator is also the bomb-aimer, and this is not so that one man can do the work of two but because the calculations which the bomb-aimer has to make, such as the height and speed of the aircraft and the direction and speed of the wind, are precisely the same as those used in navigation.

In fact, the navigator often uses the bomb-sight in the course of his navigation. Accurate navigation depends on the closest co-operation between the navigator and the pilot. When the navigator gives the pilot a new course he enters it in his log; the log is a complete record of the flight with an account of all the fixes, of the courses and speeds of the aircraft, etc.

The navigator is trained in a navigation school, and after this he goes to a bombing school, and then to an Operational Training Unit where he receives advanced instruction in company with the crew to which he is now attached.

The 24-Hour Clock

Methods of Signalling Used by R.A.F.

Communications from aircraft to ground and to sea, between land stations and between aircraft themselves, are carried on by many different methods. Outlines of those most regularly employed are given in this section.

SERVICE signalling is classified as visual and non-visual. In the first class are methods of communication by flags, lamps, and pyrotechnics; the second and larger class includes all forms employing electric impulses such as land telegraph lines (Morse sounders and buzzers, automatic telegraphy, teleprinter), radio-telegraphy and radio-telephony.

Semaphore Code

Semaphore signalling is carried out by means of flags. As will be seen from the illus. in page 92 the signaller holds a flag in each hand, and by placing the flags in the appropriate position signals the letters of the alphabet. The signaller must operate against a proper background in order that the distant reader can distinguish the letters.

This form of signalling is appropriate to ground work only. It is not practicable between air and ground. When this form of signalling is being used on the ground it is usual for the reading signaller to keep his eye on the distant signaller and call out the message to an assistant who writes the message down.

Expert semaphore signallers can under favourable conditions pass messages at speeds in the neighbourhood of 12 words per minute.

Morse Code

The Morse code, as shown in page 113, consists of combinations of shorts and longs (generally referred to as dots and dashes). Unlike the semaphore code, which is applicable only to flag signalling, the Morse code has a great variety of applications, in addition to flag signalling.

When used for flag signalling, a single flag is used by the signaller and it is waved through short and long arcs of a circle to represent the dots and dashes of the Morse code. The background is important, and the signallers are usually provided with a white flag for use against a dark background and a dark blue flag for use against a light background. As in semaphore signalling it is usual for the reading signaller to call out the message to an assistant who writes the message down. Morse flag signalling is somewhat slower than semaphore, but it is possible to read Morse in conditions when semaphore signals cannot be clearly read.

Signalling Lamps

As has been said, Morse can be transmitted by many methods. The signalling lamp is one of these. The most commonly used signalling lamp in the Royal Air Force is known as the Aldis lamp. This consists of a port-

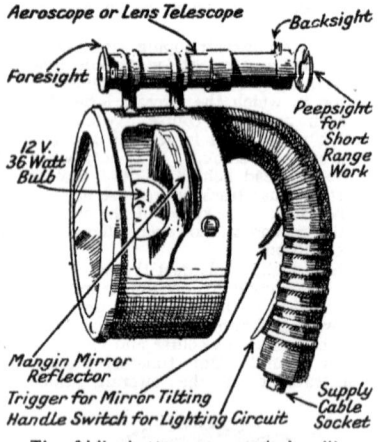

The Aldis battery-operated signalling lamp shown diagrammatically.

able lamp connected to a battery on the aircraft or on land. The lamp is provided with a handle having two triggers. One trigger is held down to close the electric circuit and light the lamp. The lamp thus burns continuously whilst signalling, but the second trigger is operated by the signaller causing a pivoted reflector inside the lamp to articulate. The beam of the lamp is thus moved through an angle of 9° and the receiving signaller sees the light only when the second trigger is depressed. This is called the "mark." When the

SECTION 2. G

trigger is released a " space " is indicated. A characteristic of the lamp is that it may be used either in daylight or darkness, but, of course, the ranges are considerably greater in darkness. The lamp may be used for signalling from the ground to an aeroplane in daylight even though the aircraft is only just visible. In order that the receiving aeroplane may be kept in the field of the lamp a telescopic sighting device (the aeroscope) is fitted to the lamp. The signaller keeps this sight close to his eye during the whole of the message. (See Fig. 3.) This form of signalling is particularly useful to aircraft of the Coastal Command for communicating with shipping.

Land Line

The simplest of all forms of land line communication is by telegraph key and sounder. When the Morse key is operated the sounder situated at the distant end produces a sound which is very similar to the original sound of the key, that is, a succession of clicks. For example, the letter A, which in Morse is represented by ·—, is heard on the sounder as four clicks, the first two clicks being separated by a short

KEY TO THE MORSE CODE

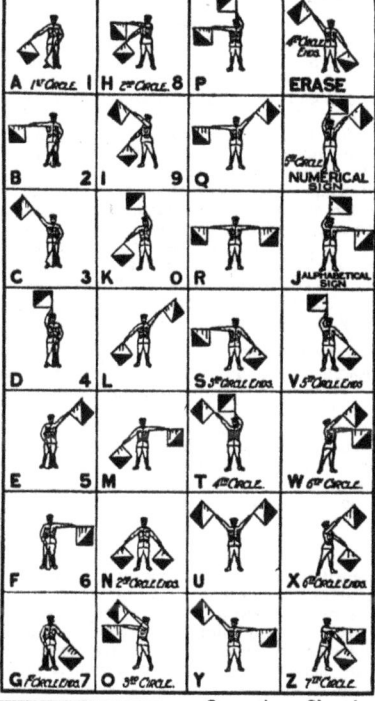

Letters

A ·—	K —·—	X —··—
A' ·—·—	L ·—··	X' —··—·
B —···	M ——	Y —·——
B' —···—'	N —·	Z ——··
C —·—·	N' ——·——	
C' —·—·—	O ———	**Figures**
Ch ————	O' ———·	1 ·————
D —··	P ·——·	2 ··———
E ·	P' ·——·—	3 ···——
E' ·—··	Q ——·—	4 ····—
F ··—·	R ·—·	5 ·····
G ——·	S ···	6 —····
H ····	T —	7 ——···
I ··	U ··—	8 ———··
J ·———	U' ··———	9 ————·
	V ···—	0 —————
	W ·——	

PUNCTUATION AND SPECIAL SIGNS USED IN PROCEDURE

Nneral (also Decimal Point)	··—··	Parentheses (brackets)	—·——·—
Con	——·——·	Inverted Commas	·—··—·
" Ill Stop "	·—·—·—	Underline (also Block Letters)	··——·—
Coma	·· ·· ··	Commencing Sign	···—·
Seicolon	—·—·—·	Erase	·········· (about ten times)
Inrrogation (also Repeat)	··——··	Separative Sign	····
Examation, etc.	——··——	Long Break Sign	—···—
Astrophe	·————·	Ending Sign	·—·—·
Hhen	—····—	Fraction Separation Sign	·—··—
Oque Stroke	—··—·		

Semaphore Signals

Phonetic Alphabet

To avoid errors in spelling out names, etc., over the telephone.

A —Ac
B —Beer
C —Charlie
D —Don
E —Edward
F —Freddie
G —George
H —Harry
I —Ink
J —Johnnie
K —King
L —London
M —Monkey
N —Nuts
O —Orange
P —Pip
Q —Queen
R —Robert
S —Sugar
T —Toc
U —Uncle
V —Vic
W —William
X —X-ray
Y —Yorker
Z —Zebra

interval of time and the second two by a longer interval of time. In practice the reading of the Morse sounder becomes as easy as understanding everyday speech. Experts can read at speeds up to 30 words per minute.

From this simplest form of telegraphy many complex systems have developed, including combined telegraph and telephone apparatus. One form of field equipment consists of a portable telephone set equipped with a transmitting key and a buzzer.

Since this combined set is adapted to field working with varying, and possibly bad, line conditions, telegraphy by means of the buzzer is often possible when telephony is impossible.

Radio-Telegraphy

Radio-telegraphy is used in the Royal Air Force for communication between aircraft and ground stations and also between ground stations themselves. The design of the equipment for use in aeroplanes presents special problems, since it is essential that weight be reduced as far as possible, and owing to the limited space available the dimensions must also be reduced. The equipment in the aeroplane comprises a valve transmitter, supplied with the necessary current from the aeroplane electrical supply, a multi-valve receiver and an aerial which is used for either transmission or reception. The radio operator receives the Morse signals in his headphones and uses a telegraph key for transmission. The radio stations on the ground which transmit to the aeroplane use considerably more power than the transmitters in the aeroplane, for the receiving operator in the aeroplane has many difficulties to contend with, not the least of which is noise. The ground transmitters for communication from point to point on the ground are much more elaborate, have very large aerial systems, and are complete with remote control apparatus to enable them to be operated by an operator situated several miles away.

Radio-Telephony

Radio-telephony differs from radio-telegraphy in that instead of transmission and reception of Morse, speech is transmitted and received. Broadly, it may be said that the carrier wave, instead of being started and stopped in the short, and longs of the Morse code, is modulated by means of a microphone. At the receiving end the human voice is reproduced. Radio-telephony is used to a considerable extent in the Royal Air Force. It has many advantages, notably absence of the necessity for trained telegraph operators. In a single seater fighter where the pilot is the only occupant, it is almost the only method that can be used. The pilot's helmet is equipped with earphones, and he wears a mask microphone. There are many communication systems for which it is not suitable, however. It is not used for long distance point to point communications (see Automatic Telegraphy).

Automatic Telegraphy

This system makes use of the Morse code. At the transmitter end a paper tape is punched, generally by being passed through a perforator which has a typewriter keyboard. Each Morse symbol is formed by a pair of punched holes. The pair corresponding to a dot is disposed in one way on the tape, whilst the pair corresponding to a dash is disposed in another.

An automatic transmitter pulls the tape through at a very high speed, and as the

Pupils at a Signalling School taking down messages from the Morse sounder, which is extensively used in Service work. *Cecil Bean*

punched holes pass electrical contacts they cause impulses to be transmitted down a line. At the other end of the line a high-speed recorder is connected which has an electric or clockwork motor pulling a paper tape at high speed past an electrically operated inking device actuated by the received impulses, reproducing the original message in Morse code.

The speed of transmission over the line may be as high as 300 words per minute. Automatic telegraphy can be used with radio transmission.

Teleprinter

The teleprinter is a device which enables a message to be typed on a typewriter keyboard and instantly recorded in typescript at a distant point. The transmitting teleprinter and receiving teleprinter are normally connected by line. Briefly the teleprinter operates in the following manner:

A key is depressed and sets up a combination of small levers. These levers are associated with electric contacts in such a way that a number of impulses are sent down the line. The impulses are not all in the same direction. Actually, each letter consists of the same number of impulses, but the direction of the impulses is arranged in a characteristic order. For example, for the letter M, the sequence is three impulses in one direction and four in the other.

At the receiving teleprinter a given group of impulses causes a group of small levers to take up positions corresponding to the positions of the small levers at the transmitting end, and arrests the rotary movement of a type wheel, bringing the required type letter ready to print on the paper tape. Thus, the depression of any key at the transmitting end results in the printing on the tape at the receiving end of the appropriate letter within a fraction of a second.

Pyrotechnics

This term embraces many forms of signalling used in the Service, such as the cartridge signal, distress signal rockets, landing flares, reconnaissance flares, etc., but it is the first that is most used.

The cartridge is pretty much the big brother of the ordinary sporting gun cartridge, and its construction is very similar. The body of the cartridge is made of rolled brown paper and is waterproofed externally with paraffin wax. One end of the body is lined with thin sheet steel, and this is secured into a brass base by means of a compressed paper or strawboard wad. Into this base is fitted a percussion cap, which, when struck, produces a flash which ignites the powder charge. The gases formed by the explosion force the filling out of the case. At the same time the flash from the burning charge ignites the priming composition and in turn ignites the star or contents of the cartridge.

According to the requirements of the Service, the contents of the cartridges are made up to produce single or changing colour stars as well as different lengths of time of burning.

The standard size of these signal cartridges is slightly over 3 inches long; they weigh from 4 to 6 oz. according to the nature of the contents.

PIGEONS OF THE R.A.F.

Two pigeons are carried in aircraft of certain Royal Air Force Stations of the Coastal and Bomber Commands whilst engaged in operational flying over the sea, as a means of emergency communication in the event of W/T failure or when aircraft are forced down in the sea.

Pigeons so carried are first thoroughly trained on land, and also trained by being liberated from aircraft in the air.

Pigeons before being issued to operational aircraft are fitted with message containers of bakelite containing an S O S message form, partially completed, giving the particular Station to which the aircraft belongs, the number of the aircraft and the date of issue to the aircraft.

Should an emergency arise, the crew completes the S O S message, giving the location, message and time. Should the aircraft crew not have time to complete the S O S form as above, a white strip is provided on the outside of the container on which a map reference may be written to indicate the position of the aircraft in difficulties without the necessity of removing the S O S message from the container.

Each Royal Air Force Station equipped with a Pigeon Service is provided with a trained staff consisting of one corporal and two airmen, whose practical experience as private pigeon fanciers suits them for this particular work.

Their duties would consist of looking after pigeons awaiting service, fitting the message containers with partially prepared S O S messages inside to each pigeon, the issue of two pigeons to each aircraft leaving on operational flying, keeping watch for pigeons returning to the Station from the aircraft, and the removal from returned aircraft of pigeons not used during operations, etc.

On the return of a pigeon with an S O S message from an aircraft in distress, the loft personnel immediately delivers the message to the Station's Signals Officer and necessary action is taken.

Homing pigeons are carried in R.A.F. bombers for use in case of forced landing. Here the wireless operator is handling one of the birds.

PRINCIPLE OF THE SLIDE RULE

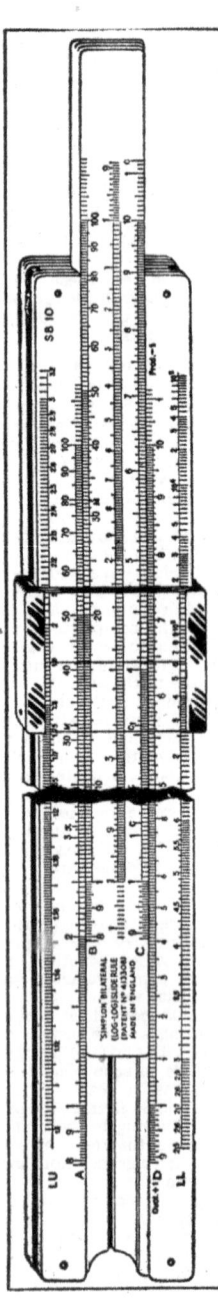

This instrument enables arithmetical computations to be performed quickly by mechanical means. There are four principal scales: **A** and **D** on the rule itself; **B** and **C** on the **slide**. The illustration of a typical slide rule (above) also shows Log-log scales (LU and LL) on top and lower edges respectively. Scales A, B, C, D are, in effect, tables of logarithms plotted out to scale on the rule. A and B are alike.

Multiplication. This and division may be carried out on either upper scales (A and B) or lower scales (C and D). The lower scales enable more accurate working, but the upper ones are generally used where possible. An example is given in Fig. 1. Two numbers are multiplied by adding together the distances corresponding to those numbers on rule and slide. Thus, $2.5 \times 3 = 7.5$: Set 1 on B under 2.5 on A; move cursor line over 3 on B; read result (7.5) under cursor line on A. The position of slide, etc., is shown in Fig. 1.

Division. Performed by **subtracting** the distance representing the divisor on one of the scales from the distance defining the dividend on the other adjacent scale. Fig. 2 illustrates an example: $7.65 \div 4.5 = 1.7$. Set cursor line over 7.65 on D; slide 4.5 on C under the cursor line: read result 1.7 on D under 1 on C.

Squares and Square Roots. Readings on A are squares of exactly opposite readings on D, so that squares and roots may be read off directly.

Cubes and Cube Roots. A number may be raised to the third power by continued multiplication. See Fig. 3: $1.5^3 = 3.375$. Set 1 on C to 1.5 on D: move cursor line over 1.5 on B; read result 3.375 under cursor line on A. In finding the **cube root of 27** we should move the cursor line over 27 on A: draw out slide (to the right in this case) until the same number (3) comes under the cursor line on B which registers simultaneously on D under 1 on C.

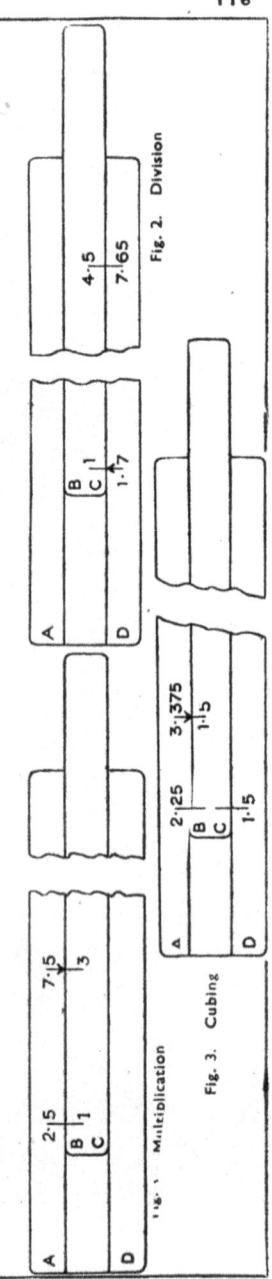

Fig. 1. Multiplication

Fig. 3. Cubing

Fig. 2. Division

Illustrations by courtesy of Dargue Bros. Ltd., Halifax

116

Meteorology and the R.A.F.

Adequate information and expert advice on the weather are essential to the success of R.A.F. operations. It is denied to the enemy. The Meteorological Office provides both information and forecasts as here stated in brief.

THE personnel of the meteorological service are comprised in two broad categories—Meteorological Assistants and Forecasters.

Meteorological Assistants plot weather charts, make meteorological observations, attend to and read recording instruments, determine the wind at different heights, and the height of the cloud. The weather chart is an outline chart of the region in which the Assistant is working and shows the coast, certain height contours and a series of circles which are situated at the positions of stations from which reports are received. Each station is identified by a number which is printed upon the chart and also appears in the message. On this chart the observations from the different stations (received in a figure code) are plotted.

In the British Isles charts of this nature are prepared at intervals of about every 3 hours seven days a week. The purpose is to produce a weather chart of the area which can be used by the Assistant's superior officer for the preparation of aviation forecasts.

Forecasters utilize charts and observations made by Assistants to prepare forecasts and to explain to R.A.F. officers the meteorological situation over the area with which they are concerned and the changes and developments which will take place in it.

When the observations have been plotted and scrutinized the Forecaster must complete the charts, draw the isobars, insert the "fronts" and diagnose the meteorological situation. He must examine the significance of the observations in their relation to each other and of the charts in their relation to the preceding charts, and must arrive at sound conclusions as to what succeeding charts will be like, because he is concerned not only with the subsequent meteorological conditions at a single place but with the weather over large areas during substantial periods of time and at different levels.

The Forecaster must issue forecasts at set times for the general guidance of those concerned with flying operations and route forecasts for projected flights. But he must also keep the meteorological information received constantly under review in relation to the flying which is in progress or contemplated, and must take prompt action to ensure that any of this information, or advice based upon it, which is relevant to the flying programme is brought to the notice of appropriate R.A.F. personnel.

The organization of the supply of meteorological information to the Royal Air Force has three main divisions: that for meeting the needs of the Home Commands; that to supply the needs of Commands overseas; and the organization for meeting the requirements of special routes such as the transatlantic one.

The service organization which has been adapted to meet the requirements of the Home Commands is of a dual character: the Central Forecast Branch and the R.A.F. (Command and Group Stations) Branches.

Central Forecast Branch. This Branch is the nerve-centre of the organization. It is responsible for the collection of the observations which constitute the raw material of the meteorological "factories," and for their distribution throughout the whole organization.

It is responsible for the management of the meteorological stations which make observations and furnish reports from places other than Royal Air Force aerodromes, and, above all, it is responsible for deriving from the study of the observations and the charts based on them the general deductions about future weather.

These observations are coded in a figure code designed to concentrate the information into the shortest possible message.

Collection of these messages from a wide network of stations is completed in a few minutes. As soon as it is completed the messages are distributed in one collective message at high speed to all the meteorological stations at the different Commands, Groups and aerodromes. By this means an instantaneous picture of the meteorological conditions over the whole country is available every hour within a short time of the observations being made.

At the Central Station while the observations are being collected and distributed they are also being plotted on blank outline maps according to a system which enables practically the whole of the information to be shown on a single map. Actually there are several maps, and on some of them only a selection of the information is shown in order that a broad picture may be obtained over a wider area. It is from a study of these maps that the Forecaster prepares his analysis and his prognosis of the meteorological situation.

The analysis and forecasts made by the meteorologists at the central station are distributed regularly throughout the day for the information and guidance of the meteorologists at the stations at

Commands, Groups and aerodromes. It is on the deductions which the meteorologists make at the central station that the meteorological advice given to the Royal Air Force is largely based.

Command and Group Stations. The function of the meteorological stations at Commands and Groups is primarily to give personal advice to the air staff in connexion with specific operations either projected or in progress, and to give necessary guidance to the meteorological staff at aerodromes in the Groups.

It is essential to the air staff at Commands and Groups to know if an operation which has been planned will be practicable or effective in the weather conditions which will exist at the time during which the operation is to take place. For this purpose they require to know not only the conditions which are anticipated along the route or in the area of operations, but also the conditions which will exist at the aerodromes, to which the aircraft return.

This is one of the most difficult problems with which the meteorologist has to deal —the problem of forecasting the conditions of cloud, weather, and particularly of visibility, on aerodromes at some time during the night, which is still a long way ahead of the time at which his advice is required.

The information required by the crews of aircraft is not merely general information as to whether the operation will be practicable, but more precise information as to actual conditions along the route, over the target and on their return.

The information they require is information about the cloud — about the wind at the level at which they will fly—the freezing level in the atmosphere and about fronts— warm fronts— regions in which there may be very extensive and deep clouds changing from the tenuous cloud with a visibility of 1,000 ft. or more, to dense and very turbulent rain clouds—or cold fronts—regions of violent disturbance with strong ascending currents producing heavy rain or hail and thunder and lightning.

The air staff at Groups and particularly at Stations also require to know at a glance meteorological conditions at aerodromes all over the area in which they are interested.

Another duty of one of these Branches is to give advice and information required by Balloon Command and its stations for the operation of Barrage Balloons—information about thunderstorms and upper winds of great significance.

Overseas Branch. This Branch includes a technical and administrative staff at the Air Ministry and at the Headquarters of Overseas Commands and technical staff at subordinate formations and aerodromes. The work of the meteorologist in Overseas Commands is broadly similar to that at home.

The idea that there is no "weather" in tropical countries is a mistaken one. The phenomena there are frequently more intense then they are in temperate regions. There may be hurricanes or squalls or violent thunderstorms, or fogs, or, perhaps worst of all, violent sandstorms.

The Beaufort Scale of Wind Force

Beaufort No.	General Description of Wind	Specification of Beaufort Scale — For Use at Sea	Specification of Beaufort Scale — For Use Inland	Velocity Limit abt 30 ft. above level ground
0	Calm	Sea like a mirror	Smoke rises vertically	M.p.h. Less than 1
1	Light air	Ripples with appearance of scales, but without foam crests	Wind direction shown by smoke drift but not by wind vanes	1–3
2	Slight breeze	Small wavelets, still short but more pronounced. Crests glassy appearance, do not break	Wind felt on face, leaves rustle, ordinary vane moved by wind	4–7
3	Gentle breeze	Large wavelets. Crests begin to break. Foam glassy appearance. Perhaps scattered white horses	Leaves and small twigs in constant motion, wind extends light flag	8–12
4	Moderate breeze	Small waves, becoming longer; fairly frequent white horses	Raises dust and loose paper; small branches are moved	13–18
5	Fresh breeze	Moderate waves, taking more pronounced long form; many white horses. (Chance of some spray)	Small trees in leaf begin to sway	19–24
6	Strong breeze	Large waves begin to form, white foam crests more extensive elsewhere. (Probably some spray)	Large branches in motion, whistling in telegraph wires	25–31
7	High wind	Sea heaps up, white foam from breaking waves begins to be blown in streaks along direction of wind. (Spindrift begins)	Whole trees in motion	32–38
8	Gale	Moderately high waves of greater length, edges of crests break into spindrift. Foam in well-marked streaks along direction of wind	Breaks twigs off trees; generally impedes progress	39–46
9	Strong gale	High waves. Dense streaks of foam along direction of wind. Sea begins to "roll." Spray may affect visibility	Slight structural damage occurs; chimney pots removed	47–54
10	Whole gale	Very high waves, long overhanging crests. Foam, in great patches, blown in dense white streaks along direction of wind. Surface of the sea takes white appearance. Rolling becomes heavy and shock-like. Visibility affected	Trees uprooted; considerable structural damage	55–63
11	Storm	Exceptionally high waves. Sea completely covered with long white patches of foam lying along direction of wind. Edges of wave crests blown into froth. Visibility affected	Very rarely experienced; widespread damage	64–75
12	Hurricane	Air filled with foam and spray. Sea completely white with spray; visibility very seriously affected	—	Above 75

DEFINITIONS OF TERMS GENERALLY USED
IN THE AIR SERVICE

Abeam (on the Beam).—Directly at right angles to the fore and aft line.
Ab Initio.—From the beginning.
Administrative Service.—A branch of the Royal Air Force of which the primary duty is to supply fighting units with what they require, or to perform some necessary service for them.
Advanced Base.—A base in combined operations sufficiently close to the zone of operations to permit supplies, etc., being sent direct from it to that zone. It may also be used for storing supplies, concentrating reinforcements, and establishing hospitals, rest camps, etc.
Advanced Landing Ground.—A place, usually nearer the enemy than the air stations, where aeroplanes can land and take off.
Aeroplane includes amphibians, seaplanes, landplanes.
Air Base.—A locality where a maintenance organization of air force fighting units is situated. Aircraft may, or may not, operate therefrom, but there will normally be aerodrome facilities.
Aircraft.—Includes aeroplanes, kites, gliders, balloons, kite balloons, airships.
Air Force Commander.—The Air Officer Commanding-in-Chief when air forces are engaged in a primary role in a theatre of operations; or the Air Officer Commanding when the air forces are attached to, and acting in a secondary role with, naval or army forces.
Airframe.—An aeroplane without an engine installed.
Airman.—A warrant officer, an N.C.O., an aircraftman, or an apprentice of the Royal Air Force.
Air Station.—A place at which Royal Air Force operational units are accommodated, and from which they operate.
Air Stores Park.—A maintenance unit organized to facilitate rapid distribution to, and holding a reserve of spares and stores for, fighting units. It may hold motor transport, but does not hold aircraft.
Air Striking Force.—A force composed primarily of bomber units and established, either permanently or temporarily, to operate independently.
Amphibian.—An aircraft of the seaplane type which has, in addition to floats or a boat hull, wheels which can be let down when it is desired to alight upon or take off from the land or an aircraft carrier.
Anchorage.—Position where a seaplane can lie at anchor.

Bow (on the).—A direction midway between ahead and abeam.
Box-Barrage.—Anti-aircraft barrage which completely encloses an area as protection from attack by enemy aircraft.
Briefing.—Giving final instructions before going out on a raid.

Cadre Squadron.—An R.A.F. squadron comprised partly of regular and partly of Special Reserve personnel.
Communications.—Roads, railways, inland waterways, air routes, or other facilities in a theatre of operations suitable as a route for the movement of men, animals, or material.

De-icing.—Freeing aircraft from ice.
Depot.—A maintenance unit which holds stores and spares for the air force, including aircraft and motor transport.
Drift, to.—To move sideways over the ground or water. Not to be confused with skidding or side-slipping. The movement of a seaplane " making leeway " (*see* leeway) is also termed drifting.
Drogue.—A canvas cone, so arranged that it resists passage through the air when towed.
Echelon.—A formation of parallel units facing the same direction, successively on the flank and to the rear of one another.
Embarkation Officer.—The officer appointed to superintend embarkation and disembarkation at a port.
Establishment.—The number of officers, airmen, civilians, aircraft, and transport included in a unit's authorized organization.
Fathom.—A length of six feet.
Fix.—The position of an aeroplane or ship found by means of two or more bearings or angles of terrestrial objects, or by astronomical observations.
Flight.—In peace 3 machines; varied in war-time.
Floatplane.—A seaplane fitted with an undercarriage and floats for the purpose of taking off from and alighting upon the water.
Flying Boat.—A seaplane without alighting carriage, but with hull in form of a boat.
Fore and Aft.—Line between stem and stern.
Formation (Tactical).—The disposition relative to one another of aircraft flying together.
Group.—A formation consisting of a number, not fixed, of wings.
Guys.—Ropes used for working derricks or other moving spars.
Head of Service.—The senior officer of an air force service in the theatre of operations.
Headquarters.—A unit, or part of a unit, upon the establishment of which are borne the Commander, his staff, and assistants of all ranks.
Imprest.—An advance of public money for expenditure on the public service, e.g. payment of airmen, local purchases, etc.
Intercommunication.—The means of transmission of orders and information, by which the close cooperation of all forces in the field is ensured.
Kedge Anchor.—An auxiliary anchor, or an anchor used for an auxiliary purpose, e.g. to haul round stern.
Knot.—A speed of one nautical mile an hour.
Landfall.—When land is first reached after crossing water.
Landing Place.—In a combined operation, a place selected for beaching craft or building piers.
Lee Side (Leeward).—The side sheltered from the wind or sea; opposite to weather side.
Leeway.—Lateral movement to leeward.
Maintenance.—Maintenance of air forces in the field consists of supplying their requirements in technical material. It includes the repair, overhaul and salvage of unserviceable material, and the proper care of equipment within units.

Definitions of Terms

Midships.—Lying midway between the stem and stern in the fore and aft line or midway between starboard and port in the athwartship line.

Mobilization.—The process by which an armed force passes from a peace to a war footing.

Mooring Bridle.—Lines attached to two or more points on a seaplane so as to distribute the tension of the mooring line.

Near Miss.—A bomb or bombs dropped very near the target.

Open Anchorage.—An anchorage exposed to the effects of wind and sea.

Pitch, to.—Angular motion about the lateral axis. A loop is a complete revolution about that axis.

Porpoising.—Undulatory movements of a seaplane about its lateral axis when taxi-ing.

Port & Starboard.—The left-hand side, as seen by a pilot looking forward, is the Port Side; the right-hand side, as seen by a pilot looking forward, is the Starboard Side.

Port Detachment.—A unit whose duty is to arrange for, and facilitate, the clearance of air force material from a dock area.

Power Dive.—To dive on the objective with engine full on.

Quarter (on the).—A direction midway between astern and abeam.

Radius of Action.—The greatest distance an aircraft can fly in a straight line, under given conditions, while retaining sufficient fuel to return to its starting point.

Refilling Point.—For material other than ammunition :—the place where articles hitherto carried in bulk are reloaded in detail for units.

Routeing.—Laying down the routes to be followed by ships or convoys.

Salvo.—A number of bombs dropped all at the same time.

Seaplane.—An aeroplane other than an amphibian designed to take off from and alight upon the water. It may be a floatplane or a flying boat.

Ship-plane.—An aircraft designed for taking off from, or alighting upon, decks of a carrier.

Squadron.—In peace 12 machines (3 flights with one in reserve). Under war conditions the number varies.

Staff.—The air force staff is organized in three main branches:
 (a) The air branch, which deals with the employment of the fighting units and the execution of operations.
 (b) The personnel branch, which deals with the administration, discipline, reinforcement and evacuation of personnel.
 (c) The equipment branch, which deals with the supply and maintenance of all war materials and includes the movement staff which controls all movement. Movement of air forces is subject to direction by the air branch in the actual execution of operations as distinct from routine movement.

Starboard Side.—The right-hand side, as seen by a pilot looking forward.

Stick.—Bombs released one after the other at certain intervals predetermined by the bomb aimer.

Stores.—Material other than supplies.

Straddle a Target.—A number of bombs dropped in a straight line at certain intervals across a target, the first falling on the near side and the last on the far side.

Supplies.—Food, forage, fuel, petrol, oil, light, disinfectants, and medical comforts.

Target Area.—The area in which the target is situated.

Tides :
 Flood Tide.—A rising tide.
 Ebb Tide.—A falling tide.
 Spring Tides.—Those tides which rise highest and fall lowest during the lunar month. They occur just after full and new moon.
 Neap Tides.—Those tides which rise least and fall least during the lunar months. They occur just after the first and last quarters of the moon.
 Range of Tide.—The difference between the heights of high and low water.
 Rise (or height) of Tide.—The height to which the tide rises above the level of low water.
 Tide Tables.—A publication from which the times and heights of high and low water can be calculated for any locality.

Transport.—The portion of an organized unit, formation or service, of which the primary duty is conveyance of personnel or material.

Units.—The smallest number of men and material grouped together under one commander for both command and administration. The smallest units of the air force are squadrons. A unit has a war establishment of which the whole or the components have been authorized.

Weather Side.—The side on which the wind blows. The opposite to lee side.

Windward.—Direction from which the wind blows in relation to a definite point.

Wing.—The smallest administrative formation in the air force. The number of squadrons in a wing is normally two, three, or four, but this may be increased in special circumstances.

PETROL AND OIL

Gallons to Tons.—For converting petrol and oil gallons to tons :

Factor : $\dfrac{\text{Petrol Gallons}}{300} = \text{Tons}$

$\dfrac{\text{Oil Gallons}}{240} = \text{Tons}$

	lb.
One 2-gallon can of petrol weighs	19¾
One 4-gallon tin of petrol weighs	35½
One 5-gallon drum of lubricating oil weighs	54

Water in Petrol cans and Oil drums

	lb.
One 2-gallon petrol can of water weighs	23¼
One 4-gallon petrol can of water weighs	42¾
One 5-gallon oil drum of water weighs	60

Special Training and Equipment

SECTION 3

A. Photography in the R.A.F.

Types of camera used for air photography by the Royal Air Force, with a description of processing methods and apparatus.

ALTHOUGH the air camera has been used by the Air Force since early in the last war, the period between 1914 and the present day has seen a fundamental change, both in the design of the camera itself and in the manner in which it is used. From a cumbersome hand-operated affair of mahogany and brass mounted outside the fuselage, the air camera has developed into a compact instrument, operated and warmed by electricity, which requires only the adjustment of a dial and the turning of a switch to set it working without further attention for anything up to two hundred and fifty exposures.

Standard Air Camera

The standard air camera used for most purposes is the Type F.24, which is normally loaded with 56 ft. of 5¼-in.-wide film, giving 125 exposures 5 in. square. The film used is either superspeed panchromatic, fine-grain panchromatic or infra-red, according to the type of photograph to be undertaken. The camera is usually carried in a fixed mounting, adjustable for either vertical or oblique photography, and when used with the electric camera control and driving motor is entirely automatic in operation. The control is adjusted to give the correct interval for the height and speed of the aircraft, to maintain the necessary overlap between successive exposures, while the motor resets the focal plane shutter and winds the film on after each exposure. Owing to its relatively light weight and compact form, the F.24 camera can also be used in a hand-held mounting for oblique photography.

The F.24 is designed on the unit system, which not only allows any unserviceable part to be replaced without the whole camera being returned for repair, but also allows the appropriate lens to be fitted for whatever type of work is to be carried out. Similarly, on a long photographic mission it is a simple matter to replace an exposed film magazine with a fresh one with the minimum delay.

As photography may have to be carried out at heights as low as 200 ft. or as high as 35,000, a range of lenses is available varying in focal length from 3¼ to 20 in., while for special tasks use is sometimes made of lenses with focal length up to 40 in. At great heights the use of a short focal length lens would certainly permit a vast area of country to be covered with a single exposure, but the resulting scale would be too small to reveal those details which betray the enemy's activities; the long focal length is therefore essential to give a scale large enough for detailed interpretation of the photographs. At very low altitudes, on the other hand, it is necessary to use a short focal length lens in order to cover an adequate amount of ground.

The greatly increased heights at which photography is now commonly carried out have brought in their train certain difficulties not previously encountered. Chief of these was the effect of extreme cold, which caused contraction of the camera mechanism, gumming of the lubricant and consequent risk of binding of the moving parts. At the same time it was discovered that the celluloid film base became extremely brittle at low temperatures, while trouble was experienced through condensation of moisture on the lens and within the camera. All these difficulties have been largely overcome by enclosing the camera in an electrically heated jacket and placing over the lens a heated flat of optically worked glass, which serves at the same time as a colour filter.

Developing and Printing

F.24 films are developed, fixed and washed in a spool-type tank, the film being wound to and fro between the spools as development proceeds. In the earlier type the spool unit was lifted from tank to tank for the various processes, which could be done only in the dark room, but a new type is now being introduced in which the spools are mounted in a single light-tight tank. Once the film has been loaded into this tank the whole process may be carried out in daylight.

Investigation is also being carried out with an entirely automatic film-processing machine, which has yielded very promising results. The exposed film is fed into one end of the machine and emerges at the other as a dry negative ready for immediate printing.

In addition to the normal hand-printing machine used in all photographic sections, use is also made of automatic multi-printing machines similar to the automatic film-processing machine.

Night Photography

Night photography is now playing an increasingly important part in R.A.F. operations, and although circumstances caused the night camera to be brought into general use before its technical development had been perfected, it is now proving its value in every night raid over Germany.

The design of this camera, which is a modified version of the F.24 day camera, set a difficult task for the technical staff, since successful results can be obtained only through the most accurate synchronization of the camera shutter and flash bomb, it being necessary to protect the sensitive film as far as possible from the effects of searchlights and anti-aircraft fire, while ensuring that the flash itself is not missed.

The night photographs which have been published in the Press in recent months give a measure of the success which has been achieved.

Cine Gun Camera

An entirely different type of camera now in wide use is the 16-mm. cine gun camera, which is used not only for training new pilots in air gunnery, but also for recording the results of actual air combat with the enemy. These cameras, which, like the F.24, are electrically warmed and operated, are generally mounted internally within the wing of the aircraft, and are connected directly to the gun-firing mechanism so that they come into action automatically when the guns are fired. With these cameras many very striking films have been obtained, showing the devastating effects of the fire of our multi-gun fighters. (See page 126.)

The technical staff of the R.A.F. have had many opportunities of comparing captured German cameras with our own, and of using them in the air. These comparisons have shown beyond all question that not only are our own cameras smaller, lighter and more compact than the German types, but that they are technically superior and yield far better results in use.

How to Read Air Photographs

Aerial photographs do not provide a record for all to read. Their value is obvious, but the problem of interpretation is a matter for specialist study. Here the principles of the job are made clear.

THE problem of interpreting aerial photographs varies according to what the interpreter is looking for. If it is a photograph of open country, then it is necessary to find where it is on the map. This is not easy, and it may take a beginner half an hour. But the interpreter can never afford to take his time; all his work has to be done at full speed so that the operational staff can have the information as soon as possible.

With every photograph he has to calculate the scale so that he may be able to find the exact size of every object, and he has also to orientate the print. If there are shadows he can find the North fairly easily, because he will know the time of day when the photograph was taken. But if there are no good shadows his task is more difficult; he may have to ask the meteorologists which way the wind was blowing at the time and then find the direction of the wind in the photograph as shown by smoke or by waves. If there is a church in the picture the interpreter will be lucky, because churches always point the same way.

If he is looking for ships or aircraft the interpreter has to be able to recognize their type, and it is only after a great deal of practice that he will know that a tiny speck on the ground is a Heinkel 111, or a line a quarter of an inch long a battleship of a particular type. Scale may be a help, and this can be calculated from the focal length of the lens combined with the height at which the photograph was taken. But the calculation may not be absolutely right and a very small error in the height may be very misleading.

Spotting a Battleship

Thus it will be necessary to know the distinguishing features of scores of different kinds of aircraft and of as many ships. It was by such accurate knowledge that a particular battleship under construction was recognized when nothing could be seen in the photograph except the reflection of its superstructure in the water. The rest of the ship was hidden by a dark shadow, but eventually it was proved that a number of details recognizable in the superstructure could only belong to one battleship.

Reading Air Photographs

It is often necessary to detect industrial targets. It is not very easy to distinguish one industrial plant from another, and the interpreter will usually have to know a great deal about them before he can do so. Sometimes it will only be from the smallest of details that he can find out what is being made under the roof of a particular factory. The general type of industry can be inferred from the height of the buildings and the capacity of a works from its size and sometimes from the railway sidings, but it is only after long practice that the estimate will be at all accurate.

No knowledge of the enemy's industries will come amiss, and it is essential to know all about the natural resources of each district. Besides this, the interpreter must know all about camouflage and be able to pick out the most vulnerable part of any plant. When the R.A.F. began to bomb targets in Germany the photographic interpreter was given a new job, the recognition and assessment of damage. Before aerial photographs can be properly understood it is necessary to remember the scale, often no larger than that of many maps. A factory may be ruined and all its machinery smashed, but from the air there may be nothing showing except a minute hole in the roof. To recognize damage is at least as difficult as any other kind of photographic interpretation. There may have been a very serious fire, but if the roof of the building failed to collapse there may be nothing to see from the air except that the ground round the building is discoloured.

It is useful to have photographs of a town both before and after bombing; the interpreter can then look out for small changes which may mean a great deal of damage. In winter snow is apt to conceal what has happened to the target. Without a very sharp stereoscopic pair of photographs it is hard to tell the difference between a hole in a roof and a patch where the snow has melted. Shadows are an important clue—a broken shadow generally means a broken building—but the very long shadows of winter may cover up

A bombing attack on the synthetic ammonia works at Chocques, near Béthune. 1, bombs bursting on power house; 2, gasholders damaged; 3, railway sidings and rolling stock; 4, probably a benzol and by-product plant. Close examination reveals many further important details.

a good deal of damage. With all these difficulties the interpreter must be very cautious, for he must not mislead the Operational Staff by claiming damage which is uncertain.

SOUND, LIGHT & WIRELESS WAVES

Sound. Sound travels at the rate of 380 yards per second. Four beats of the pulse to 1,000 yards is a fair rough calculation.

Light. Velocity 186,325 miles a second. From the sun to the earth, 92,900,000 miles, would only take approximately 8 minutes, 17 seconds.

Wireless Waves or Aether vibrations travel at 186,325 miles, or 300,000,000 metres, per second.

The Armament of British Aircraft
An Outline of Gunnery and the Air Gunner's Work

Here we follow in brief the development of guns mounted on fighting machines from the Lewis gun of the last war to the eight and twelve-gun armament of Spitfire and Hurricane and the shell-firing gun. Notes are included on fire-power, the camera gun and the cine camera gun.

AT the beginning of the last war aircraft on reconnaissance had no other weapon of defence than the pistol or at best the rifle. There were no gun sights and the pilot or observer took aim as though with a shot gun.

Experiments had been made with the mounting of machine-guns in aircraft, mainly with the object of attacking forces on the ground rather than for defence. But it was not until the Lewis gun was adopted by the Army that this method had any success. The Lewis gun was a light and compact weapon, but the early mountings were very simple, no more than sockets in various accessible positions into which the gun was dropped according to the direction of fire required. The sighting was equally primitive. Guns mounted in this way are "free" guns.

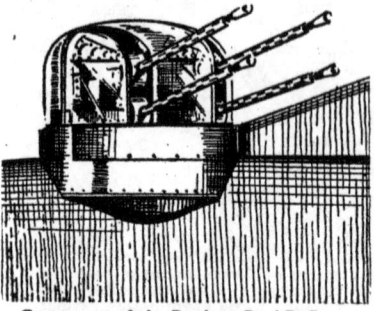

Gun turret of the Boulton Paul Defiant, a night-fighter put into service to intercept enemy bombers.

At the same time experiments were being made with the "fixed" gun, that is, a gun fixed in the aircraft and firing directly ahead; to aim a gun of this kind the pilot has to manoeuvre the aircraft into the required position. But at this time there was a serious drawback to the use of such guns, at any rate in tractor aircraft with the airscrew in front; the gun had to be mounted outside the radius of the airscrew, since otherwise the bullets would strike the airscrew and damage it.

In those days machine-guns were seldom altogether reliable and were apt to jam; if the gun was mounted outside the airscrew disk it was usually inaccessible and if it jammed could not be set right. Various mountings were devised to enable the gun to be withdrawn into the cockpit for reloading or for rectifying a stoppage, but none was very satisfactory, so attempts were made to bring the gun closer inboard and to armour the airscrew. The enemy produced a mechanism which enabled the engine to control the firing of the gun so that its fire was withheld when the blades of the airscrew passed through the path of the bullet. Later many devices of this nature were invented.

Guns of the kind are still in use in all Air Forces, but at the present time there is less need for them than in the past. Machine-guns are now more reliable and less likely to jam. Moreover, the modern fighter carries eight guns, and if one should jam it matters much less than when an aircraft carried only one or two guns.

There were equally important improvements in the use of "free" guns. In 1915 a mounting was produced in which the gunner stood in the centre of a ring which ran on rollers and carried an arm which could be elevated or depressed; lateral and vertical direction could be controlled by one movement. Thus the gunner was able to swing his gun rapidly in any given direction and follow all the manoeuvres of the enemy.

Mountings of this kind lasted for many years. They were usually carried in open cockpits which exposed the gunner to the full blast of the airflow. But as the speed of aircraft increased it was obviously necessary to give the gunner some protection and transparent domes were put over the cockpit. Moreover, the greater speed of aircraft increased the physical effort required for the handling of these mountings; these installations were, in any case, limited to one or occasionally two guns because the gunner was physically incapable of handling more.

The need for power-driven mountings became evident and power-operated turrets were rapidly developed. In manual installations it was often physically impossible to swing the gun into the airflow and so the field of fire was apt to be severely limited; power-driven turrets got rid of this limitation and at the same time allowed the mounting of four guns. Meanwhile, the rate of fire of the machine-gun was increasing; the early machine-guns fired about six hundred rounds a minute, but this rate has now been doubled. Thus, instead of a single-gun installation firing

Aircraft Armament — SECTION 3. B

Upon the alertness and sure aim of the gunner in his turret may depend the lives of all in the big bomber. Here he is seen on guard.

'Tail-end Charlie,' as the rear gunner of a long-range bomber is nicknamed, has a lonely vigil, and may be nine or ten hours in his turret.

600 rounds a minute, we now have a twelve gun installation with an output of 14,400 rounds a minute, and these can be brought to bear over a very wide field of fire.

Another advantage of power-operated turrets is in the kind of gun that can be used in them. The old installations could not take continuous or belt-fed guns because they were too cumbrous for a man to handle. Thus they had to take magazine-fed guns, the magazines of which held only about a hundred rounds. When the magazine had been emptied it took some time to fill it again, and during this period, even though it might be only a few seconds, the aircraft was most vulnerable to a determined attack. In power-operated turrets there is no restriction on the use of belt-fed guns and fire can be maintained until the full supply of ammunition (1,000 rounds or more per gun) has been exhausted.

Together with the gun the gun sight has developed: as was said before, it did not exist in the earliest stages of air warfare. But it soon became apparent that there was an urgent need for a sight which gave correct aim by making allowance for the enemy's speed, and at the same time some component of the sight was wanted to allow for the speed of the

The fighter's machine-guns have a very rapid rate of fire, and the magazines must be loaded with long belts of cartridges, as here illustrated.

Aircraft Armament

gunner's own aircraft. It was not until 1916 that such a sight was invented, and after that it remained the standard form of sight until quite recently. In fact this kind of sight is still used by the Air Forces of many nations. This, and a similar form of pilot sight, was used by the R.A.F. until about 1933, when they were replaced by optical sights of the reflector type, in which the sighting graticule as seen by the pilot or gunner consists of a luminous ring against the sky; this gives the minimum obstruction to the gunner's line of sight and field of view. By controlling the illumination of the sight the ring can be dimmed for use at night, which prevents dazzle.

The Air Forces of every country have made constant experiments in the calibre of guns. It was recognized that the ·303 inch gun was effective against aircraft without armour protection, but that against armour larger calibres would be necessary.

For obvious mechanical reasons a gun of larger calibre cannot have the same rate of fire as the smaller machine-gun, though the damaging effect of each single projectile is greater. Moreover, the gun is much bigger and therefore more difficult to instal; the ammunition is heavier, so that a smaller quantity can be carried and it is bulkier, so that this also is more difficult to instal.

Careful experiment was necessary before the advantages of the smaller weapon could be weighed against those of the larger. The one was easily installed and had a high rate of fire; the other fired fewer but more lethal projectiles. Larger guns were experimentally installed before the end of the last war, both by the French and by ourselves, and guns of 37 mm. and even of 75 mm. calibre were tried. Because of the difficulty of sighting in air combat when the gunner's aircraft and his target were both rapidly manoeuvring, such slow-firing guns with their necessarily inaccurate sights were temporarily abandoned.

Ammunition for the ·303 calibre gun is usually a mixture of ball, with plain ammunition, armour-piercing, incendiary, and tracer, the tracer being included as an aid to sighting. Explosive ammunition was effectively used in air combats in the last war when aircraft were fragile by comparison with those of today, but against modern metal structures it is of little value unless the projectile is above 20 mm. calibre.

Fire-power of British Fighters

Some of the latest Hurricane fighters of the R.A.F. are armed with twelve machine-guns, which are capable of an aggregate rate of fire of 14,400 rounds a minute. Others have four 20 mm. cannon.

This remarkable combat photo (taken with a cine camera-gun on a Spitfire) shows the stream of fire directed by British fighters at two Heinkel IIIs which are caught in their converging lines of bullets.

These twelve deadly bullet streams spurt from the guns when the pilot presses a button on his control stick, and they converge on a single point. Woe betide a German aircraft caught in this enormous concentration—sufficient to rip off a wing as though a circular saw had cut through it. Three kinds of bullets are fired in these machine-guns—ball, incendiary and armour-piercing.

If the pilot has got the enemy correctly in his sights a two or three seconds' burst of fire from his guns is often all that is needed to bring him victory.

This terrific fire-power of the British fighter has forced the Germans to protect their men and the vital parts of their machines with heavier protective armour plating.

Some people think that the increasing use of cannons in aircraft means that the machine-gun is out of date. But that is not so. The machine-gun still has a very important role in air fighting. It is like the infantry man's bayonet—unsurpassed for in-fighting.

Ciné Camera-Guns

Another development in British fighters is the ciné camera-gun, which takes a film of the target every time the guns fire. This makes it possible to confirm the accuracy of the pilot's shooting and the type of machine attacked.

This, loaded with 16-mm. ciné film, is fitted in the wings of Hurricanes and Spitfires alongside the guns. A ciné photographic record of the engagement is automatically registered as long as the guns continue firing.

The camera is useful in another way—for training a new pilot to shoot straight. When he first starts learning to fight in the air he carries a camera-gun instead of a real one. When the film is run over it shows him any mistakes he has made.

The next stage in his training is firing at a ground target—with real bullets this time. From this he graduates to shooting at targets in the air towed by another aeroplane.

This part of the training is very important because the "kick"—or recoil—from eight guns firing at the rate of 9,600 rounds a minute is so great that it slows up a Hurricane or Spitfire by as much as 30 m.p.h. Unless the pilot knows what is going to happen when he presses the button he will find himself thrown off balance and his shots going wide.

Bombs and Bombing Warfare

Following is a brief note on the development of the bomb in war and its use today A popular misconception is cleared up. See also Section IV.

IT was just before the last war, at Eastchurch, that the Royal Naval Air Service began experiments in dropping projectiles from the air. The projectiles were hand grenades, which were thrown over the side of the aircraft with a rough and ready aim. As the grenades grew in size into bombs, and became no longer manageable by hand, mechanical racks for their release were fixed beneath the aircraft. This was at the beginning of the war.

For some time bombing continued to be made from low heights and aiming remained a matter of guesswork. As operational heights and the speed of aircraft increased guesswork was replaced by bomb sights. These first bomb sights had certain tactical disadvantages—notably that they limited attacks to two directions only, upwind and downwind. But war pushed the science of bombing quickly ahead and sights were soon evolved which removed these limitations and gave full scope to the bomb-aimer.

Today there are fully automatic bomb sights which may be said to "think" for themselves and require the minimum of manipulation by the bomb-aimer. They are used for level attacks. For other forms of attack, such as dive-bombing, more is left to the pilot's judgement, aided by devices for accurate sighting.

In 1916 bombs of about 16 lb. were dropped even on such massive targets as battleships. As the carrying capacity of aircraft increased, so heavier bombs were dropped, until by the end of the war bombs of two thousand pounds and over were used.

Not only did the weight go up, but bombs had begun to be designed for specific purposes. For instance, in attacking a submarine, bombs with a very high explosive content are needed, the lethal effect being obtained by the underwater shock of the explosion. Such a bomb would fail in its purpose if it had the thick case necessary for a bomb designed to pierce armour.

Between these two extremes of bombs with thick and thin cases lie many other types of explosive bomb. Besides these, incendiary bombs of many different kinds have been developed during the same period, the incendiary medium

Lying flat, the bomb-aimer sights his target through the aperture of the bomb sight. To view this photograph, hold flat above the head.

SECTION 3. C — **Bombs and Bombing**

Bombs being moved out to action position on the mobile racks of a Sunderland flying-boat of the Coastal Command.

ranging from light oils to phosphorus and magnesium compounds.

The bombs must have suitable fuses, detonators, and other devices for exploding them. Some targets are best attacked by bombs which explode on impact, and for these an instantaneous fuse is needed. Other targets must be attacked by bombs which will not explode until they have penetrated well inside, and this calls for a fuse with a delayed action. A fuse with a much longer delay may be used in time bombs intended to dislocate traffic or suspend activity until the bomb has either exploded, been made harmless, or removed.

Bombs are of many shapes. The ideal shape is the perfect streamline which assists the accuracy of aim. But this shape may not be the best to effect damage on the target or it may not ensure that the bomb has the optimum explosive content for its purpose. Some bombs have come to be popularly known as "aerial torpedoes"; there is as yet no such thing as an aerial torpedo, though naval torpedoes are, of course, launched from aircraft into the sea.

The chief purpose of early military aircraft was reconnaissance, but when their possibilities as long-range artillery—that is, as bombers—were recognized the need for aircraft specially designed was soon appreciated. The first bomber intended for long-range work came into service about the middle of 1918. After the war economy held up the development of these specialized aircraft. Some ten years ago specialization was resumed, and with the introduction of all-metal monoplanes the high capacity modern bomber, long range, armour protected and heavily gunned, became possible. Recently 1, 2, 4 and 8 thousand pound bombs of greatly increased explosive effect have been used.

SECTION 3. D

How the Life-Saving Parachute Works

Everyone, in or out of the Service, has read stories of air crews "baling out" and is therefore aware of the invaluable part played by the parachute. This short account makes clear its operation. A note is added on the life-saving jacket.

As is well known, a parachute is a piece of apparatus introduced primarily for the purpose of saving life in the air, but parachutes are also used for dropping supplies and stores from the air.

The type in use today has been part of the essential flying equipment, for a considerable time, and because its efficient functioning has inspired absolute and implicit confidence in the wearer, it has saved a great many lives.

All life-saving parachutes are similar in that, when opened in the air, they take the form of a canopy or large umbrella of fabric by which the wearer descends slowly to earth supported by a system of lines attached to a body harness.

The parachute at present adopted as standard equipment for the R.A.F. is the Irving type. It is almost exclusively manually operated. There are three sizes, all identical as to the design of the silk canopy and rigging lines, but enclosed in several kinds of pack and attached to the body of the wearer by harness of different types specially designed to meet various requirements.

There is, however, a further type of equipment which is composed of a combined flying suit and parachute harness. The suit is of the standard one-piece type with modifications and the special lining, and has built into it a parachute harness of silk cord or webbing and fabric arranged to take the two-point detachable pack.

This two-point detachable pack type is the one normally issued to all other personnel flying in aeroplanes apart from the pilot. His is the seat type pack. All are fitted with quick-release harness from which the wearer is able, if necessary, to release himself instantaneously on landing by operating the release attachment.

As can be imagined, the care and maintenance and packing of parachutes is very responsible work, and it is only

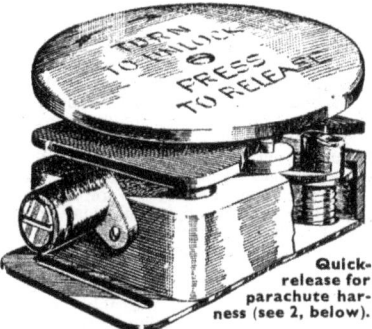

Parachutes   SECTION 3. D

Quick-release for parachute harness (see 2, below).

entrusted to trained personnel. The following is a brief outline of the manner in which a parachute opens.

The first act is of course the pulling of the rip cord. Immediately the locking pins are withdrawn from their cones all the four flaps of the pack cover fly open under the action of the pack opening elastics, accelerated by the spring frame of the auxiliary parachute, causing it to spring rapidly away from the pack. As the auxiliary becomes filled with air it pulls the canopy, air passes up to the apex of the canopy, becomes compressed, extends the periphery and allows more air to enter and completely fill the canopy out to its proper shape.

It may appear that all this takes a long time, and it possibly seems so when "baling out," but actually the time taken for the canopy to open completely from the pulling of the rip cord is approximately two seconds.

The rate of descent of persons of average weight in temperate climates is approximately 21 feet per second, and it is only slightly increased in tropical climates. The shock on landing at these speeds is about the same as jumping freely from a height of nine or ten feet.

Another item of life-saving equipment is known as a stole, a sort of inflatable waistcoat, something on the lines of superior and stronger "water wings," which is issued to all flying personnel whose operations

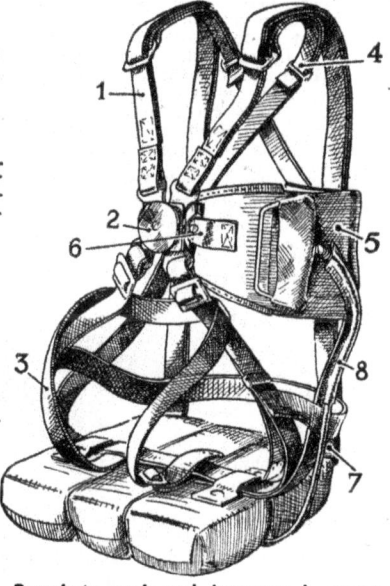

Parachute pack and harness: 1, upper front suspension strap; 2, quick-release box (see detail above); 3, leg loop; 4, adjusting strap; 5, waist belt; 6, tongue for quick-release box; 7, main suspension strap loop; 8, rip cord.

are mostly concerned with over-water patrols or operations.

These waistcoats (known to air crews as "Mae Wests," see Glossary of Slang) are capable of keeping a man's head above water for a very considerable time.

Balloons and the Balloon Barrage   SECTION 3. E

The silver objects which crowd the skies on fine days over great cities have beneath them an important R.A.F. organization. Something of it is told here as well as of the work on individual balloons.

DURING 1917 a small balloon barrage was flown in London to counter what was becoming a rather serious danger—the night raider. It consisted of a total of only 30 balloons and a considerable quantity of wire, and in practice was not very valuable. Only one German bomber flew into it, with the result that the entire barrage collapsed. Today, our balloon barrages present a very different picture. Nearly every important town has its own balloons.

The balloon barrages have certainly achieved their purpose. They have prevented dive bombing. They have kept enemy aircraft at a height from which they cannot bomb accurately. And, perhaps most important of all, they have kept the enemy aircraft at heights at which they can be most effectively dealt with by the heavy anti-aircraft guns.

The organization responsible for our balloon barrages is the Balloon Command. Great Britain is divided into geographical areas, each of which has a Balloon Group. These are divided into a number of Balloon

Balloons

Centres, which, in turn, control the balloon squadrons in their areas. While the squadrons are the operational units, the Centres are the depots which supply all equipment and carry out all repairs and maintenance.

It is here, too, that the airmen, temporarily withdrawn from their war sites, are brought up-to-date with the latest methods of balloon handling and ground defence. In many of the towns and cities the airmen of the Balloon Command form an integral part of the ground defences; every airman is trained in musketry and un-armed combat, and every balloon site is a strong point.

The flying of balloons is not restricted to land sites. Balloons flying from drifters, barges, and other craft form part of the defences against mine-laying aircraft at the majority of our great ports. The crews of these ships, though leading a lonely life, have an exciting time. Frequently attacked by gunfire from low-flying aircraft, they have shot down several enemy aircraft with the machine-guns with which they are armed. Balloons are also flown very successfully in convoys, and are taking an active part in the Battle of the Atlantic. These balloons, while mostly manned by naval and merchant service personnel, are all serviced and maintained by the R.A.F. The balloons flown from land are larger than those flown from ships.

A specially prepared gas-tight fabric made of two-ply rubber-proofed cotton forms the envelope of the balloon, which is strongly reinforced at the points where the anchor ropes and main cable are attached. The envelope is given an aluminium powder finish to reflect the heat of the sun. Some 600 separate pieces of fabric, amounting to over 1,000 yards of 42-inch material, are used in making one balloon.

The balloon is inflated in the following manner. On removal from its canvas container it is spread flat on the ground with the anchor ropes stretched out taut and the fins laid out on each side. Then three or four ballast bags are attached to the anchor ropes.

On the trailer attached to the winch lorry are a number of cylinders containing hydrogen under pressure. A canvas hose joins an inflation sleeve on the balloon to the valve caps on the cylinders, which are connected ten at a time, and as the balloon fills the anchor ropes, which have hitherto been kept taut, are gradually released sufficiently to ensure an even tension over the upper surface of the envelope, and to allow the gas to distribute itself evenly throughout the gas-bag. Were this not done the balloon might rise unduly at one end, dragging the ballast with it. A rip cord is provided to open a panel and deflate the balloon if it becomes unmanageable, either during inflation or at any other time when it is on the bed.

The balloon is never completely inflated, because allowance must be made for expansion, since the air pressure decreases the higher the balloon rises. The three fins are not filled with gas; they have a large air scoop which allows air to enter and fill them, keeping the nose of the balloon in the wind, and so enabling it to fly on an even keel.

High winds are the balloon's greatest enemy, for a sudden tremendous pull may snap the cable or a gust may tear the fabric. Repairs are speedily carried out in repair shops by members of the R.A.F. and W.A.A.F., using electrically operated sewing machines. During stormy weather there is always fire danger from electric discharges; often during fine weather there is an accumulation of static electricity over the balloon, but normally this runs to earth through the cable.

The balloons have to be hauled down and frequently "topped up" with gas, owing to losses due to hard battling against high winds and excessive expansion caused by the heat of the sun.

The "hospitals" in which damaged balloons are treated are large sheds capable of housing several balloons when inflated. Much of the fabric repair work is done by the W.A.A.F. Complete spare balloons and parts are also kept in these hospitals.

Originally part of the Auxiliary Air Force, the balloon squadrons were taken over by the R.A.F. in September, 1939.

Letting up a barrage balloon; the operator in the winch lorry is protected by a strong iron grating above his head.

Air Sea Rescue of Airmen

Details of the Service instituted by the Royal Air Force to save airmen who have been forced down in the sea.

As the life of a trained pilot is the most valuable asset of the R.A.F., the responsibilities of the Directorate General of Aircraft Safety, of which Air Sea Rescue is a branch, become of vital importance to the Service.

Fighters are sent on daily sweeps over enemy territory. Bombers attack targets deep behind the enemy lines. Coastal Command aircraft convoy our ships, hunt submarines and keep our sea lanes open. Any one of these aircraft may be forced to call upon the resources of this service, because all of them have to fly over water to carry out their tasks.

A complex organization is necessary to help a pilot in distress. Aircraft have to be sent out to locate him and watch over him until he can be picked up. Surface craft must be ready to proceed at a moment's notice to the place where he has been found. Ancillary equipment has to be provided so that he is supplied with all he needs until rescued.

This means close cooperation with the Royal Navy, who alone are in control of surface craft. For this reason the organization of this branch of the Directorate General of Aircraft Safety is made up of a Senior Air Force and Senior Naval Officer.

To facilitate the carrying out of the functions of the rescue service the British Isles are divided into four geographical sections. Each of these is watched over by a group of officers. It is their task to institute searches and notify the Naval Authorities where boats are required.

Reports may be received from a number of sources that an aircraft has been forced to land on the water. The watch-keepers may act on an SOS direct from the aircraft in distress or on a signal sent from an accompanying aircraft. They may be notified by a member of the Royal Observer Corps, the Coast Guards, the Coast Watchers, or even the general public that something untoward has happened over the sea. In every case they will mobilize whatever is necessary to rescue the aircrews as quickly as possible.

Today all aircraft, even the single-seater fighters, are equipped with a collapsible dinghy. In the case of the larger type of aircraft these dinghies may be stowed in various ways, while the fighter pilot carries his as part of his parachute harness. The dinghies are made of a rubberized yellow silk fabric and inflated with CO_2 (carbon dioxide). Topping up pumps and leak stoppers are provided in case any enemy bullets have injured the dinghy. Bomber and Coastal Command aircraft also carry pyrotechnic signals and first-aid kit.

All ships afloat are potential rescue craft. However, first call is made on the

If by the aid of their inflated dinghy the airmen manage to reach one of these brightly painted rescue floats, some of which are anchored 25 miles out, they can remain in safety and comfort for a lengthy period. Behind is a high-speed A/SR launch.
Photo. Fox

Air Sea Rescue

Collapsible dinghies inflated by a cylinder of carbon dioxide are part of a fighter pilot's harness. Larger ones carry two men with leak stoppers, arm paddles, rations and signals.

H.S.L.s (high-speed launches) of the Air Sea Rescue Service, supplemented in case of need by M.L.s or any other Naval craft available. The Royal National Lifeboat Institution have a splendid record of past rescues. Fishing trawlers and even destroyers have been used by the Royal Navy to bring back aircrews once they were located by search aircraft.

Searches off shore are carried out by Lysander aircraft piloted by specially trained crews. These aircraft are equipped with dinghy-dropping gear, which enables the pilot in case of necessity to drop an extra dinghy to airmen in the water. Farther out aircraft from Bomber or Coastal Command are used to locate distressed aircrews. As many as six Hudsons have been used on square searches in an endeavour to locate a Bomber crew forced down on its return from an operational flight over Germany.

Besides these duties the Directorate General continually endeavours to find improvements to the ancillary equipment already in existence and to devise new means to lighten the lot of airmen in the sea. Working in close cooperation with various technical branches of the R.A.F. many aids which will be of great value both to the aircrews and to those charged to locate them are under consideration.

A number of rescue floats, brightly painted in red and yellow, have been anchored on strategic positions off the coast. These floats, some of them as far out as 25 miles, are equipped with all the necessities to make a lengthy stay as comfortable as possible. Bunks are provided, there is a cook-stove, emergency rations of all kinds, clothing and even cigarettes and games have not been forgotten. All channel-marking buoys are now rigged with a man-rope and a ladder, so that an airman can climb easily on to them and find safety inside the cage. There again he will find a strong oak box with the usual sort of equipment to tide him over the time of waiting, including a yellow flag which he can make fast to the outside of the cage to make his presence known.

All these means have enabled the Air Sea Rescue Service to give back to the R.A.F. a considerable number of airmen who are now able to aim further blows at the enemy, while enemy pilots who have been rescued are safely lodged in prisoner-of-war camps.

An H.S.L. (high-speed launch) of the Air Sea Rescue Service which has just rescued an airman from the dinghy alongside. A Lysander is flying over.
Photo, Topical Press

Vital Work of the Ground Staff

It is the men on the ground who keep the aircraft in the air. Before a bomber or fighter can take off it is checked up and tested by keen specialists who leave nothing to chance. While the ground mechanics have but little chance of glory theirs is an arduous task of vital importance.

PERHAPS the most obvious example of the importance of ground-work is the heavy bomber. Our bombers have long flights in bad weather, they cross the Alps, stand up to severe punishment during the course of operations, and still come home. Consequently much depends on work carried out by ground crews and those in charge of them.

Each bomber has its flying crew and its ground crew, made up of men who are skilled in their particular job.

The ground crews of a bomber squadron are in charge of a Flight Sergeant. Individual crews of particular aircraft are in charge of a corporal, usually possessing the trade qualifications of "Fitter One," the highest grade of any trade in the Royal Air Force. Under his supervision are two engine fitters, two aircraft riggers, one wireless mechanic, one electrician, one instrument repairer and one armourer.

A Flight normally consists of eight or ten aircraft, and exercising general supervision of these ground crews is a sergeant of each trade who is directly responsible to the Flight Sergeant and who acts as technical adviser in case unusual difficulties arise.

When the crews report at the hangars each morning, they are detailed to their duties, which generally means a complete daily inspection of aircraft.

The fitters examine the engines, checking pipe lines for security, inspecting magnetos, looking for leaks in any of the components, and going over fuel, oil, and coolant tanks. In addition, the variable-pitch airscrew must be examined and tested for its full range of movement.

This task is done while the engine is running.

Oil pressures, and the temperatures of oil and coolant are checked and the revolutions of the engines per minute. These with an examination of the boost pressure are only a few of the items that must be noted before a final clearance is given.

During this time the riggers examine the airframe. The freedom of movement of the controls is seen to and any slackness taken up. The hydraulic system of the undercarriage is looked into. Tire pressures, oil levels in air compressors, the fabric and metal surfaces are carefully searched. These surfaces must be particularly examined for tears and corrosion and the entire aircraft seen to be cleared of all oil and dust.

Meanwhile, the wireless operator tests his receiving and transmitting sets, accumulators may need to be recharged, or coils to be replaced. The wiring is followed through, and the system tested with a ground station.

Wireless is of great importance. On its perfect working much may depend. It must be capable of receiving and sending the vital signals that bring some aircraft safely home.

This Hurricane fighter has come in for refuelling during a pause in an aerial battle; every minute tells, and the ground staff gets to work almost before the pilot climbs out.

Work of Ground Staff

All the electrical installations are tested. These include bomb circuits, intercommunication for the crew to speak from one post to another inside the aircraft. They are thoroughly tried out by the electrician, and signal lamps, batteries and circuit fuses are tested.

The instrument repairer sees that all flying and navigational equipment is in order, and this is no small part of the general scheme of maintenance. There are engine speed indicators, directional gyros, rate of climb indicators, instruments showing angle of bank, compasses and air speed indicator, and others showing engine temperature and pressure gauges.

Last, but of no less importance, the armourer sees that all bomb releases are working well. He tests the hydraulically-operated gun turrets, cleans all the machine-guns (which are many), sees that bombs are properly housed and correctly fused, and that all safety devices are in position.

When all these details have been attended to, the respective tradesmen sign the maintenance form, which states that all equipment has been tested. This form is taken to the Flight Sergeant, who satisfies himself that all is correct before he, too, signs the certificate which immediately places the aircraft as ready for flight.

Taking Off and the Return

The time arrives for the aircraft to be made ready for take-off. Electrical starters are wheeled out, rations are put aboard, emergency rations are stowed near the collapsible dinghy, in case the aircraft has to be abandoned.

Then come the flying crew, and the armourer gives a final check to bombs and guns. The engines are started. The Captain tests the controls, runs up the engines, and assures himself that all is in order before signing the maintenance form. Chocks are waved away, and the aircraft takes off on its journey into the night. There may be a run of twelve hundred miles, non-stop, before it.

The ground staff have not yet finished. The Flight Sergeant details a crew to stand by in readiness, in case any aircraft should have to return because of unforeseen circumstances, which is a rare occurrence, compared with the number of sorties that are sent out.

Towards dawn the reception crew is ready and waiting. A faint hum of engines is heard in the distance — the first one back. Work begins again.

Each member of the ground crew looks after his own job. The aircraft lands, and taxies to the reception crew. The flying crew alights, and the ground crew takes over. The "kite" is theirs again. A "faults" book is kept at hand in which the Captain notes any faults met with on the flight, and which must be rectified before the next trip.

The ammunition boxes of this Spitfire are being reloaded with fresh belts after a flight; meanwhile, the 'plane is refuelled by other men.

Another aspect of maintenance work is the servicing and cleaning of guns after a combat, seen in progress here at a fighter station.
Photos: British Official

Work of Ground Staff

The Flight Sergeant and the senior N.C.O.s in charge of each trade inspect the aircraft. Naturally, there are times when urgent repairs must be made. Aircraft may have been hit by anti-aircraft fire. Sometimes the fabric is stripped from the undersides of the main or tail planes—still they reach home; but before they go out again that damage must be made good. Photographs are taken for future reference.

Petrol, oil and coolant consumption is recorded so that the performance of the engines may be watched.

If special jobs call for more expert workmanship than the Flight personnel can give, there is a special Flight of highly skilled workmen, representative of all trades, and called the "Service Flight," from which men can be called to deal with the emergency.

When all is finally completed, the aircraft goes through the daily inspection and an air test prior to its next operational flight.

Workmanship is of a highly skilled character, and supervision is very strict.

Looking After the Fighters

Practically the same routine applies to the fighter squadrons, although with them the trips are not so long, and the aircraft are smaller. But to make up for that difference, the rate of servicing is accelerated. During the day, when the fighters are in action, work is fast and furious; but just as precise. Hours are long, but nobody minds.

When an alarm goes, the message goes through by telephone to the Flight Sergeant, who sends the individual crews to their aircraft. Meanwhile the pilots are racing to take off. Generally the ground crews win the race, and the engines are started before the pilots are ready to climb into the cockpit. Seconds are precious.

After action, when the fighters come back, they taxi to the ground crews, tankers come alongside and fuel up. The armourers rearm the guns, the rigger changes the oxygen bottles and fits the starting motor to the aircraft so that it can be started up at once.

The rigger then closes the gun holes with fabric. This is done in order to keep the guns clean, and to keep the aircraft 100 per cent efficient in the air until the guns are fired.

Another member of the crew searches the aircraft for bullet holes, the electrician goes over the wiring, and the wireless mechanic tests the radio set. In five minutes the aircraft has been gone over; the allowance is 7 minutes, but it is usually less. One squadron, whose aircraft all landed almost at the same time, was serviced in 8½ minutes.

Should the damage be other than superficial and major repairs be necessary, replacement aircraft are brought out to fill in the blanks.

At nightfall, the daily inspection takes place in a manner similar to that of the bomber aircraft.

Ground crews eat when they can. They put work first, and are keen rivals of each other, with a great pride in their aircraft, and a close fellowship with the flying crews. They share the triumphs and the disappointments, and are excited or downcast accordingly. The "kite" is theirs.

Refuelled, bombed-up and with magazines recharged, this Whitley bomber is being handed over by the ground staff to her crew.

Parachute and Air-Borne Troops

These notes on the newest methods of war from the skies are based upon the work of the R.A.F. in cooperation with the Army. They include a sidelight on the famous descent in Southern Italy on February 10-11, 1941.

SOME ten years ago the Russian Army began to experiment seriously with the dropping of troops from aeroplanes by parachute, and some spectacular photographs were published later, showing hundreds of parachutists in the air at once. Alone out of the other Powers the Germans copied the Russian innovation, but adopted a rather different technique, which gave to the new arm its full advantage of surprise and novelty.

Soviet troops were dropped from aircraft during the Russo-Finnish war, but with little success: isolated, they were surrounded and mopped up by the Finns before they had time to do much harm. Russia seemingly had not then learnt that parachute troops were not merely a glorified infantry to be dropped down among the enemy, but a new sort of soldiers who, properly trained and equipped and dropped behind the enemy's line, could inflict enormous material and moral damage.

The Nazis dropped saboteurs by parachute in Norway to cut communications and occupy key points such as road and railway junctions. Owing to the snow and the rugged nature of the terrain they were not uniformly successful—but they showed what could be done, and the Germans learnt many valuable lessons from the brief campaign.

By the time that the Nazis invaded the Low Countries the new arm had been improved. Some 2,000 were landed in Holland, mainly at Rotterdam and The Hague, where Nazi sympathizers met them and gave them aid and directions. Though many groups were wiped out by the Dutch defence, others fulfilled their allotted roles —acting as the advance guard of larger formations that followed in troop-carrying aircraft. The parachutists occupied previously selected landing grounds, not only aerodromes, but large flat meadows, sports grounds and similar places. These they made ready for the arrival of the Junkers-52 transports.

The parachutists were all specialists or technical troops, comprising engineers, signals personnel, linguists, intelligence men. They were well armed with novel short-range automatic rifles, and a number had folding bicycles. Some were waterside men who could handle boats or barges, work bridge gear, act as pilots, etc.

But the chief feature of the new technique was the shock and surprise it occasioned; the war was no longer some distant happening with a front where conflicts took place and a region at the rear where things were reasonably quiet and peaceful. Enemy troops could now descend in the very midst of cities, could even capture the municipal offices, power stations, waterworks; could seize hostages and menace even the sovereign—all miles from the frontier where troops were defending the land against an invader.

As part of her defence against "paratroops" and against air-borne soldiers in larger formations, Britain took speedy steps to deal with possible malcontents or Nazi sympathizers who might smooth the way for aerial invaders. Then, too, by the embodiment of the Home Guard the country gained a mobile and vigilant force with local knowledge who watched night by night for parachutists and served in a hundred other useful ways. But the military authorities did much more than prepare defences, for, in collaboration with the Royal Air Force, they began to train British soldiers and officers as parachute troops.

The R.A.F. produced the equipment and evolved the methods of training and parachute descent; it also taught air

At certain R.A.F. stations British parachute troops are trained, the Army and R.A.F. collaborating. A "jumper" on his way down.

technique to the Army personnel selected as trainees. The Army for its part attended to the weapons and the tactical training of the paratroops, and worked out the special organization for fighting on the ground.

Jointly the R.A.F. and the Army thus trained and organized the Special Air Service troops, about which the public heard for the first time in February, 1941, when it was disclosed that parachute soldiers had landed in Southern Italy.

British paratroops are drawn from various regiments; they wear a distinguishing badge of a white parachute between blue wings. All are specially picked men: keen, determined and with a high degree of intelligence. Physical fitness, of course, is essential, for if all goes well on the descent the landing is made with an impact like that from a jump to ground from a height of ten feet. And all may not go well: there are fences, hedges and trees to reckon with, and wind may make the parachute drift and swing.

British paratroops wear proper uniform and are not dropped down in disguise like the agents and saboteurs of the Nazis. They wear special helmet and boots to protect them until landed. An outer overall also is worn, to ensure that none of their equipment shall catch in any part of the aircraft when they drop out.

If the ground defences are agile and vigilant, paratroops are very vulnerable just before and just after landing. Encumbered with their parachute and its harness, bewildered perhaps by the descent and needing some minutes to get their bearings and prepare their weapons, they may be picked off by riflemen or machine-gunned where they stand.

Troop transport by aircraft has been extensively developed and practised. A party disembarking from a Bristol Bombay transport 'plane.

The aircraft, too, must run great risks. Yet, despite these risks, determined and well-planned attacks will succeed and may effect a great deal. For Britain before she is ready to embark on large-scale offensives against the enemy with his enormously long coastlines, paratroop operations offer a means of local attack on vital points—the enemy may be paralysed locally by well-directed expeditions such as that on Southern Italy by a chosen band of British soldiers.

Not much may be revealed yet about this interesting operation, but a few details are included from an account given by an R.A.F. officer who helped to organize and prepare the attack, and who accompanied the paratroops to their landing point and watched them drop down.

The flights were long ones, made at night over hostile territory in bad weather. The projected landing points were just mere "pin-points," to reach which needed extremely careful navigation. The night was clear, with a full moon above patches of white cloud.

In planning this operation a landscape model had been used to give the troops an idea of the country and enable them to find their way on the ground. All the men were got down, and the watchers in the aircraft saw them moving off together to their job, giving a last flash with their torches as the 'planes passed overhead on the way back to their far-away base. The spirit and efficiency of the men were wonderful, and as they got into the aircraft at the take-off they sang a song they had made up for the occasion.

Armed and equipped, British troops are seen in a transport 'plane during exercises early in 1939.

BOOKS OF AERONAUTICAL INTEREST

Author	Title	Publisher	Author	Title	Publisher
———	Bomber Command	H.M.S.O.	Fokker, A.	Flying Dutchman	Penguin Series
———	The Battle of Britain	H.M.S.O.	Fraser, C.	Story of Aircraft	T. Y. Cowell Co., New York
———	Meteorological Glossary, A.P. 897	H.M.S.O	Fraser, S.	Air Chevrons	A. H. Stockwell
———	The Weather Map, A.P. 893	H.M.S.O.	Gardner, S.	A.A.S.F.	Hutchinson
———	R.A.F. in Action	A. & C. Black	Garnett, David	A Rabbit in the Air	Chatto & Windus
A. H. S.	Customs of the Service	Gale & Polden	———	The Grasshoppers Come	
"Ajax"	Air Strategy for Britons	Allen & Unwin	———	War in the Air	
Allan, W. J. D.	Air Navigation	Pitman	Golovine, N. N.	Views on Air Defence Air Strategy	Gale & Polden
Ashmore, E. B.	Air Defence	Longmans Green	Gossage, E. L.	The Royal Air Force	William Hodge
Austin, A. B.	Fighter Command	Gollancz	Graves, C.	The Thin Blue Line	Hutchinson
Baring, M.	R.F.C. H.Q.	Bell	Grey, C. G.	British Fighter Planes	Faber & Faber
Beckles, Gordon	Birth of a Spitfire	Collins	———	A History of the Air Ministry	Allen & Unwin
Blake, W. T.	Today with the R.A.F.	Cassell	Halstead, I.	Wings of Victory: A Tribute to the R.A.F.	Drummond
Brewer, G.	Ballooning	Air League			
Brimm, D. J., etc.	Aircraft Engine Maintenance	Pitman	Hammerton, Sir J. A. (Ed.)	A B C. of the R.A.F.	Amalgamated Press
Brunt, D.	Meteorology	Oxford University Press	Harben, N. Roy	Complete Flying Course	C. Arthur Pearson
Buchan, William	R.A.F. at War	Pilot Press	Haslett, A. W.	Radio Round the World	Cambridge University Press
Charlton, L. E. O.	War Over England	Longmans Green	Hewitt, J.	An Elementary Air Navigation Course	John Hamilton
———	Our War in the Air	Dent			
Chatworthy, G. K.	Examples in Elementary Air Navigation	Pitman	Johns, W. E.	Air V.C.s	John Hamilton
Chichester, F.C.	Astro Navigation	Allen & Unwin	Jones, H. A. For Vol. I see Raleigh, Sir W.	The Official History of the War in the Air, Vols. II to VI	Clarendon Press, Oxford
———	Ride on the Wind	Hamish Hamilton	Jones, J. I. T.	An Air Fighter's Scrapbook	Nicolson & Watson
———	The Spotter's Handbook	Allen & Unwin	———	King of Air Fighters	Nicolson & Watson
Clydesdale and McIntyre	The Pilot's Book of Everest	W. Hodge	Jordanoff, A.	Through the Overcast	Funk & Wagnalls
Davies, J. H.	A Modern Flying Course	John Hamilton	Keith, C. H.	Flying Years	John Hamilton
Douhet, G.	La Guerre de L'Air	Les Ailes, Paris	Kermode, A. C. and Haddon, J. D.	An Introduction to Aeronautical Engineering: Vol I. Mechanics of Flight Vol. 2. Structures Vol. 3. Properties and Strength of Materials	Pitman
E. E. B.	Winged Words	Heinemann			
Eliot, G. F.	Bombs Bursting in Air	Revnal & Hitchcock, New York			
Falls, Capt. Cyril	The Nature of Modern Warfare	Methuen			
"Fighter Pilot"	Campaign in France	Batsford			
Finch, R.	The World's Airways	London University Press	Kermode, A. C.	Aeroplane Structure	Pitman
Foertsch, H.	The Art of Modern Warfare	Oskar Piest	Kermode, A. C.	Flight Without Formulae	Pitman

A SELECT LIST OF WORKS OLD AND NEW

Author	Title	Publisher	Author	Title	Publisher
Kermode, A. C. and Haddon, J. D.	The Mechanics of Flight	Pitman	Reyner, J. H	Short Wave Radio	Pitman
Kiernan, R. H.	Captain Albert Ball, V.C.	John Hamilton	Rhys, E.	Flying Shadow	Faber & Faber
———	The First War in the Air	Peter Davies	Robertson, F. A. de V.	British Aviation	Longmans Green
Kingsford, A. R.	Night Raiders of the Air	John Hamilton	Rourke, L.	Men Only in the Air	C. Arthur Pearson
Kingston-McCloughry, E. J.	Winged Warfare	Jonathan Cape	Shephard, E. C.	Air Force of Today	Blackie & Sons
Leeming, J. F.	Airdays	Harrap & Sons	———	Great Flights	A. & C. Black
Lehmann, Russbueldt	Germany's Air Force	Allen & Unwin	Shurlock, H. M	600 Questions and Answers on R.A.F. Law	Gale & Polden
Lester, R. M.	Weather Prediction	Hutchinson	Slater, Hugh	War into Europe	Gollancz
Lewis, C.	Sagittarius Rising	Davies	Slessor, J. C.	Air Power and Armies	Oxford University Press
Logan, M.	Flying Simply Explained	Pitman	Spaight, J. M.	The Sky's the Limit	Hodder & Stoughton
Lyle, N.	Simple Flying for Simple People	Angus & Robertson	———	The Battle of Britain, 1940	Bles
McCudden, J. T. B.	Flying Fury	John Hamilton	Spaulding, O. L.	Ahriman: A Study in Air Bombardment	World Peace Foundation, Boston
MacMillan, N.	The Art of Flying	Duckworth	Summers, J. K.	Practical Air Navigation	Pitman
———	Best Flying Stories	Faber & Faber	Surgeoner, D. H.	Aircraft Radio	Pitman
———	The Chosen Instrument	John Lane, The Bodley Head	———	First Principles of Flight	Longmans Green
———	Air Strategy	Hutchinson	Sutcliffe, R. C.	Meteorology for Aviators	H.M.S.O
Manning, W. O.	'Flight' Handbook	Flight Publicity Co., Ltd.	Swoffer, F. A.	Learning to Fly	Pitman
Mickie, A. A.	Their Finest Hour	Allen & Unwin	Tangye, N.	Teach Yourself to Fly	English Universities Press
Mittelhoar, W.	Flying Adventures	Blackie & Sons	Taylor, P. G.	Pacific Flight	J. Hamilton
Monks, Noel	Squadrons Up	Gollancz	Teichman, F. K.	Airplane Design Manual	Pitman
Orlebar, A. H.	Schneider Trophy	Seeley Service	Tredrey, F. D.	Pilot's Summer	Duckworth
Parsons, E. C.	Flight into Hell: The Story of the Lafayette Escadrille	John Lane	Turner, C. C	How the Air Force Defends Us	Allen & Unwin
Pemberton-Billing, Noel	Defence Against the Night Bomber	Hale	———	The Old Flying Days	Sampson Low
Pick, W. H.	A Short Course in Elementary Meteorology, A.P. 850	H.M.S.O.	Vauthier P.	La Doctrine de la Guerre du General Douhet	Berger-Levrault
Pierce, W. O'D.	Air War: Its Psychological, Technical and Social Implications	Modern Age Books	Walker, R.	Flight to Victory	John Lane
			Weems, P. V. H.	Air Navigation	McGraw Hill
Pollard, A. O.	Epic Deeds of R.A.F.	Hutchinson	Whitehouse, A. G. T.	Hell in the Heavens. The Adventures of An Aerial Gunner in the Royal Flying Corps	W. & R. Chambers
———	The Royal Air Force	Hutchinson	Wilkinson, S.	Lighter Than Air	A. H. Stockwell
Preston, Capt. R. L.	How to Become An Air Pilot	Sampson Low	Williamson, G. W.	A Primer of Flying	Pitman
Raleigh, Sir Walter	The Official History of the War in the Air, Vol. I	Clarendon Press, Oxford	Wimperis, H. E.	Defeating the Bomber	Dent
			"Wing Adjutant"	Today With the R.A.F.	Cassell
For vols. ii-vi see Jones, H. A.			Winter, R. A.	Dive Bomber	Harrap

PHYSICAL UNITS AND THEIR EQUIVALENTS

GENERAL

One ft.-lb.	=	1 lb. raised 1 ft. high.
One H.P. minute	=	33,000 ft.-lb. in one minute.
" " "	=	42·4 B.Th.U.s per minute.
One H.P." hour	=	1,980,000 foot-lb. in one hour
" " "	=	2,545 B.Th.U.s
" " "	=	0·746 kilowatt hours.
" " "	=	746 watt hours.
One 1·33"H.P.	=	1 kilowatt
One ton of water	=	35·962 cubic ft.
" " "	=	224 galls.; 217 galls. salt.
Water's maximum density	=	39·2°F. fresh freezes at 32°F
Salt Water	=	Freezes at 27° F.
" "	=	At 39·2°F. 64 lb. weight.
Fresh Water 1 cu. ft.	=	62·4 lb. weight.
" " 1 cu. in.	=	0·0360 lb. weight.
" " 1 cu. ft.	=	6·2288 galls.
Fresh Water, 1 gall.	=	10 lb. weight at 62°F.
Salt Water, 1 gall.	=	10·3 lb. weight at 62°F.
1 lb. per sq. in.	=	A column of water 2·305 ft. high.
0·0361 lb. per sq. in.	=	A column of water 1 in. high.
0·490 per sq. in.	=	A column of mercury 1 in. high.
532·5 grains	=	Weight of 1 cubic ft. of air at 62°F.
1 lb. of air	=	13·146 cubic ft. at 62·0°F.
15 lb. per sq. in.	=	The mean weight of a column of air 1" □ and 45 miles high.

SOUND

V = Velocity (feet), T = Time (secs.), t = Temperature of air in deg. F.
D = Distance in feet the sound travels in time T.

$V = 1089·42\sqrt{1 + 0·00208\,(t-32)}, D = 1089·42T\sqrt{1 + 0·00208\,(t-32)}$

Example—6·5 secs. after a flash has been seen thunder is heard.

$D = 1089·42 \times 6·5\sqrt{1 + 0·00208\,(t-32)} = 7,300$ ft. = 1·38 miles.

LIGHT

Speed = 186,330 miles per sec. 92,399,000 miles in eight minutes (time taken for the sun's light to reach the earth).

HEAT

One small Calorie	=	One gramme of water raised 1 deg. C.
One large Calorie	=	One kilogram of water raised 1 deg. C
One large Calorie	=	3·968 B.Th.U.s.
One small Calorie	=	3·08 foot-lb.
One large Calorie	=	3,090 foot-lb.
" " small Calorie	=	4,200 joules
One B.Th.U.	=	4·20 joules.
" " "	=	1 lb. of water raised 1 deg. F
" " "	=	778·8 foot-lb.
" " "	=	1,055 joules.
" " "	=	0·252 kilogram calories.
One therm	=	100,000 B.Th.U.s.

ELECTRICITY

One volt	=	Pressure to force current of 1 amp. through resistance of 1 ohm.
One ampere	=	Amount of current to deposit ·00111800 grammes of silver per second from a solution of silvernitrate.
One milli-ampere	=	One thousandth of an amp.
One micro-ampere	=	One millionth of an amp.
One ohm	=	Resistance to allow current of 1 amp. to pass at pressure of 1 volt.
One micro-ohm	=	One millionth of an ohm.
One megohm	=	One million ohms.
One joule	=	One Watt second, ·24 G.C.
" " "	=	·74 foot-lb.
One watt	=	One volt × one amp.
" " "	=	·238 gramme-calorie sec.
" " "	=	3,600 joules.
One watt hour	=	3,414 B.Th.U.s.
One kilowatt	=	1·34 H.P.
" " "	=	1,000 watts, 1 B.O.T. unit.
One kilowatt hour	=	3,600,000 joules.
" " "	=	1·34 H.P. hours.
" " "	=	3,414 B.Th.U.s.
One coulomb	=	The unit of quantity.
" " "	=	The current of 1 amp. flowing for 1 sec.
One farad	=	Unit of capacity. A condenser of one farad capacity would be raised to a difference of pressure of one volt by a charge of one coulomb.

Elements of Air Fighting
A. Notes on Tactical Methods

In this last Section we consider the application in air warfare of the various forms of training. Attack in formation and by individual machines is outlined. A war record of The R.A.F. is added.

WHEN theory is put to the test of war experience it is usually found to be faulty. But although there were many false predictions about the form that air fighting would take in the war which began in September, 1939, the Royal Air Force was not far out in its preparations.

In fact, the tactical methods that had been developed for the use of British fighters and the special defences that had been provided for our bombers were found in practice to be extremely effective. The very first engagement of the war showed that the high-speed aircraft of 1939 were as well able to engage in a prolonged dog fight with the enemy as those of the earlier period. The higher speeds did introduce certain novelties, but they did not prevent the machines from maintaining contact with one another for fairly long periods.

Air Fighting at Dunkirk

Air-fighting methods may be said to have developed in two sharp steps during the war against Nazi Germany. There was first the Continental campaign and then the Battle of Britain. The evacuation of Dunkirk was really an intermediate period so far as the air fighting was concerned.

In the early stages of the war the Royal Air Force detached elements, which were known as the Advanced Air Striking Force and the Air Component, to operate with the British Expeditionary Force in France. These elements were equipped with such aircraft as the Hawker Hurricane fighter and the Fairey Battle bomber, and there were also Westland Lysander army co-operation machines.

A great deal of reconnaissance, photographic and other work was done from the outbreak of war until the time when France collapsed. This work was mainly the concern of the Fairey Battles and it was then that British airmen came into conflict for the first time in numbers with the German fighters.

The Battles found the Messerschmitt 109 to be an aircraft of fairly good fighting capabilities, though it was soon recognized that it was far below our own fighters in technical quality. When large numbers of the German fighters were able to make contact with relatively small formations of our Battles they did considerable damage, but when our Hurricane fighters were present the damage was all done to the enemy machines.

This was the time when tactical methods were being tried and when theories were receiving their first real test. The German bombers when working over France, either on reconnaissance or on actual raids, were not fitted with power-operated gun turrets in the manner of the British heavy bombers, but they had gun positions from which they could sweep wide arcs of the sky.

Our fighter pilots, however, found that these machines were unable to resist them when they managed to make contact, and at this time British successes began to mount and to give some faint indication of how the tactical balance lay.

The German reconnaissance and bombing machines came over usually at great heights, and right in the early stages it was recognized that air war had been pushed up to much greater altitudes than anything previously seen. Combats were common at heights of over 25,000 feet, and later on they were to become common at even greater heights.

Tactical Methods, Old and New

Fundamentally the tactical methods used by the Royal Air Force pilots were the same as those developed in the earlier war. This was really inevitable, because the machines they were using employed the same principle, that is to say, the fighters had guns fixed in position so that they fired

SECTION 4. A — Elementary Air Fighting

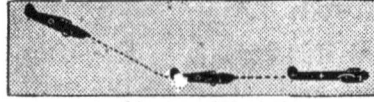

Attacking on a flat course.

forward in the line of flight. Consequently a firing position for a fighter in this war, as in previous wars, is with the nose pointing directly at the enemy aircraft. One slight difference did, however, begin to emerge, more in the combats between our fighters and the German shipping raiders round the coasts of Britain than in France, and this concerned the approach made by the fighter to the machine it proposed to try to shoot down. The modern fighters, with their vastly better streamlining than the older ones, gathered speed quickly in a dive and, having gathered it, they shed it very slowly. This was in contrast to the earlier types which gathered speed relatively slowly and shed it very quickly.

The consequence of this was that our pilots found that they had to approach enemy bombers on a fairly flat course instead of in a steep dive, because otherwise they gave themselves too short a period for bringing effective fire to bear between the time they came in range and the time they had to break off through being close to the enemy machine.

Mass Air Fights

All these early combats involved small numbers of aircraft and often there were individual duels between pairs of machines. It was not really until the Norway campaign that the use of aircraft in mass began to be noticeable. The Germans here used their troop carriers and had operating fairly large numbers of bombers and fighters, and this was the reason that we found it impossible to establish our own air bases in Norway. When the evacuation of Dunkirk came the full employment of mass formations was seen. The Germans flung in vast numbers of bombers in preparation for the movement of their troops across France, and they sent out big forces of fighters to attempt to deal with our fighters over the beaches of Dunkirk.

This Dunkirk evacuation, therefore, marks the turning-point between the individual combats with the employment of few aircraft on each side, and the mass battles which were later to develop over Britain.

The Battle of Britain was fought mainly by very large formations, and the Germans used often 500 aeroplanes in the day and, at least once, more than 1,000. Our fighters were still not working in such big concen-

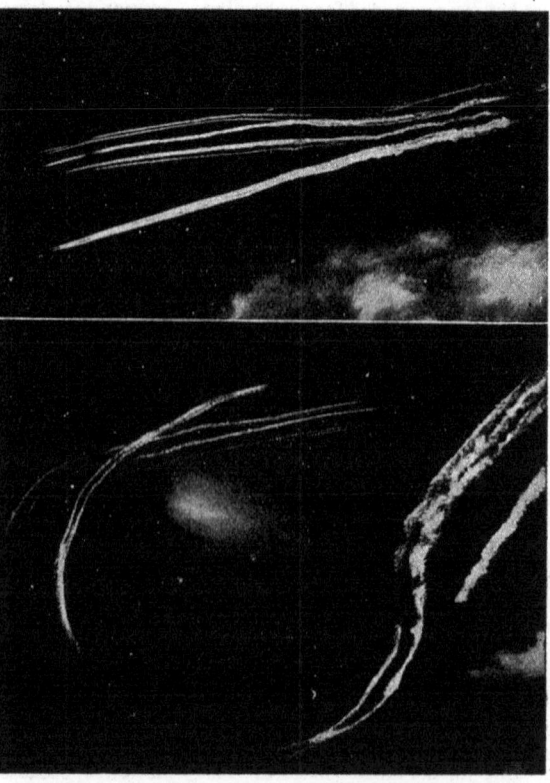

Aircraft manoeuvring in combat frequently leave trails such as these, photographed at 8.48 a.m. on Nov. 17, 1940. Top, our fighters in hot pursuit catch up with the Nazis (upper five streaks). Lower photo, British fighters dive into the 'scrap.'

trations as this, but they were used in greater forces than at any previous period. As is now well known, they inflicted two crushing defeats upon the German air force, first in August and then in September, and both these defeats were due not only to the fine quality of our airmen, but also to the superior technical standard of their aeroplanes and the extremely careful training which is an essential part of the plan of the Royal Air Force.

Attacking in Formation

We may now discuss some of the detailed points of air fighting. Mention of the more advanced tactics is prohibited, and accordingly a general survey is presented rather than a detailed statement of actual methods.

The basis of the fighting formations is the group of three machines flying in a V (see Formation Flying, pages 120–121), and this V arrangement is built up and is still the basis of the largest formations.

The reason is that the leader of a V is clearly defined and those on either flank are in an excellent position to watch his movements and to follow them without delay. In short, the V formation, whether of three machines or thirty-six or more, is the handiest and the best fitted for fighter manoeuvre in the air.

The defence of Britain is based on a complex organization which begins with the detection and recognition of enemy aircraft and ends with the moment when a British defending fighter formation comes in sight of the enemy machines in the air.

Between these two stages there are innumerable steps, but they are all so arranged that the time lost is reduced to a minimum. When bomber speeds go up to perhaps 300 miles an hour it is obvious how important is the saving of time in all defence preparations.

On the fighter aerodromes there are "readiness" squadrons which have their machines out and the engines warmed up, and which have their pilots in rest-rooms close to the machines and all ready dressed with their life jackets and flying kit, so that on a signal being received they can get away very quickly. The actual instructions are often issued by means of loud-speakers and the pilots then act on them.

When they are in the air they are able to communicate with one another by radio, and in this respect air fighting in the present war is more complicated and more highly organized than it was in the previous war. The squadron leader can give his orders and can talk to the members of his team.

If it be assumed that the squadron has taken off and is in a position from where it can see the enemy formation, the next succeeding steps become fairly clear.

The formation leader decides upon the method of attack he will use. There are many methods and the pilots can be informed which one to make by an appropriate order. After they have received that order they may engage the enemy, and then it is likely that something approaching a dog fight will ensue.

In that event the cohesion of the formation is necessarily reduced and there must be a great deal of individual fighting. But the principle still obtains that the formation must work as such for as long as possible, and considerable effort has been made in devising means and in training men so that formations can act as a team even after they have become embroiled with the enemy.

The problem is one of the utmost difficulty, and it says much for the Royal Air

Two scouts patrolling rear of fighter squadron, usually in S-form.

Force methods that its team work is certainly more highly developed than that of any other air force in the world.

The Attack by Individual Pilots

We may now step down from the general movements of the formation and note the typical experiences of an individual in it. He has taken off in his single-seat fighter and climbed with his formation, keeping accurate station all the time by "dressing" on the machine next to him in the direction of the squadron leader. The aircraft may be flying in flights in line astern, which would mean that there would be groups of three machines each one in V one behind the other. At the tail end of the formation it has been usual to detail two aircraft to make S-turns on both flanks. Their job is to keep a watch for enemy attacks from the rear and enable the formation to be warned in time to anticipate such attacks.

All air formations are vulnerable from the rear, but especially the single-seat

SECTION 4. A — Elementary Air Fighting

fighter formations, whose guns all point forward. Moreover, the single-seat fighter pilot cannot look round easily enough to study the sky well to the rear and to be sure that no attack is coming from that direction.

These two end machines, therefore, fly all the time at a higher speed than the main formation, and by making continuous S-turns are able to keep a good look-out to the rear.

If an enemy formation is now sighted the fighter formation will increase speed while its leader determines the form of attack he will make.

The attack of an individual pilot may be delivered from three-quarters on either

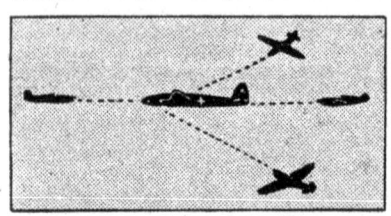

Front, rear and beam attacks are made, depending on type of bomber.

flank or from directly astern of the enemy. On a few occasions nose-on attacks have been made and they have sometimes been successful. This is very remarkable when it is considered how high the combined speeds of modern aircraft may be. But the nose-on attack has the advantage that the fighter may be shooting at the enemy from a direction against which the enemy is virtually unarmed.

Aircraft armour is mainly concerned with protecting the crew, the fuel tanks, and vulnerable points of the aircraft against bullets coming from the rear. The nose-on engagement has the merit that the fighter's fire, if it is correctly aimed, is more likely to take effect than from the rear.

But the commoner form of attack is still from the rear. The pilot of the fighter

A fighter must have the nose of the plane in line with the enemy before firing a burst.

Enemy fighter patrol above a bomber formation.

approaches on a long, shallow dive with engine on and comes up to firing position. He takes sight by means of a reflector sight which gives a clear image of the enemy machine on a glass screen. The range at which he will open fire is dependent upon his own judgement and the circumstances of the battle. Effective fire is certainly possible, however, with the modern eight-gun equipment at much greater ranges than it was with the earlier two-gun equipment.

The fighter pilot will give the enemy a burst by pressing the firing button on the top of the control stick and thus bringing into play all eight Browning machine-guns.

The high rate of fire of these guns is such that the pilot must husband his resources in ammunition and make sure that every time he presses the firing button there is a good chance of obtaining a hit on the enemy.

Enemy fighter patrol above and behind, protecting rear; arrow shows weak spot in defence of bomber formation.

Often the fighter pilot, in going through the manoeuvres that have just been described, faces fire from the rear guns of the enemy aircraft. He can partly evade this fire by careful selection of his line of approach, but he will probably have to face some of it at some stage in the attack. He also has to be constantly on the alert for enemy fighter attack from the rear.

The German bomber squadrons which came over by day during the big Battle of Britain in 1940 were nearly always escorted by powerful contingents of fighters flying above them. It was the duty of these fighters to watch the bombers and if they saw them being attacked immediately to plunge down and to engage the attackers.

The fighter pilot's task, therefore, in shooting down an enemy bomber is a difficult one, and his attack must be swift and sure if it is to succeed and if he himself is not to be shot down by enemy fighters coming in from the rear while his attention is engaged.

In cases where fighter meets fighter, the combat often takes a rather different form. If two individuals are singled out

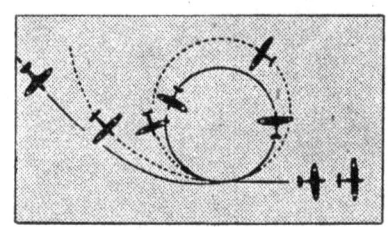

Inside turn to bring guns to bear on the opponent.

they will often circle for some time seeking to gain a firing position, each one turning on the smallest possible radius in order to try to come up behind the other. If one manages to turn inside the other and to gain a firing position, the machine in front will have to make a rapid manoeuvre to try to escape and reverse the positions. This is the dog fight as known since the earliest days of air fighting.

The Attack on Big Bombers

Something must now be said about the air fighting which takes place when large bombers are involved. This is usually night fighting. At the opening of the war the very large bomber was tried as a day machine, but it was found to be too vulnerable to fighters and ever since it has been devoted to night work.

The large British bombers have power-operated multi-gun turrets in front and rear, and these are used for combating fighter interference.

Drastic efforts have been made by both sides to solve the problem of night fighting and to enable the defensive machines to find raiders during darkness. These attempts have secured a measure of success, but night fighting is not (and is not likely to become) so intensive a business as day fighting.

Our bomber crews, when they fly over enemy territory, have to remain on the alert all the time for enemy fighters, and if an enemy fighter approaches they must engage it with one of the multi-gun turrets. These turrets have been most successful. They enable four guns to be swung quickly, even when the aircraft is moving at high speed and the wind pressures are great.

They are used not only in the bombers but also in certain specialized fighters such as the Boulton Paul Defiant, which is a turret fighter whose armament is concentrated in the power-operated dorsal turret immediately behind the wings. A turret is also used in the Bristol Blenheim fighter, which is a development of the Blenheim bomber.

The Power Turret

The correct use of a multi-gun turret is a difficult business and requires intensive training. Air gunners achieve a very high degree of proficiency in this work and can bring extremely accurate fire to bear even when the target is moving across their field at a high rate.

The multi-gun turret is one of the things which has given the Royal Air Force an advantage in certain kinds of air fighting. It is especially valuable for protecting the big bombers at night.

In the future, air fighting may be expected to develop along the lines already indicated. There are, at the time that these notes are being compiled, no indications of drastic novelties, although it is worth mentioning that the introduction of cannon, or shell-firing automatic guns, in our fighters as well as in those of the enemy, is likely to affect the manoeuvres of combat and probably to cause a general slight increase in the average ranges at which firing takes place.

These cannon have become necessary, as the armour of aircraft has been developed to resist machine-gun fire. In this respect the development of air fighting appears to be following somewhat on the

Gun turret in Defiant showing axes of fire.

lines of the development of sea fighting. But in most other respects it takes it own individual way and is not strictly comparable with previous war experience in the other arms.

Air fighting in the future will be conducted by even faster, quicker-climbing and more heavily armed aircraft, but so far as can be seen at the present time it will follow much the same principles as have here been laid down.

The Methods of Formation Flying
Their Application to Air Fighting

Complementary to the preceding article on tactics in air fighting and also to the earlier section on flying training and practice (see pages 75 to 80), this article considers the fundamental principles of military formation flying.

FORMATION flying was devised in order to allow groups of aircraft to work together in a coherent manner. The sizes of formations have shown a steady growth from the beginning of military aviation, but the principles governing their shape and use remain the same despite this increase.

A Service formation is based on a leader, and there is always a sub-leader designated who takes over supposing the leader should fall out. In a V formation, which is perhaps the commonest, the machines are numbered from 1, which is the leader, backwards alternately on either side of the V, the even numbers being on the right and odd numbers on the left.

Station-keeping is a duty which calls for a good deal of concentration on the part of the pilots, and a fairly elaborate air drill has been evolved by the Royal Air Force with appropriate orders for developing efficiency in this. There are close formations and open formations, and for drill purposes the close formation is used. For war flying the machines may be more extended. In formation flying, as in all previous work, ground instruction runs parallel with air instruction.

In order to keep formation each pilot has to watch the machine upon which he is " dressed." Confidence has to be developed in the pilot in flying in close to other machines. The method used is for each pilot to juggle with the throttle.

The leader of the formation maintains a speed which is well within the scope of all the aircraft in the formation and they take up their positions on the leader, and by constantly using the engine throttles and giving a shade more power or a shade less, according to whether they are about to fall behind or to get too far ahead, they can maintain station with surprising exactness.

Formations sometimes take off as such, and this is perhaps the most satisfactory way. But they may also be formed in the air and this method must also be thoroughly mastered by all Service pilots.

Sometimes landings are made in formation, and it will be understood that the efficiency with which large numbers of aircraft can be handled depends upon the efficiency of the individual pilots in working together in this way without trouble and without mistakes.

The essential thing about a formation is that the manner in which the aircraft are " dressed " upon the leader should be clearly settled. In a V formation it is obvious that the aircraft on the right arm of the V must dress by the left, each one going by the movements of the aircraft next on its left front, and those on the left arm must dress by the right.

In line astern the conditions are equally obvious. In line abreast the dressing, whether by the centre or by the right or left, is clearly defined. The V formation with three aircraft, a leader and two flank machines, is simplest and also the tactical unit in battle. A squadron in Flights in line astern will present the spectacle of groups of three machines, each one in V, in line one behind the other.

Hawker Hurricanes in V formation. The familiar wedge formation has important offensive and defensive advantages

Formation flying at 200 miles an hour is no more difficult than formation flying at 100 miles an hour, for the things with which the pilots are concerned are relative movements between the aircraft and not absolute movements.

Concentration and sound judgement of distance are the requirements if a close formation is to be held accurately. For war purposes extremely close formations are unsuitable. The aircraft are too limited as to individual manoeuvre and the claim on the pilots' attention for position keeping is too great. For war purposes the formation is rather more open and rather more elastic, and this enables the pilots to watch the sky more thoroughly and, if necessary, to take evasive action against anti-aircraft fire.

Some details are given in the previous section of the method adopted for protecting the tail end of formations of single-seat fighters (*see* page 143). Two aircraft are detailed to fly in S bends on the flanks.

Turns are particularly difficult to make without disrupting the formation yet without making a wide radius sweep. For turning the long narrow formation as it might be called—that is, the one with the aircraft arranged in line astern or at the most in Flights in line astern— is the most convenient. The wider the formation—the greater the distance over which its front spreads—the more troublesome the turning.

Cross-over turns were developed by the pilots of the war of 1914–18 in order to overcome this difficulty. It was an especially great difficulty for those earlier pilots because their aircraft had much narrower speed ranges than the aircraft of today.

In the cross-over turn, the leader sweeps round on as small a radius as he believes to be feasible, while the aircraft spread out at the ends of the V cross-over, changing their stations so that the ones that were on the right flank are on the left and vice versa.

A moment's thought will reveal the value of this cross-over move in turning in formation. It gives a short cut to the aircraft which would otherwise have the widest sweep to make, while it extends the distance which must be flown by the aircraft on the inside of the curve.

The distances to be covered by aircraft on the inner and the outer flanks are thus levelled up, and the formation can make its turn on a relatively small radius without being broken up and without the risk of some aircraft straggling behind the main body.

Hurricanes flying in close formation. Air drill and formation flying are essential to the handling of aircraft in numbers.

The Royal Air Force during peacetime did a great deal of close formation flying practice, the reason being that it instils flying discipline and accustoms pilots to judging distances and intervals.

In the future it is likely that there will be considerable developments in formation flying. As air forces grow in size, so the need to devise methods of using large numbers of machines together also grows.

EAGLE SQUADRONS, R.A.F.

First formed officially on Oct. 8, 1940, from American volunteers, some of whom had already fought in the Air Force of France. Commanded by Squadron-Leader W. E. G. Taylor, formerly of the U.S. Naval Air Service and later an Air Line pilot ; he came to England in 1939 to join the Fleet Air Arm.

The Hon. Commanding Officer, Col. Charles Sweeny (who enlisted in the French Foreign Legion in 1914), was one of the group of Americans who formed the famous Escadrille Lafayette to fight for France in the air during the war of 1914–18. A colonel in the American Army, he holds the commission of Group Captain R.A.F.

The personnel of the Eagle Squadron included Americans of varied callings, drawn from all parts of the U.S.A. Trained as squadrons in March, 1941, they became part of Fighter Command as Nos. 71, 121 and 133.

In September, 1942, the three squadrons were formally handed over by the C.-in-C. Fighter Command to the Commanding General, Fighter Command, U.S. Army Air Force.

SIMPLE TABLE OF TRIGONOMETRICAL FUNCTIONS

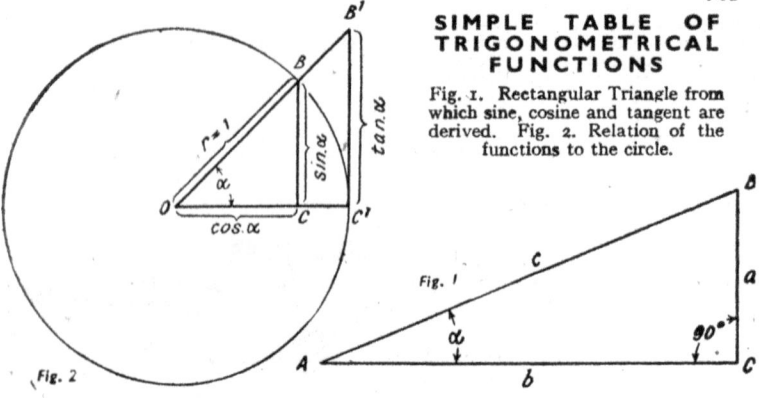

Fig. 1. Rectangular Triangle from which sine, cosine and tangent are derived. Fig. 2. Relation of the functions to the circle.

Deg.	L'gth of Arc	Chord	Sine	Tan.	Cotan.	Cosine			
0	0	000	0	0	8	1	1·4142	1·5708	90
1	·0175	·0174	·0175	·0175	57·2900	·9998	1·4018	1·5533	89
2	·0349	·0349	·0349	·0349	28·6363	·9994	1·3893	1·5359	88
3	·0524	·0523	·0523	·0524	19·0811	·9986	1·3767	1·5184	87
4	·0698	·0698	·0697	·0699	14·3007	·9976	1·3640	1·5010	86
5	·0873	·0872	·0872	·0875	11·4301	·9962	1·3512	1·4835	85
6	·1047	·1047	·1045	·1051	9·5144	·9945	1·3383	1·4661	84
7	·1222	·1221	·1219	·1228	8·1443	·9925	1·3252	1·4486	83
8	·1396	·1395	·1392	·1405	7·1154	·9903	1·3121	1·4312	82
9	·1571	·1569	·1564	·1584	6·3138	·9877	1·2989	1·4137	81
10	·1745	·1743	·1736	·1763	5·6713	·9848	1·2856	1·3963	80
11	·1920	·1917	·1908	·1944	5·1446	·9816	1·2721	1·3788	79
12	·2094	·2090	·2079	·2126	4·7046	·9781	1·2586	1·3614	78
13	·2269	·2264	·2250	·2309	4·3315	·9744	1·2450	1·3439	77
14	·2443	·2437	·2419	·2493	4·0108	·9703	1·2313	1·3265	76
15	·2618	·2610	·2588	·2679	3·7321	·9659	1·2175	1·3090	75
16	·2793	·2783	·2756	·2867	3·4874	·9613	1·2036	1·2915	74
17	·2967	·2956	·2924	·3057	3·2709	·9563	1·1896	1·2741	73
18	·3142	·3129	·3090	·3249	3·0777	·9511	1·1756	1·2566	72
19	·3316	·3301	·3256	·3443	2·9042	·9455	1·1614	1·2392	71
20	·3491	·3473	·3420	·3640	2·7475	·9397	1·1471	1·2217	70
21	·3665	·3645	·3584	·3839	2·6051	·9336	1·1328	1·2043	69
22	·3840	·3816	·3746	·4040	2·4751	·9272	1·1184	1·1868	68
23	·4014	·3987	·3907	·4245	2·3559	·9205	1·1039	1·1694	67
24	·4189	·4158	·4067	·4452	2·2460	·9135	1·0893	1·1519	66
25	·4363	·4329	·4226	·4663	2·1445	·9063	1·0746	1·1345	65
26	·4538	·4499	·4384	·4877	2·0503	·8988	1·0598	1·1170	64
27	·4712	·4669	·4540	·5095	1·9626	·8910	1·0450	1·0996	63
28	·4887	·4838	·4695	·5317	1·8807	·8829	1·0301	1·0821	62
29	·5061	·5008	·4848	·5543	1·8040	·8746	1·0151	1·0647	61
30	·5236	·5176	·5000	·5774	1·7321	·8660	1·0000	1·0472	60
31	·5411	·5345	·5150	·6009	1·6643	·8572	·9848	1·0297	59
32	·5585	·5513	·5299	·6249	1·6003	·8480	·9700	1·0123	58
33	·5760	·5680	·5446	·6494	1·5399	·8387	·9543	·9948	57
34	·5934	·5847	·5592	·6745	1·4826	·8290	·9389	·9774	56
35	·6109	·6014	·5736	·7002	1·4281	·8192	·9235	·9599	55
36	·6283	·6180	·5878	·7265	1·3764	·8090	·9080	·9425	54
37	·6458	·6346	·6018	·7536	1·3270	·7986	·8924	·9250	53
38	·6632	·6511	·6157	·7813	1·2799	·7880	·8767	·9076	52
39	·6807	·6676	·6293	·8098	1·2349	·7771	·8610	·8901	51
40	·6981	·6840	·6428	·8391	1·1918	·7660	·8452	·8727	50
41	·7156	·7004	·6561	·8693	1·1504	·7547	·8294	·8552	49
42	·7330	·7167	·6691	·9004	1·1106	·7431	·8135	·8378	48
43	·7505	·7330	·6820	·9325	1·0724	·7314	·7975	·8203	47
44	·7679	·7492	·6947	·9657	1·0355	·7193	·7815	·8029	46
45	·7854	·7654	·7071	1·0000	1·0000	·7071	·7654	·7854	45
			Cosine	Cotan.	Tan.	Sine	Chord	Length of Arc	Deg.

'Briefing' the Bomber Crews

It is the natural aim of the ambitious R.A.F. recruit to become a member of an air crew. Whether his hopes are set on piloting or bombing, he will find this first-hand account of an Operations Room Conference immediately before a raid of direct interest and appeal.

MOST people know that when parties go to law their respective counsel are "briefed"—that is, given a summary of the facts of the case and points of law, prepared by the solicitors on either side. The solicitor points out what he considers are weak points in the opponent's case, and indicates chinks in the armour through which that case may be weakened or made to fail. He also warns of dangers.

Something of the same sort happens when bomber crews are briefed for a night's operations, but here the analogy stops, for the bomber's "brief" includes precise details of the intention of the operation, explicit instructions regarding the manner in which it is to be carried out, and information about alternative targets that may be attacked if circumstances should prevent the primary object from being attained.

Earlier in the day in question the C.O. of the Station will be ready in the Operations Room waiting for orders about the night's targets to come through. With him will probably be the Wing Commander and the Intelligence Officers.

On the receipt of the orders quite a complicated human machinery is set in motion. The armourer must see to the provision of bombs for the jobs in hand (their character will depend on the sort of targets to be attacked). Weather forecasts must be prepared by the Meteorological Officer. The Medical Officer and the Signals Officer are notified about the coming operation. Scores of aircraftmen will take a hand in getting the bombers ready, down to the last detail.

The Station Intelligence Officer gathers together information about the precise targets for that night. If it is a group of factories that is to be bombed, plans will be got out from files where such information has been painstakingly collected over a long period in readiness for just such an opportunity as may occur that night. The ground defences will be described. Vulnerable points will be marked—the power stations whence the electric motors draw their current; transport lines on which the works depend for their raw materials. Landmarks by which the pilots may check their position are marked on maps; others near the target are indicated by which the works may be definitely identified.

To supplement all this information and to get a last check upon it the station I.O. gets into touch with the Group Intelligence Officer to see if the latter has any fresh news about the target area.

The bulk of the work of preparing the aircraft is done by the ground staff, but the crew none the less keep a sharp eye on the various tasks to see that nothing is left undone. The crew will probably consist of men who have flown together many thousands of miles and have achieved that close and perfect cooperation that

In the Briefing Room, where the air crews gather some hours before a raid is to start, precise information is given about the night's operations, and specially vulnerable points are indicated.
Photo, British Official: Crown Copyright

SECTION 4. C — Briefing the Bombers

The gunner of an R.A.F. bomber booked for duty that evening checks up at the blackboard where the names of the crews are posted.

is so necessary. It will include the captain, second pilot, observer-navigator-bomb-aimer, wireless operator and gunners.

At a time which has been appointed they gather in the Operations Room for the actual briefing by the Squadron Commander. He reads the operation order, and gives particulars of the time, route to be followed, kinds of bombs that have been loaded, and any special instructions.

Next the Wing Commander takes up the story. Probably he has been over that particular part of enemy territory and can give hints based on personal experience. Then the Intelligence Officer brings out his maps and goes over the route on them, pointing out landmarks and drawing attention to prominent features by which landfalls can be recognized. Barrages and strong points in the ground defences are indicated; many valuable hints are imparted. Questions are answered, and any doubtful matters elucidated.

The Group Captain adds a few words about the job from his own viewpoint, and the briefing is finished. The crew have a couple of hours before the "take-off," and they go to get a meal. But first the navigator must work out their courses; and the captain, too, has last-minute jobs of importance that could not have been done until after the briefing.

The crew musters by the big bomber and at the prearranged minute the aircraft goes off. Once in the air, its wireless operator signals the control room, giving the code identification letter and the time of take-off. Thereafter nothing more will be heard of the aircraft for some hours, until the captain sends a code signal telling that the task has been completed. For only if he is in dire need will he otherwise break the silence. He is constrained to secrecy like the commander of a warship in face of the enemy, and a message to his base might give away valuable information. All being well, in the early hours of the next day the bomber will signal its approach, and will land a few minutes later.

SPECIMEN COMBAT REPORT

The following is part of a combat report from which certain particulars as to date and so forth are omitted.

WHILST leading Green Section on a patrol S. of London I noticed A/A fire just West of London and on investigation I noticed a force of some forty enemy aircraft which I could not identify. I just put my Section into line astern. I made towards A/A fire when two Me. 109s appeared to my right. I accordingly turned and attacked them. I gave one a burst and it half rolled and dived vertically to 12,000 feet when it straightened out. I had dived after it and as soon as it finished its dive I recommenced my attack. I was going faster than the E/A and I continued firing until I had to pull away to the right to avoid collision. The E/A half rolled and dived vertically, with black smoke coming from underneath the pilot's seat it seemed.

I followed it down until it entered cloud at about 6,000 and had to recover from the dive as E/A was then going at approximately 480 m.p.h. I then made my way through the cloud at a reasonable speed and found the wreckage of E/A burning furiously.

It was painted yellow from spinner to cockpit.

I climbed up through cloud and narrowly missed colliding with a Ju. 88, which was on fire and being attacked by numerous Hurricanes. Unfortunately, I could not make further contact with the enemy and returned to base.

I had taken off from ———, at 11.30 and landed at 13.50 hours.

Signature

O.C. { Section.......... Green
{ Flight .... B.
{ Squadron

R.A.F. Record: Three Years of War
A Chronological Summary of Great Achievements

In this appreciation of the heroic exploits of airmen and air staff in the period September 1939 to September 1942 by an unofficial air correspondent, an attempt is made to present an abstract of the achievements—unequalled in history—of the fighting Commands in the main theatres of war. It is necessarily restricted to the Royal Air Force.

THREE years of air warfare have crowded into the Annals of the Royal Air Force a multitude of operations, trials and achievements unequalled by anything in history. Each of the eight Commands has worked with magnificent tenacity in facing the supreme and often overwhelming tasks which have been set it. Even in the darkest hours British pilots and air crews have shown their unmatched powers in offence as well as defence.

First Blows, September, 1939

The first blow struck at the enemy by the R.A.F. occurred soon after the declaration of war when Bristol Blenheims flew out from England in the late afternoon of Monday, September 4, 1939, and from a moderate height attacked warships at Brunsbüttel and Wilhelmshaven. Another form of air action was carried out on the same day when the R.A.F. made reconnaissance and leaflet-dropping flights over Northern and Western Germany. The leaflets were spread by night and from a great height. Later, night reconnaissance flights were made over Berlin, Prague and other Eastern objectives. In the opening days of the war Hawker Hurricane fighters and Westland Lysander army co-operation machines, as well as Fairey Battle aircraft, operated from their bases in France.

A large proportion of the R.A.F. personnel and stores was transported to France by air, and machines and their crews flew over immediately to take up war stations there. These units in France were maintained and fed by air for some twelve days after the outbreak of war, and flying hospital units were made available. In Britain home defence squadrons were ceaselessly at the ready, awaiting the moment to intercept reconnaissance and bomber aircraft of the Luftwaffe.

First Raids on Britain, October, 1939

The enemy opened his attacks on this country with a raid on the Firth of Forth area. This was on October 16, 1939. Five minutes after the raid warning had sounded R.A.F. fighters made contact with the enemy off May Island at the entrance to the Firth of Forth. Four German bombers were shot down, three by Hawker Hurricanes, flown by pilots of the Auxiliary Air Force, and one by A.A. guns.

Coastal Command Patrols, 1939

The Germans were also very active over the North Sea, and here, too, R.A.F. fighters as well as aircraft of the Coastal Command were constantly on patrol and frequently in action. In the first few months of the war, as is the case today, the Coastal Command consistently maintained vigil over the North Sea and the Atlantic Ocean, flying by day and by night, often in the most hazardous weather.

The Avro Anson, the Lockheed Hudson and the Short Sunderland four-engined flying boat did wonderful work in reconnoitring enemy harbours or tracking enemy ships and U-boats, and there were instances when Nazi submarines were successfully bombed by aircraft of the Coastal Command. The Sunderlands also figured in a number of notable rescue operations when merchant seamen, stranded in open boats after torpedo attacks, were spotted from the air, picked up by the flying boats and flown to British ports.

A.A.S.F. in France, to March, 1940

Meanwhile, the operations carried out by the British Air Forces in France became more extended, and though they were on a relatively small scale there were frequent occasions when R.A.F. fighter pilots in the Advanced Air Striking Force were able to reveal their mettle and the efficiency of the Hawker Hurricane and its eight-gun armament. One of the first officers to show outstanding ability in combat while in France was Flying Officer E. J. ("Cobber") Kain, a New Zealander, who was mentioned in dispatches in February, 1940, and was decorated in March with the Distinguished Flying Cross. Unhappily, Kain was killed in an air crash three months later. In March, 1940, the R.A.F. carried out the first heavy raid on targets in Germany, when Bomber Command squadrons equipped with Vickers Wellingtons, Handley-Page Hampdens and Armstrong-Whitworth Whitleys attacked the seaplane base on the island of Sylt.

Norway and Denmark, April, 1940

April 9, 1940, was the day on which the enemy invaded Denmark and Norway, and within a few hours R.A.F. bombers had attacked enemy cruisers in Bergen Fjord. One vessel was hit. Thereafter Coastal Command bombers were daily in action

R.A.F. OPERATIONS SCANDINAVIAN CAMPAIGN

Date	German losses	British losses
April, May, June, 1940	56	55

bombing German aircraft grounded at Bergen; and low-flying attacks were carried out at Stavanger, Trondheim and elsewhere by Blenheim aircraft. Raids were also made on the large Danish aerodrome at Ry on the shore of Lake Salten Langso, North Jutland.

Belgium and Holland, May, 1940

On May 10, 1940, the Germans' invaded Holland and Belgium and the major Western offensive began. The R.A.F., which had been continually in action over the North Sea, over the Atlantic, over the British coastline, over Germany and Norway, was now engaged in an unequal struggle in the Low Countries. Blenheims of the Bomber Command swept over Holland to destroy Nazi troop carriers at Rotterdam. Fighters of the Advanced Air Striking Force, speeding over Dutch territory from their stations in France, fiercely attacked road transports and troop columns, and many German aircraft fell to the guns of the Hurricanes. Air support to the limit was given to ground forces. Every available British aircraft took part in the desperate operations over the Netherlands, and many acts of unrecorded gallantry were carried out hourly. On Tuesday, May 14, 1940, the Dutch Commander-in-Chief, General Winkelman, ordered his troops to cease fire, but the R.A.F. continued its attacks with unabated zeal.

Battle of France, May, 1940

At the same time developments in France were reaching a critical stage. After a period of comparative inactivity the bombers and fighters of the R.A.F. were incessantly in action, giving support to the French forces at Sedan, and elsewhere, by combating German dive-bombers and fighters and by carrying out a widespread offensive on the enemy's road and rail communications and other objectives. In the last days of May the situation for the Allies became daily more grave. The enemy was exerting more and more pressure to reach the Channel ports, the Belgian Army had given up the struggle, and the French were being overwhelmed by the enemy's mechanized power. In the Battle of France the work of the R.A.F. by day and night was maintained with a spirit of gallantry and devotion to duty unsurpassed in history. Pilots were flying without rest to such an extent that on landing they fell exhausted and could be aroused only with difficulty.

The first awards of the Victoria Cross to airmen in the present war resulted from an action in this period. They were made to Flying Officer D. E. Garland and Sergeant T. Gray, who showed the most conspicuous bravery in a raid on a bridge over the Albert Canal, near Maastricht. At all costs it had to be destroyed, and when the order came through every crew in Garland's and Gray's squadron volunteered for the task. Five crews were selected and set out for the target, which they attacked through a tornado of fire. The bridge was destroyed, but four of the five aircraft did not return to their base, including that piloted by Flying Officer Garland.

Dunkirk, May 29-June 4, 1940

The bitter struggle reached a further critical stage when the British Expeditionary Force was on the coast at Dunkirk and the great evacuation was in progress. The Luftwaffe was then fighting in conditions in which it had every tactical advantage, while the R.A.F. went into battle with tremendous handicaps. The enemy, with his great superiority in machines, bombed and gunned the British troops and the heterogeneous ferry fleet of ships and boats. The assaults were continuous, and enemy bombers and dive-bombers went into action with an immense screen of fighters. The Nazi machines had a great number of aerodromes at their disposal near at hand. On the other hand, the British fighters had to come from their stations in England and also in France in much smaller numbers, and, being short-range aircraft, they had to return over comparatively long distances for more fuel and more ammunition. British airmen, like the soldiers and sailors, were hard pressed and fighting against terrible odds to the limit of their power.

In addition to Spitfires, Hurricanes and Boulton-Paul two-seater Defiants, Coastal Command Lockheed Hudsons swept into this intense conflict. The fighter pilots went out on as many as four patrols every day. Again and again enemy bombing attacks on men on the beaches and

R.A.F. OPERATIONS
WESTERN FRONT (including Dunkirk)

Date	German losses	British losses
September, 1939 –March 1940	24	7
April, 1940	13	3
May, 1940	701	271
June, 1940	219	98
Total	957	379

in the ferrying craft were countered by the R.A.F., and, by June 4, 603 Luftwaffe machines had been destroyed by the Fighter Command in combats over Dunkirk. It was thus estimated that the R.A.F. had inflicted losses amounting to 4 to 1.

In the House of Commons Mr. Winston Churchill stated that there was a victory inside the deliverance at Dunkirk; in a tribute to the R.A.F. he said, " May it not also be that the cause of civilization itself will be defended by the skill and vision of a few thousand airmen?"

During and immediately after the period when the R.A.F. fought furiously to aid the beleaguered forces at Dunkirk, our bombers continued to attack the enemy at points in Norway, Holland and in his own country. In Germany, oil refineries, fuel depots and the Ruhr were bombed.

Middle East War, June-Aug., 1940

On June 10 Mussolini declared war on Great Britain and France, and on the following day the R.A.F. of the Middle East Command went into action against

R.A.F. RAIDS ON ITALY AND SICILY

Number of attacks between 12/6/40 and 3/9/41	42
Number of objectives between 12/6/40 and 3/9/41	32
Main Targets	
Turin (17), Milan (8), Genoa (5).	
Targets in Sicily—Messina, Syracuse, Cape Passero, Catania, Palermo.	

the Italian Air Force and ground forces. Our bombers assaulted aerodromes both in East Libya and Italian East Africa, and on June 11, 1940, R.A.F. night bombers raided Turin. These operations were the prelude to the ever expanding air war in the Mediterranean and Middle East. There followed remarkable long-distance raids by our home-based bombers on Milan, Turin and Genoa. Over the Mediterranean the R.A.F. were successful, too, in sinking a number of Italian submarines; and throughout July and August our fighter pilots, most of them equipped with the obsolescent Gloster Gladiator biplane, dis-

played a most pronounced superiority over the Italians in daily encounters over Libya.

First Year's Results

By September 3, 1940, the anniversary of the outbreak of war, the R.A.F. had destroyed a total of 3,594 enemy aircraft, and between August 11 and August 31 alone 1,035 machines of the Luftwaffe and 17 of the Regia Aeronautica were shot down, while the British Air Force losses amounted to 335.

Battle of Britain, Aug.-Oct., 1940

By September, too, the Germans had gathered momentum in their great onslaught against Britain. The mass day attacks over this country started on August 8, 1940, and diminished on October 30, 1940, and during that period the R.A.F. showed for the second time its unsurpassed skill, power and will to shatter the enemy. From dawn till dusk the Hurricanes and Spitfires of the Fighter Command were in battle; from dawn to dusk they sent German bombers and fighters to their doom.

Attacks on Germany and Invasion Ports, Autumn, 1940

At the same time the Bomber Command continued to strike Germany with unchanging resolution. Berlin was bombed for the first time on August 25, and then the Ruhr, aerodromes in German-occupied Holland and Belgium, and the invasion ports were the targets night after night. Many raids by Bristol Blenheims on the ports of Boulogne, Calais, Ostend, Dunkirk and Veere were made in daylight. These raids were part of Britain's defensive plan

BIG DAYS IN THE BATTLE OF BRITAIN

Aug.	German	British	Pilots Saved	Sept.	German	British	Pilots Saved
8	60	16	3	1	29	15	9
11	60	26	2	2	66	20	12
12	61	13	1	4	57	17	12
13	78	13	10	5	38	20	9
14	31	11	12	6	46	19	12
15	181	34	17	7	103	22	9
16	74	22	14	9	52	13	6
18	150	22	12	11	89	24	7
24	50	19	12	15	185	25	14
25	54	13	4	18	48	12	9
26	47	15	11	25	26	4	3
28	29	14	7	26	33	8	5
30	62	25	15	27	133	34	17
31	93	37	26	30	48	22	12

Note.—To save space, only days on which 20 or more German machines were destroyed are included. The totals for August are: German 1,110, British 310: September: German 1,114, British 311.

FIGHTER COMMAND OPERATIONS TWO YEARS
(In Britain and Home Waters)

Date	German losses	British losses	Pilots saved
Oct. '39–May '40	57	1	—
1940			
June	24	—	—
July	237	50	6
August	1,101	297	149
September	1,089	319	168
October	246	118	67
November	221*	53	28
December	51	9	8
1941			
January	26	1	—
February	36	6	—
March	71	6	1
April	112	3	—
May	207	18	5
June	52	2	1
July	47	1	—
August	15	—	—
Sept. 1–3	2	—	—
Total	3,594	884	439

* Including 20 Italians

BOMBER COMMAND OPERATIONS TWO YEARS

		Total
Raids on Germany—3/9/39 to 3/9/41		1,778
Targets attacked do. do.		241

Main targets		No. of attacks		
		1/1/40–31/12/40	1/1/41–3/9/41	Total
Aachen	AB	8	5	13
Berlin	ABDE	34	14	48
Bremen	ABCD	52	31	83
Cologne	BDE	53	39	92
Dortmund	ABDEF	20	3	23
Dortmund-Ems Canal	C	15	1	16
Duisburg	BC	35	13	48
Dusseldorf	ADE	20	23	43
Emden	CDF	26	30	56
Essen	BF	33	8	41
Gelsenkirchen	BDF	39	3	42
Hamburg	BCDE	58	17	75
Hamm	BF	79	2	81
Hanover	BCDE	27	13	40
Kiel	CD	32	22	54
Mannheim	BD	34	10	44
Osnabrück	BF	34	4	38
Wilhelmshaven	CD	34*	18	54
		633	256	891

*+ 2 (September, 1939)

Key to objectives bombed: A—aerodromes, aircraft factories; B—railways, marshalling yards; C—naval bases, shipyards, harbours, ships, canals; D—oil refineries, dumps, fuel works; E—munition and chemical works, power plants, blast furnaces; F—ammunition dumps.

to check invasion, but soon our strategic bombing attacks grew in intensity. Compared with the number in action in 1941, the R.A.F. bombing force was then small; yet by meticulous planning heavy blows were made on the weakest points in the enemy's war machine. The numerous attacks on the marshalling yard at Hamm, the first heavy raid directed against the naval base at Kiel, and against the Dortmund-Ems Canal will always rank as the Bomber Command's great achievements in this period.

For his work in the raid on the Dortmund-Ems Canal, Flight-Lieutenant R. A. B. Learoyd, pilot of a Hampden aircraft, was awarded the Victoria Cross and was thus the third airman in the present war to be so decorated. Another recipient of this coveted award was Sergeant J. Hannah, gunner of a Hampden.

Greece, Oct.–Dec., 1940

On October 28, 1940, another enemy campaign was opened—Italy's invasion of Greece. And to that country were sent units of the R.A.F. to assist the small but highly efficient Air Force of our Allies in their struggle against the aggressors. Thus did Britain find herself grappling with the foe in yet one more field of war. Blenheim bombers and Gloster Gladiator biplane fighters formed the equipment of the British air component in Greece, and, as was shown in all other quarters, they operated with consistent efficiency in spite of inferiority in numbers and maintenance difficulties.

Air Raids on Britain, Oct.–Dec., 1940

After the huge losses they had suffered during their mass raids by daylight on Britain the Germans intensified their night attacks, and once again the R.A.F. was facing a problem that appeared to be without solution. But great developments in new aircraft, new equipment, and systems for night defence were being pressed on behind the scenes.

At the same time our own bombing strength was rising, and in the month of November concentrated attacks were made

Enemy tanker off French coast set ablaze by the R.A.F. bomber now circling its sinking victim.
British Official: Crown Copyright

on Berlin, Duisburg, Bremen, Cologne, Gelsenkirchen, Hamburg, Leuna, Düsseldorf, Hamm, Stuttgart and many other objectives.

On November 16 the announcement was made of the award of the Victoria Cross to Flight-Lieutenant D. J. Nicholson, a fighter pilot. The last month of the year was marked by heavy blows made by the R.A.F. on Italians in Libya and Albania and on Italian ports and industries.

Enemy Shipping, 1940-41

The Bomber Command and Coastal Command based at home carried out many brilliant exploits in December, raiding enemy ships off the coasts of Holland,

R.A.F. Record

SECTION 4. D

COASTAL COMMAND OPERATIONS THREE YEARS

Miles flown on operational sorties—approximately. 50,000,000 (Above does not include distances covered by units away from home bases.)	
Attacks on U-boats, approx.	400
Sorties on Convoy escorts exceed 30,000	
Daily Patrols to protect shipping cover routes from Arctic to Africa, Norway along European coast line to Pyrenees	Area 600,000 sq. miles

Outstanding Actions	Date
Two Sunderlands rescue crew of torpedoed *Kensington Court* in Atlantic...	21/9/39
U-boat sunk by Hudson (first attack on sub.)...	8/12/39
Altmark prison-ship located by three aircraft ...	11/2/40
Bismarck tracked by Hudsons, Sunderlands and Catalinas	23-27/5/41
U-boat attacked and captured by Hudson	7/9/41
Cooperation in St. Nazaire three-Services raid	27-28/3/42
Daylight raid over Paris, Tricolour dropped on Arc de Triomphe from Beaufighter	12/6/42

France, and Norway, and attacking ports in occupied territory. The long-range flights of Coastal Command aircraft operating to protect convoys had reached a total of 16,500 by the beginning of 1941; and by the beginning of September, 1941, the tonnage of enemy supply ships sunk or seriously damaged by the Coastal Command amounted to 240,000. The number of assaults on German naval units totalled 710.

BOMBER AND COASTAL COMMANDS' COMBINED OPERATIONS ON GERMAN-OCCUPIED COUNTRIES (1940—3/9/1941)

Raids on objectives in France, Belgium, Holland and Norway		1,770
Targets attacked in France, Belgium, Holland and Norway		397

Main targets	No. of attacks		
	1/1/40– 31/12/40	1/1/41– 3/9/41	Total
Boulogne	69	45	114
Brussels	15	—	15
Cherbourg	24	45	69
Havre	30	18	48
Lorient	38	12	50
Ostend	52	27	79
Rotterdam	27	44	71
St. Omer	10	9	19
St. Nazaire	3	11	14
Schipol	35	1	36
Stavanger	32	—	32
Texel	26	2	28
Waalhaven	18	—	18
Zeebrugge	13	4	17

The long record of achievements of the Coastal Command is distinguished by such episodes as the detection of the *Altmark*, the *Scharnhorst*, the *Lützow* and the *Bismarck*. In the prolonged action which ended with the destruction of the *Bismarck*, brilliant and decisive parts were played by Hudson, Sunderland and Catalina aircraft. In these operations, Sunderland flying-boats flew for 12 hours at a stretch while the Catalinas reconnoitred for over 20 hours.

Daylight Sweeps over France, 1941

On January 10, 1941, bombers with over a hundred fighters as escorts swept the French coast. It was the first big offensive sweep carried out in daylight. By February many of the Fighter squadrons were re-equipped with a new make of Vickers-Armstrong Spitfire, and through the great rise in British output and American aid the strength of the R.A.F. was steadily mounting. New night-fighter squadrons went into action

FIGHTER AND BOMBER COMMANDS' COMBINED OPERATIONS
(Attacks on Enemy and Enemy-Occupied Territory)

Date	Enemy losses	British losses	Personnel saved
January, 1941	6	20	1 crew
February	11	50	2 crews
March	16	45	—
April	18	92	1
May	31	67	2
June	183	160	6
July	231	256	13
August	126	265	10
September	2	13	—
Total	624	968	32 + 3 bomber crews

with the Douglas Havoc and the Bristol Beaufighter. On the night of February 15, 1941, Bomber Command carried out a remarkable long-range flight, flying as far as Cracow, the distance being 1,750 miles. In March further power was given to the R.A.F. when the new four engined bombers were in action, and the most powerful bombs ever used were carried. In the Middle East the enemy was being hammered from the air with ceaseless intensity. In April and May our daylight operations over occupied France, Holland and over Germany itself were made with great persistency.

Night Defence, May, 1941

The growth in the effectiveness of Britain's night defences stood out well in the early summer of 1941. In the first ten days of May the Germans made further heavy attacks on ports, industrial towns, and London. From May 1 until May 10 the Luftwaffe lost at least 116 bombers, and on the last night no fewer than 33 German aircraft were destroyed. In offensive sweeps over Northern France, from the middle of June until the end of August, 450 enemy aircraft were shot out of the sky.

Daylight Raids on Germany, July–August, 1941

Blenheim bombers carried out during the summer a number of magnificent daylight raids over Rotterdam, Cologne, Bremen, Knapsack and other targets, flying with the greatest daring at tree-top level. Several raids marked the introduction into action at about the same time of the Boeing Fortress when it flew in the sub-stratosphere. And two more pilots of the R.A.F. were decorated with the Victoria Cross: Acting Wing-Commander H. I. Edwards, D.F.C., who made an outstanding daylight, low-flying raid on Bremen on July 4; and Sergeant J. A. Ward, who acted with conspicuous bravery while returning from a night raid on Münster on July 7. Ward climbed on to the wing of a Wellington to extinguish a fire near the starboard engine when the machine was flying at 13,000 feet.

Middle East, 1941

In the Middle East the Imperial Air Forces continued to fight with increasing strength. British airmen who had been in combat with an enemy of far greater numerical strength served there with characteristic initiative and courage. They

R.A.F. OPERATIONS—MIDDLE EAST 1940–1941

Date	Theatre of War	Enemy Losses	British Losses	Personnel saved
1940 June	African fronts	41	6	—
July–Sept.	,, ,,	144	23	—
Oct.–Dec.	,, ,,	194	30	—
1941	All Middle East Theatres of War			
Jan.	,, ,,	272	18*	1
Feb.	,, ,,	339	27*	2
March	,, ,,	368	19*	4
April	,, ,,	252	58*	5
May	,, ,,	223	62*	5
June	,, ,,	216	65*	7
July	,, ,,	133	28*	3
August	,, ,,	134	25*	4
1940 Oct.–Dec.	Greece and Albania	52	19	—
1941 Jan.–July	,, ,,	249	†	
Total		2617	380	31

* These figures include losses in Greece and Albania.   † Losses unknown.

AWARDS—FIRST THREE YEARS 1939–1942

Total Awards 5,335

R.A.F.

V.C. 9   D.S.O. 158 (12 with bar)
D.F.C. 2,209   D.F.M. 1,618
(171 with bar)   (28 with bar)
A.F.C. 368 (6 with bar)   A.F.M. 84   M.C. 14

W.A.A.F. and R.A.F.

M.M. 50   G.C. 2   G.M. 67   O.B.E. 99
M.B.E. 151   B.E.M. 289

fought over the Western Desert, Greece, Eritrea, and Abyssinia. They were in battle in Iraq and Syria and Iran. They scoured the sky over the Mediterranean Sea, locating and attacking enemy ships, submarines and aircraft in an area which amounts to about half a million square miles. As time passed the strength of the R.A.F. grew swiftly in the Middle East and in every other theatre.

GREAT EVENTS OF THE THIRD YEAR

Momentous events involving the R.A.F. in many great enterprises lay ahead when the second year of the war had drawn to a close. Throughout the twelve months ending in September, 1941, the strength and resources of Britain's air arm had been growing. The gigantic Empire Air Training Scheme had successfully met the call for more and more trained flying personnel and technicians. The output of aircraft, including several new types, had been satisfactorily geared up and research and development had been unceasingly pursued. But the entry of Japan into the conflict early in December, 1941, made a deflection of our air strength unavoidable.

Nevertheless the home-based Operational Commands continued to extend without respite the air offensive against Germany. Our fighter sweeps over occupied France, which began in 1941. were continued with the greatest dash and daring. At night, in face of severe weather conditions, our bombers penetrated far into Germany. With Russia in the war a new purpose was added to the night raids. The assaults on many Nazi targets (such as ports and U-boat bases) were part of the Battle of the Atlantic; others were made to disrupt the economic structure of Germany, and to help the Soviet by checking the flow of Nazi war supplies to the Eastern Front via the Baltic.

British Air Superiority

A rise in our air superiority in the West became discernible early in 1942; the work of our bombers, fighters and fighter-bombers over Northern France, Holland and Belgium was carried on with such frequency that it became a regular routine.

BOMBER COMMAND OPERATIONS
RAIDS ON GERMANY—THIRD YEAR

Date	No. of Targets	No. of Attacks	Main Objectives
Sept., 1941	30	18	Cologne, Karlsruhe, Berlin, Stettin.
October	28	15	Cologne, Ruhr, Hamburg, Stuttgart.
November	12	19	Berlin, Essen, Lübeck.
December	8	14	Wilhelmshaven, Cologne, Emden.
Jan., 1942	6	15	Bremen, Hamburg, Münster
February	9	14	Kiel, Mannheim.
March	12	7	Ruhr, Cologne, Lübeck.
April	8	19	Ruhr, Rostock, Hamburg, Cologne, Augsburg (day-raid).
May	5	7	Cologne (1,000-bomber raid), Essen, Ruhr.
June	5	16	Ruhr, Bremen, Emden.
July	14	27	Danzig, Lübeck, Saarbrücken.
August	18	14	Saarbrücken, Karlsruhe, Flensburg, Munich, Bremen.
Sept., 1–3	2	2	Flensburg.
Total, 12 Ms.	157	187	

Sept. 1939–Sept. 1942 213 towns were attacked. Places most frequently attacked were :—

Cologne (110)   Kiel (70)   Düsseldorf (50)
Bremen (101)   Wilhelmshaven   Osnabrück (44)
Hamburg (93)   (69)   Hanover (44)
Hamm (85)   Mannheim (56)   Gelsenkirchen
Emden (80)   Duisburg (55)   (42)
 Berlin (53)   Dortmund (39)

In this period the total losses in Europe of Bomber, Fighter, Coastal and Army Co-op. Commands were :—
Fighters, 551. Other aircraft, 758.
Axis Losses, 731.

In pressing on with its sweeps, frequently at extreme range over enemy territory, Fighter Command held the balance in its favour and a constant toll was taken of Luftwaffe interceptors. From September, 1941, until September, 1942, more than 600 M.E. 109s and F.W. 190s were destroyed in air combats over France by our intruding fighter aircraft. Nearly forty enemy machines were destroyed over German territory by aircraft of Fighter Command engaged in offensive operations in darkness. During the same period (September, 1941–September, 1942) our fighters accounted for 60 German aircraft intercepted during daylight or darkness over Britain. All told, the enemy lost 200 aircraft as a result of the combined efforts of the R.A.F. night-fighter squadrons and A.A. batteries. In all, Fighter Command accounted for about a thousand aeroplanes of the Luftwaffe in the third year of the war—equal to 80 full-strength squadrons.

Three Years' Toll of Enemy Raiders

From the time war broke out until September, 1942, British fighter pilots serving in home-based units destroyed no fewer than 4,000 enemy aircraft in the daytime ; and more than 700 fell to the cannon and guns of R.A.F. fighters operating at night. These are truly astonishing totals. In 1942 units of the United States Air Force were based in Britain, and some time after they had been established here their bombers went into action by carrying out daylight raids on targets in Holland and France. In these assaults R.A.F. Fighter Command co-operated, and our Spitfires flew in great force to escort the American Bostons and Flying Fortresses.

R.A.F. in the Dieppe Raid

The first operation of this kind took place on July 4, and a few weeks later, on August 18, Fighter Command undertook its greatest enterprise of the year when it held the skies for the combined operations at Dieppe. On that historic day R.A.F. fighters flew continuously into the zone of action from dawn till dark, and in so doing carried out 2,500 sorties.

Hammering Enemy Warships at Brest

In the first few weeks of 1942 one of Bomber Command's main tasks was the hammering of the "Scharnhorst," "Gneisenau," and "Prinz Eugen," as they lay in the harbour of Brest. Night after night our heavy and medium bombers flew over that target, probably the most heavily defended key-point in the West.

On the night of March 3 Bomber Command struck its heaviest blow on targets in Occupied France. A strong force bombed the immense Renault factory near Paris, inflicting tremendous damage which robbed the enemy of one of his most

BOMBER AND COASTAL COMMANDS MAIN OBJECTIVES, OCC. COUNTRIES
THIRD YEAR (Sept., 1941—Sept., 1942)

Town	No. of Attacks
Abbeville	14
Boulogne	24
Brest	40
Calais	15
Cherbourg	24
Dieppe	12
Dunkirk	34
Havre	43
Ostend	29
St. Nazaire	22
Total	257

Other towns attacked :—Amiens, Antwerp, Béthune, Caen, Commines, Flushing, Grenvilliers, Ghent, Hazebrouck, Lannion, Lens, Lille, Lorient, Mazingarhe (near Béthune), Morlaix, Nantes, Poissy, Billancourt, Rotterdam, Rouen, Zeebrugge.

SECTION 4. D R.A.F. Record

FIGHTER COMMAND OPERATIONS THIRD YEAR OF WAR
(In Britain and Home Waters)

Date	German Losses	British Losses
Sept., 1941	9	—
Oct.	23	1
Nov.	18	—
Dec.	13	2
Jan., 1942	10	3
Feb.	10	—
March	7	—
April	30	—
May	34	—
June	35	—
July	55	—
August	42	1
Sept. 1-2	4	—
Total	290	7

important sources of supply. Five days afterwards, in daylight, Boston bombers attacked the Matford works at Poissy, near Paris, whence the Germans had been obtaining a vast number of army lorries.

These operations and a number of raids made on objectives in Germany during March revealed in some measure the rising bombing strength of the R.A.F. at home. An assault on Essen early in March was in fact made on a heavier scale than the Luftwaffe's raid on Coventry. A little later hundreds of bombers flew to Rostock and blasted the town where stood the Heinkel aeroplane works, the Neptune shipyards and other vital targets. Halifaxes, Stirlings, Lancasters, Wellingtons, Manchesters and Hampdens were used in this great attack.

Thousand-Bomber Raids

In May, Short Stirling four-motor bombers flew right across Germany to attack the great Skoda armament works at Pilsen in Czechoslovakia. On the night of May 30-31, when the moon was full and the sky was clear, Bomber Command made the greatest air attack the world had ever known—the "thousand-plus" raid on Cologne. In ninety minutes Stirlings, Halifaxes, Lancasters (all four-engined giants), and Wellingtons, Whitleys and Hampdens dropped 3,000 tons of bombs— high-explosive and incendiaries. The German defences were "saturated," and A.A. guns and searchlights became impotent; the enemy's location system was overwhelmed, and his fighter aircraft could do little. On the next night (June 1) one thousand and thirty-six R.A.F. bombers thundered over Essen.

Reconnaissance photographs showed plainly the colossal havoc resulting. In Cologne it spread over an area of 5,000 acres. In each operation our losses were astonishingly small. Of the 1,130 aircraft which raided Cologne less than four per cent did not return, while in the Essen attack our losses were lighter still and six German night-fighters were destroyed by the guns of the British bombers. A third thousand-bomber raid took place on the night of June 26, when Bremen received crippling and shattering blows in an attack lasting 75 minutes. In these mammoth operations all four operational Commands played a part. Fighter, Army Co-operation, and Coastal Command aircraft went into diversionary action against enemy aerodromes and other targets as the great throng of Bomber Command units flew in to their objectives.

In spite of the magnitude of these mass assaults other bombing work of the R.A.F. in the West was not reduced. The Ruhr, enemy ports, U-boat strongholds, railway communications, and French factories working for the enemy were picked for repeated attention by strong forces numbering hundreds of machines. During June the R.A.F. went into action on 20 days and 23 nights. Sixteen attacks were made against five targets in Germany, while out of thirty-three operations against seventeen targets in occupied territory twelve were made in daylight.

R.A.F. OPERATIONS—MIDDLE EAST THIRD YEAR OF WAR

Date	Axis Losses	R.A.F. Losses	Pilots Saved
Sept., 1941	35	37	—
Oct.	15	41	—
Nov.	107	99	—
Dec.	137	145	—
Jan., 1942	51	63	12
Feb.	67	75	8
March	89	42	10
April	170	67	16
May	187	107	23
June	165	151	43
July	308	181	41
August	86	106	17
Sept.	32	21	9
Total	1,449	1,135	179

In June, too, the R.A.F. night-fighter "intruders" did fine work. They destroyed 12 Luftwaffe bombers over enemy bases and damaged a great many more.

Long-range Daytime Raids

Among the most striking features of the air offensive in the West in the spring and summer of 1942 were the daylight attacks at long range. On April 17 two formations of six Lancaster bombers, led by Acting Squadron-Leader J. D. Nettleton, flew at a height of not more than 50 feet over a thousand miles of enemy territory to attack the M.A.N. Diesel-engine works at Augsburg. It was one of the most audacious daylight raids of the war, and for his bravery and superb leadership Nettleton was afterwards awarded the Victoria Cross—the eighth V.C. to have been won by men of the R.A.F. in this war. Some three months later several Lancaster squadrons flew in broad daylight to Danzig to bomb the submarine base there. This hazardous task entailed a flight of 850 miles; three aircraft only were lost.

Coastal Command

The war over the sea was marked in the third year by the intensified efforts of Coastal Command. Its anti-submarine patrol area extended northwards to the Arctic Circle and ranged from the coast of Norway to mid-Atlantic, while operations against enemy shipping rose to unparalleled dimensions. Some units of the Command, operated from bases in North Russia, carried out the vitally important duties of convoy protection. Night after night other Coastal Command aircraft laid thousands of mines in enemy waters. Day after day Sunderlands, Whitleys and Catalinas, flying for fourteen hours and more, kept up their watch for U-boats. Over the Bay of Biscay Beaufighters and other machines sought out and fought the Arado seaplanes and long-range Messerschmitt fighters intended to provide air protection for U-boats.

Epic of Malta

In operations from its Mediterranean bases the R.A.F. worked with the same tenacity and relentless energy. Heavy bombers, fighter-bombers, fighters, torpedo-bombers, and transports of the Middle Eastern Command worked in close liaison to acquire the air mastery that was an essential preliminary requirement of the Eighth Army before the great victory over the Afrika Korps was achieved. In the epic of Malta the magnificent work of the fighter squadrons (ultimately equipped with the redoubtable Spitfire) in defending the island and protecting convoys will ever be remembered. The bombing of the enemy's supply ports and his shipping in transit across the Mediterranean went on throughout the third year of the war.

In the Far East, too, the R.A.F., in spite of many setbacks, was gathering power in these crucial months of 1942. When the fourth year of the war dawned, Britain's air arm, notwithstanding its gigantic commitments, was stronger than it had ever been and everywhere, over land and sea, the R.A.F. was on the offensive.

SUMMARY OF AXIS LOSSES

Sept., 1939—Sept., 1940	
Over Great Britain and British Waters	1,549
Over Germany and German-Occupied Territory	1,082
Middle East	125
Year's Total...	2,756
Second Year (1940—41)	
Over Great Britain and British Waters	2,080
Over Germany and German-Occupied Territory	662
Middle East	1,040
Year's Total...	3,782
Third Year (1941—42)	
Over Great Britain and British Waters	290
Over Germany and German-Occupied Territory	744*
Middle East	1,449
Year's Total...	2,483
Grand Total...	9,021

* These figures include those aircraft accounted for by the R.A.F. Fighter Wing stationed in Russia.

THE ROYAL AIR FORCE REGIMENT

It was decided early in 1942 that the Royal Air Force should undertake the local defence on the ground of its own and Ministry of Aircraft Production airfields in the United Kingdom, and that the Royal Air Force should act in this respect as the executive agent of the Army, which remains responsible for the land defence of all areas. Existing R.A.F Defence Squadrons and Flights were therefore reorganized and incorporated into a new organization known as the Royal Air Force Regiment. The Regiment is an integral part of the R.A.F and is directed and controlled through the normal R.A.F. chain of command. The formation of the R.A.F. Regiment was a logical development arising from the increasingly important part which air forces have to play in modern war.

The Commandant of the R.A.F. Regiment is Major General C. F. Liardet, C.B., D.S.O., T.D., who is also Director-General of Ground Defence at the Air Ministry. A senior officer of the Regiment is on the staff of the A.O.C. in C. of each R.A.F. Command at home and overseas; similarly, in each Group, an officer of the Regiment is appointed to the staff of the Group Commander to advise him on matters affecting the Regiment and ground defence questions.

The whole effort of the R.A.F. depends on the successful defence of its airfields. It is therefore essential not only that these airfields should be adequately protected against both ground and air attack, but that a force effectively trained and equipped should be readily available to undertake this role with speed and efficiency. The R.A.F. Regiment is not simply a defensive force. It has also to advance with the military and air units in an air offensive campaign, and to occupy and set up the local defence of the occupied airfields.

General Index

In this Index, which is designed to give quick reference to text, tables, diagrams and photographs in the "*A B C of the R.A.F.*" the titles of the main articles are indicated by bold type, thus : **Auxiliary Air Force**, 60–61. A Table of Contents in page order appears in page 2.

A

Abbreviations, 74
Accidents, flying, first aid, 29
Accountant, R.A.F.V.R., 19
Acetylene Welder, 12, 14, 57
Administrative Branch, R.A.F.V.R., 18
Administrative Group and officers, W.A.A.F., 56, 57
Advanced Air Striking Force, 141, 151
Aerial combat, photograph, 126
Aerobatics, in training, 77
Aero Engines, British, 107, 108
Aerofoils, of wings, 101
Aeronautical Engineering, School of, 38
Aeroplanes, flight and structure, 101-103
—controls, 103
—design tendencies, 98
Ailerons, 102, 103
Air-borne Troops, 136
Air Chief Marshal, badges, Plates betw. 32-33
—biographies, 46-49
Air Commodore, rank badges, Plates betw. 32-33
Air Component, 141
Air Council, 43
Aircraft, classes, 101
—markings, Plate facing 33
—Service types, Plates 81-96, 97-100
Aircrafthand, 12
—trades for, 14-15
—W.A.A.F., 57
Air Crew, 12, 14-17
Air Efficiency Award, 32
Air Fighting, 141-145
—formation flying, 146-147
Air Force, see Royal Air Force
Air Force Cross, 32, Plate f. 32
Air Force Medal, 32, Plate f. 32
Air-gunner, badge, 30
—work, 124, 125
Air Marshal, badge, Plate betw. 32-33
—biographies, 49-54
Air Ministry, 43
Air Observer School, 27
Air rank officers' cap badges, 30
Airscrews, 98
Air Sea Rescue, 131
Airspeed Oxford, 26
Air Staff, 43
Air Training Corps, 63-64
Air Vice-Marshal, badge, Plate betw. 32-33
Air War, 1939-42, 151-159
Aldis Lamp, 112
Allies, Air Forces, 38
Angle of Incidence, 101
Apprentices, Schools for, 38
Apprenticeship, 10-11, 38
Armament, aircraft, 100-103
Armament Section, officers, 18
Armourer, 10, 11, 12, 14
—training and work, 34, 134
—(W.A.A.F.), 57
Armstrong-Whitworth Whitley Bomber, 97
Army Cooperation Command, 39, 40
—planes, 87, 99
Augsburg raid, 158
Australian Air Force, Royal, 67
Automatic Telegraphy, 114
Auxiliary Air Force, 60-61
—badge, 31
Awards, R.A.F., 32, 156

B

Babington, Air Marshal Sir J. T., 49
—Air Marshal Philip, 49
Badges, R.A.F., 30-31, Plates betw. 32-33
Balfour, Capt. H. H., 44
Baling out, 37, 129
Ball, Capt. A., V.C., 32
Balloon Barrage, 61, 129
Balloon Command, 42, 61, 129
—meteorology for, 118
Balloon Fabric Worker, 57
Balloon Operator, 57
Balloon Parachute Hand, 57
Balloons, 129, 130
Balloon Squadron, A.A.F. 61, 130
Banking, 103
Barber, 12, 14
Barker, Maj. W. G., V.C., 20, 32
Barratt, Air Marshal Sir A. S., 50
Barry, Col. Smith, 7
Batman, 12, 14
Battle of Britain, 142, 144, 153
Batwoman, W.A.A.F., 57
B.E.3. biplane, 4
Beauchamp-Proctor, Flt. Lieut. A. W., V.C., 32, 69
Beaufighter, 82, 99
Beaufort bomber, 83, 99
Beaufort Scale, wind force, 118
Belgium, R.A.F. in, 152
Belgium (Free), Air Force, 38
Benevolent Fund, 71-73
Bettington, Col., 68
Bibliography, 138-9
Bishop, Lt. Col., V.C., 7, 32
Blacksmith, 12, 14
Blenheim IV, 94, 99, 145
Blériot Monoplanes, R.F.C., 5
Blind Flying, instruments, 80
Boeing Fortress, 93, 98, 100
Bomb-aimer, 127
Bomb damage assessment, 123
Bomb Disposal Squad, badge, 30
Bomber Command, 41, 154, 157
—and Coastal Command, 155, 157
—and Fighter Command, 155
—1,000-bomber raids, 158

Bombers, attacks on, 114, 115
—British, 83, 86-89, 92, 93, 98
—crews, briefed, 149
—ground crews, 133
—gunner, 150
—navigation, 111
—U.S.A., 90, 91, 100
Bombing and Gunnery School, 24
—bombing practice, 28
—bomb-sight practice, 23
—despatch room, 24
—gun-turret instruction, 23
—night-flying instruction by camera obscura, 23
—rear-gunner cockpit, 23
Bombing, technique, 127
—(1914), 6
Bomb Plotter, W.A.A.F., 57
Bombs, and Bombing Warfare, 127-128
Bomb-sight, 23, 111, 127
Books, Aeronautical, 138-9
Botha, 98
Boulton Paul Defiant, fighter, 82, 124, 145
Bowhill, Air Chief Marshal Sir F. W., 46
Boyd, Air Marshal Owen, 50
Boys, apprentice, 10-11
—University Course, 65
Bradley, Air Marshal Sir S. T., 50
Brandon, Lt., 69
Breadner, Air Vice-Marshal L. S., R.C.A.F., 68
Brest, raids, 157
Brewster Buffalo, 84
Briefing Bomber Crews, 149
Bristol Beaufighter, 82, 99
Bristol Beaufort, 83, 99
Bristol Blenheim, 8, 94, 99, 145
Bristol Bombay, carrier, 137
Bristol Engines, 107
Britain, Battle of, 142, 144, 153
—Fighter Command, 153
—first raids, 151
—raids (1940), 153, 154
British Empire, Order of, 32, Plate facing 32
Brooke-Popham, Air Chief Marshal Sir Robert, 46
Browning machine-guns, 145
Burnett, A. C. M. Sir C. S., 47
Burns, first aid for, 26
Butcher, 12, 14

C

Camber of wings, 101
Cameras, 121-122
Campbell, F O K., V.C., 32
Canadian Air Force, R., 67-8
Cannon, aircraft, 81, 126, 127, 145
Carpenter, 12
Cartridge signals, 115
Catalina, Consolidated, 95, 98, 100
Catering Branch, W.A.A.F., 57

General Index

Chamier, Air Commodore J. A. and A.T.C., 64
Chaplains, R.A.F.V.R., 18, 19
— badge, 30
Charging Board Operator, 57
Charts, air use, 110
Chesapeake, Sikorsky, 100
Ciné Camera-gun, 122, 126, 127
Ciné Operator, W.A.A.F., 57
Clerk, 12, 14
Clerk, in W.A.A.F., 57
Coastal Command, 40, 155, 159
— aircraft, 40, 42
— awards, 1939-41, 40
— navigation, 110
— operations, 151, 155, 157, 159
Cologne, great raid, 158
Combat Report, 150
Commands, Air, 39
— overseas, 43
— Tree of, 43
Commissions, R.A.F.V.R., 18
Compression Stroke, 106
Consolidated aircraft, 92, 97, 100
Control Column : see Joystick
Controls, 79, 102-3
Conversion Factors, table, 116
Convoys, protection, 155
Cook, 12, 14, 57
Cooling System, Hurricane, 104
Coppersmith, 12, 14
Correspondence Courses, 38
County Associations, and A.A.F. 60, 61
Courtney, Air Chief Marshal Sir Christopher Lloyd, 50
Cranwell, R.A.F. College, 9
Curtiss Kittyhawk and Tomahawk fighter, 85, 97, 98, 100
Czechoslovakia, Air Force, 38

D

Dauntless, Boston, 100
Davies, Adm. R. Bell, V.C., 32
Dead Reckoning, 110
Decorations, R.A.F., *Plate facing* 32
Defiant, B.P., 82, 124, 145
Definitions of Terms, 119-20
Dental Branch, R.A.F.V.R., 19
— W.A.A.F., 57
Dental Clerk Orderly, 57
Dental Mechanic, 12, 14
Dental Officer, badge, 30
D.H.2, fighter, 4
Dieppe raid, R.A.F. at, 157
Dihedral angle, 101
Dinghy, collapsible, 132
Dispenser, W.A.A.F., 57
Distinguished Flying Cross, 32, *Plate facing* 32
Distinguished Flying Medal, 32, *Plate facing* 32
Distinguished Service Order, *Plate facing* 32
Dominions, Air Forces, 66-70
— — Canadian airmen, 68
— — dual control 'plane, 70
— — Harvard aircraft, 69
— fighter pilots of S.A.A.F., 68
— Wirraway and Wackett aircraft of R.A.A.F., 66
Donald, Air Marshal D. G., 54
Douglas, Air Chief Marshal S., 51
Dowding, Air Chief Marshal Sir H. C. T., 47
Draughtsman, 12
Drill of Vital Actions, 75

Drogue Packer, W.A.A.F., 57
Drummond, Air Marshal R. M., 51
Dunkirk, air tactics at, 141, 142
— R.A.F. at, 152

E

Eagle Squadron, 147
Education, facilities, 38, 65
— officer, 38, badge, 31
Educational Services, Directorate, 38
Edwards, Act. Wing Com. H. I., V.C., 32
Electricians, 10, 11, 12, 14
— training, 34
— (W.A.A.F.), 57
Electricity, Units, 140
Elementary Flying Training School, 21
— pupils' first flight, 27
Elevator, 79
Ellington, Marshal of the R.A.F., Sir E. L., 45
EmpireAirTraining Scheme, 70
Engine Driver, 12
Engineer, R.A.F.V.R., 18
Engines, of British aircraft, 107
— U.S.A., 100
Ensign, R.A.F., *Plate facing* 33
Equipment Assistant, 12, 14
— in W.A.A.F., 57
Equipment Branch, 19
Evill, Air Marshal Sir D. C., 54

F

Fabric Workers, W.A.A.F., 53, 57
Fairey Battle, construction, 102
Fairey Battles, with B.E.F., 141
Fairey P.4/34, construction, 102
Far Eastern Command, 43
Farman Biplanes, R.F.C., 5, 6
Ferry Command, 39, 42
Fighter Command, 41, 153, 155, 158
Fighters, British types, 81, 82, 87, 99, 104-105
— ground work, 135
— U.S.A., 100
Fighting, Air, 141-145
— formation, 146
First Aid, 28
Fitters, 10, 11, 14, 133
Flags, R.A.F. *Plate facing* 33
Flaps, 76
Flight, Principles of, 101-103
Flight Lieutenant, rank badge *Plate betw.* 32-33
Flight Mechanic, 12, 14, 33
— — W.A.A.F., 58
Float, rescue, 131
Flying, Elements of, 75-80
— meteorology and, 117-118
— navigation in, 110-111
— special training, 124-128
— theory, 101-103
— training, general, 20-27, 75-80
Flying Boats, 94, 100
— U.S.A., 94, 95, 99, 100
Flying Instruction Routine, 20-27, 75-80
Flying-Officer, rank badge, *Plate betw.* 32-33
Flying Squadrons, A.A.F., 60
Flying Training Command, 42
— Miles Master aircraft, 41, 99

Fokker Monoplanes, 6
Forbes, Miss K. J. Trefusis 55
Forced Landings, 77
France, Battle of, 152
— daylight sweeps, 155, 157
— Occupied, raids, 155, 157
Forecasters, meteorological, 117
Formation, in air tactics, 143
Formation Flying, 146
Fortress bomber, 93, 98, 100
Free France, Air Force, 38
Freeman,Air Marshal SirW.R.,47

G

Garland, Fl. Off. D. E., V.C., 32
Garrod, Air Marshal A. G. R., 51
George VI, King, *Frontispiece*
George Cross, 32, *Plate facing* 32
George Medal, 32, *Plate facing* 32
Germany, daylight raids, 156
— first raids, 151
— losses, 156, 157
— parachute troops, 136
— raids (1940), 153
— — (1939-41), 154
— — (1942), 156-59
Glenn Martin Maryland, 98
Good Conduct Medal, 32, *Plate facing* 32
Gossage, Air Marshal Sir E. L.,51
Gray, Sgt. T., V.C., 32
Great War, air tactics, 6, 7, 141
— air V.C.'s in, 32
— bombing in, 6, 127
— R.F.C. in, 6
Greece, R.A.F. in, 154
Grinder, 12
Ground Gunner, 12
Ground Staff, 133-135
— importance, 29
Group Captain rank badges, *Plates* be.w. 32-33
Gunnery and Gunner's Work, 124-126
Gun-sights, 125
Gun-turrets see Turrets

H

Halifax, 91, 98, 99
Hampden Bombers, 99
Hannah, Sgt. J., V.C., 32
Harris, Air Marshal Sir A. T., 52
Harvard, training plane, 26, 69
Havoc, 84, 100, 198
Hawker Maj. L. G., V.C., 32
Hawker Hurricane, 81, 104-5, 146, 147
— with B.E.F., 141
Heat, Physical Units, 140
Henderson, Brig.-Gen. Sir David 5, 6
Hercules Engine : see Bristol
High flying, 78
Hill, Air Marshal R. M., 52
Holland, Air Force, 38
— R.A.F. in, 152
Home Commands, 38-43
Howard Wright biplane, 4
H-type Engines, 108
Hudson Catalina, 94, 98
Hurricane, see Hawker
Hydrogen, for balloons, 130

I

Indian Air Force, 69
Indian Command, 43
Initial Training Wing, 20
Insall, Grp. Capt. G. S. M.,V.C.,32
Instrument Maker 10, 11, 12

General Index

Instrument Mechanic, W.A.A.F., 58
Instrument Repairer, 12, 14, 33, 34
—work, 108
—(W.A.A.F.), 58
Instruments, Cockpit, 25, 79, 80
—Flying, 76
Intelligence Branch, R.A.F., 18
Internal Combustion Engine, 106
Italy, R.A.F. raids, 153
—air losses, 156

J
Jerrard, Flt. Lt. A., V.C., 32
Joubert de la Ferté, Air Chief Marshal Sir Philip, 48
Joystick, 102.

K
Kain, "Cobber," 68, 151
Kite, principle of, 101

L
Laboratory Assist., W.A.A.F., 58
Lamps for signalling, 112
Lancaster, Avro, 88, 99, 158
Landing, 80
Land Line, 113
Last Post, 70
Launch, A.S., Rescue, 132
Lawrence of Arabia Fund, 71
Leaflet raids, 156
Learoyd, F/Lt. A. B., V.C., 32
Leave, 36
Legal Branch, R.A.F.V.R., 19
Leigh-Mallory, Air Marshal Sir T. L., 52
Lewis Gun, for aircraft, 124
Liberator, Consolidated, 92, 100
Library, R.A.F. apprentices, 10
Liddell, Capt. J. A., V.C., 32
Life-saving jacket, 129
Light, Physical Units, 140
—Waves, velocity, 123
Lightning, Lockheed, 83
Lights Out, 70
Link Trainer, 21, 22
Link Trainer Instructor, 12, 15
Linnell, Air Marshal F. J., 52
Lockheed Hudson, 40, 96
—Lightning, 83, 100
—Ventura, 86, 100
Longmore, Air Chief Marshal Sir A. M., 48
Long Service and Good Conduct Medal, R.A.F., 32, *Plate facing* 32
Ludlow-Hewitt, Air Chief Marshal Sir E. R., 48

M
Maastricht Bridges, V.C.s, 32, 152
McCudden, Maj. J. T. B., V.C., 32
Machine-guns, aircraft, 124, 125
—R.F.C., 6.
Machine Tool Setter, 12
McLeod, Lt. A. A., V.C., 32
McNamara, Grp. Capt. F. H., V.C., 32
Maid, W.A.A.F., 58
Maintenance Command, 42
Malta, R.A.F. at, 159
Manchester, Avro, 89, 99
Mannock, Maj. E., V.C., 32
Map Reading, 109-110
Marine Craft Duties, R.A.F., 19
Marshal of R.A.F., rank badge *Plates betw.* 32-33
Martinet and Master trainers, 99

Masseuse, W.A.A.F., 58
Mathematics, 20
Maurice Farman biplane, 6
Mechanics, at work, 34
Medals, awarded to R.A.F., 32, *Plate facing* 32
Medical Branch, R.A.F.V.R., 19
Medical Grades, 12, 14-15
Medical Officer, badge, 30
Mediterranean, R.A.F. opns., 153
Mental Nursing Orderly, 12
Meritorious Service Medal, 32, *Plate facing* 32
Messerschmitt efficiency, 141
Metal Worker, 12
Meteorological Assistants, 117
Meteorological Stations, 117-18
Meteorologist, 12, 15, 117
—W.A.A.F., 58
Meteorology for R.A.F., 117
Middle East Command, 43
—air opns., 153, 156, 158
Miles Master, training plane, 21, 25, 41, 79, 99
—cockpit instruments, 79
Military Medal, 32, *Plate f.* 32
Miller, 12
Monoplane, structure, 103
Morse Code, 112, 113
Mosquito, De Havilland, 87, 99
Motor Boat Crew, 12, 15
Motor Cyclist, 12
Mottershead, Sergt., T. V.C., 32
M.T. Drivers, W.A.A.F., 58
M.T. Mechanic, 15
—W.A.A.F., 58
Multi-gun Turret, use, 145
Musician, 12
Mustang, N.A., 87, 100

N
Napier Engines, 108
Naval Air Service, Royal, 5, 7
Navigation of Aircraft, 110-111
—24-hour clock, 111
Nettleton, S/L J. D., V.C., 32, 158
Newall, Marshal of the R.A.F., Sir Cyril L. N., 45
New Zealand Air Force, 68
Nicolson, Flt. Lt. J. B., V.C., 32
Nieuport Scout biplane, 7
Night defences, 141, 155
Night-fighter aircraft, 145
—gun turret, 124, 145
—pilot climbs into, 40
Night-flying, 26
Non-commissioned Officers, 13
North, True, finding, 109
Norway Air Force, 38
Nose-on Attack, 144
Nursing Orderly, 12
—W.A.A.F., 58
Nursing Service, 59

O
Observer, 17, 27
—badge, 30
—University Short Course, 65
Observer Corps, Royal, 62
Officers, commissions, 18
—cap badge, 30
—educational facilities, 38
—W.A.A.F., 56
Oil, conversion tables, 120
Operating Room Assistant, 12
—W.A.A.F., 58
Operational Training Unit, 28

Orderly, W.A.A.F., 58
Organisation, R.A.F., 39-43
Overseas Commands, 43

P
Parachute, use, 128-129
Parachute "jumper," 136
Parachute Packer and Repairer, W.A.A.F., 58
Parachute Troops, 136
Pay Groups, 12
Pay Rates, 12, 13
—Observer Corps, Royal, 62
—R.A.F. officers, 18
—R.A.F. trades and aircrew, 13
—W.A.A.F., 58
Peck, Air Marshal R. H., 53
Peirse, Air Marshal Sir R., 53
Per Ardua ad Astra, 69
Petrol, conversion tables, 120
Photographer, 15
—W.A.A.F., 58
Photographic Duties, R.A.F.V.R., 19
Photographs, Air, 122
—Chocques, nr. Bethune, 123
Photography in R.A.F., 121
Physical Training Duties, R.A.F.V.R., 19
—Instructor, 12, 15, badge, 31
Physical Units, 140
Pigeon Keeper, W.A.A.F., 58
Pigeons, as messengers, 115
Pilot Officer, badge, *Plate betw.* 32-33
Pilots, Air Sea Rescue, 131-132
—University Short Course, 65
—wings, 31
Poland, Air Force, 38
Pole Star, and True North, 109
Police, Service, 12, 15, 59
Portal, Air Chief Marshal Sir C. F. A., 49
—preface, 3
Princess Mary's R.A.F. Nursing Service, 59
Promotion, 17
Pulse, normal, 28
Pyrotechnics, signalling by, 115

R
R.A.A.F. See Australian A.F.
Radial Engines, 108
Radiographer, W.A.A.F., 58
Radio Mechanic, 12, 15, 34
Radio Operator, W.A.A.F., 58
Radio-telegraphy, 114
Radio-telephony, 114
—Operator, W.A.A.F., 58
Rank Badges, *Plates betw.* 32-33
Reclassification and remustering, R.A.F., 17, 36
Reconnaissance, Coastal Command, 40
Reconnaissance Machines British, 98, 99
—U.S.A., 100
Record of R.A.F., 151-159
Recruits, Training, 24-29, 33-35
Rees, Grp. Cpt. L. W. B., V.C., 32
Remustering, R.A.F., 17, 36
Retractable Undercarriage, 78
Retreat (trumpet call), 70
Reveille, 70
Rhodesia, air squadron, 66
Rhodes - Moorhouse, Second - Lieut. W. B., V.C. 20, 32
Riggers, work, 133, 135

General Index

Rip Cord, for balloons, 130
—parachute, 129
Robinson, Capt. W. Leefe, V.C., 32
Rolls Royce Engines, 81, 99, 107, 108
Rooks Hill House, 71
Royal Air Force, entry, 12-15
—ensign, badge, flags, and targets, *Plate facing 33*
—history, 5-8
—maximum strength (1918), 7
—Nursing Service, 59
—organisation, 39-41
—ranks, 13, 18, *Plates betw.* 32-33
—Record, Three Years of War, 151-159
—Regiment, 159
—training, 10, 17, 20-29, 75,80, 121-137
—Volunteer Reserve, 8, 12, 29
—War Memorial, 1914-19, 72
Royal Flying Corps, 5
R/T Operator, W.A.A.F., 58
Rudder, of aircraft, 79, 102
Russia, parachute troops, 136
Ryneveld, Lieut.-Gen. Sir Pierre van, 70

S

Salmond, Marshal of the R.A.F., Sir J. M., 45
Salting Benefaction, 72
Saro Lerwick, 96, 99
Saunders, Air Commodore, 68
Scandinavia, R.A.F. opns., 151
Semaphore Code, 112, 113
Service Flying Training Squadron, 25
Service Police, 12, 15, 59
Shadow Factory Scheme, 8
Sheet Metal Worker, 12
Sherwood, Baron, 44
Shipping raids, 1940-41, 154
Shoemaker, 12, 15
Shoe Repairer, W.A.A.F., 59
Short Stirling, 90, 98, 99, 158
Short Sunderland Flying Boats, 42, 96, 98, 99
—Navigator, 111
Side-slipping, 77
Signalling Methods, 112-115
—Aldis lamp, 112
—pigeons, 115
—practice in Morse, 112
—semaphore, 113
Signal Section, R.A.F.V.R., 18
Sinclair, Rt. Hon. Sir Archibald, 44
Slang, R.A.F., 37
Sleeve-valve Engines, 106, 107
Slessor, Air Marshal J. C., 54
Slide rule, principles, 116
Solo Flying, 75
Sopwith, T. O. M., flying school, 5
Sopwith Camel, for R.F.C., 7
Sopwith Pup, for R.F.C., 6, 7
Sound, Physical Units, 140
—Waves, velocity, 123
South African Air Force, 68
Southern Cross, and True North 109
Sparking Plug Tester, 58

Special Air Service Troops, 136
Special Treatment Orderly, 12
Spinning, instruction in, 76
—diagram, 77
Spitfire, 33, 81, 99, 134
Squadron-Leader, rank badges, *Plate betw.* 32-33
Stability of aircraft, 101
Stalling, 79
Station-keeping, 146
Stirling : see Short
Stole, for life-saving, 129
Street, Sir Arthur William, 44
Struben Memorial Trust, 72
Suction Stroke, I.C.E., 106
Sutton, Air Marshal Sir B., 54
Sykes, Maj.-Gen. Sir Frederick, 5

T

Tactics, Air Fighting, 141-147
Tailor, W.A.A.F., 59
Taking Off, 79, 80
Tattoo, 70
Taurus Engine : see Bristol
Technical and Specialist Officers, W.A.A.F., 56
Technical Branch, R.A.F.V.R., 18, 33-35
Technical Training Command, 41
Technical Training Schools, 35, 38
Technician, training, 33-35
—mechanics, 33, 34
Tedder, Air Chief Marshal Sir A. W., 53
Telephone Operator, 58
Teleprinter Operator, 58
Temperature, normal, 28
Thunderbolt, 85, 100
Tiger Moth, 21, 98
Tomahawk, Curtiss, 97, 100
Torpedoman, 12, 15
Tracer, W.A.A.F., 59
Trades for Aircrafthands, table, 14-15
Trades, in R.A.F., 9, 12
—W.A.A.F., 55, 57-59
Tradesmen, 12, 13, 33
Training Command, Flying, 41
— —Technical, 41
Training, R.A.F., 10, 20-29, 33-35, 75-80
Training, Special, 121-137
Training Craft, 21, 23, 25, 79, 96, 100
—U.S.A., 100
Trenchard, Marshal of the R.A.F., Viscount, 46
Tricycle Undercarriage, 78
Trigonometrical Functions, 148
Troops, Parachute and Airborne, 136-137
Troop transport, 137
Trumpet Calls, 70
Turner, 12
Turns, diagrams, 77
Turrets, 98, 124, 125, 145
Tutorial Classes, 38

U

Undercarriages, 78
United States, planes, 83-85, 90-91, 94, 96, 97, 98, 100
University Short Course, 65

V

Vanbrugh Castle School, 71, 72
V.C.s, First Air, 32, 152
Vee Engines, 108
Vengeance, Vultee, 86, 100
Ventura, Lockheed, 86, 100
V-formation, 146
Vickers fighter (1915), 4
Vickers-Supermarine Spitfire, 81, 98, 99
Victoria Cross, 32, *Plate facing* 32
—1914-18 air awards, 32
—1939-42 air awards, 32, 152
Vigilant, Vultee, 87, 100
Vital Actions, Drill of, 75
V.R., 29, see also Royal Air Force Volunteer Reserve

W

W.A.A.F., 55-59
—awards, 156
—balloon repair, 52, 53, 106
—cap badge, 55
—cook, 56
—drummer, 55
—flight mechanic, 58
—ranks, 58
Waitress, in W.A.A.F., 59
Wakefield Benefaction, 72
Wakefield, Viscount, 73
Ward, Sgt. J. A., V.C., 32
Warneford, Flt. Sub-Lieut. R. A. J., V.C., 32
Warrant Officers, 13, badges, 31
Water, in petrol cans, 120
Watussi, S.S., 70
Weather Chart, 117
Weick, Maj. Helmuth, 57
Welder, 12
Wellington Bomber, 72
Welsh, Air Marshal Sir William Lawrie, 53
West, Wing Cmdr. F. M. F., V.C., 32
Westland Lysander, 96, 98
—A.S. rescue, 132
Whitley Bombers, 99
Whittingham, Air Marshal Sir N. E., 54
Wind, Beaufort Scale, 118
—and navigation, 111
Wing Commander, badges, *Plates betw.* 32-33
Wings, of aeroplanes, 101
Wireless Mechanic, 12, 15
—training, 34
—W.A.A.F., 59
Wireless Operator, 12, 15, 35, 133
—badge, 31
—W.A.A.F., 54, 59
Wireless Operator Mechanic, 10, 11, 12
—training, 35
Wireless Waves, velocity, 123
Women's Auxiliary Air Force ; see W.A.A.F.
Women's Royal Air Force, 55
Workshop Hand, W.A.A.F., 59
Wright biplane, 4
W/T (Slip Reader) Operator, W.A.A.F., 59

Printed in England and published by The Amalgamated Press, Ltd., The Fleetway House, Farringdon Street, London, E.C.4. Sole Agents for Australia and New Zealand : Messrs. Gordon & Gotch, Ltd., and for South Africa : Central News Agency, Ltd.

INDEX LIST OF REFERENCE TABLES

	PAGE
Abbreviations, R.A.F.	74
Aero Engines, British	108
Aircraft in Service	99-100
Air Crew, Training, Remustering and Promotion	17
Air V.C.s of 1914-18 and 1940-41	32
Allies, Air Forces	38
Badges, R.A.F.	30-31
Beaufort Scale	118
Books, Aeronautical	138-139
Command, Tree of	43
Constants, Physical and Chemical	32
Conversion Factors	16
Decorations Awarded to R.A.F. Personnel	32
Definitions, R.A.F. Terms	119-120
Eagle Squadron, R.A.F.	147
Engines, Aero	108
First Aid Notes	29
Fitness and the Human Machine	28
Morse Code	113
North, True, Methods of Finding	109
Pay, Rates of, R.A.F.	13, 18
Pay, Rates of, W.A.A.F.	58
' Per Ardua ad Astra '	69
Petrol and Oil, Quantities and Weights	120
Phonetic Alphabet	113
Physical Units and Equivalents	140
R.A.F. Operations, 1939-1942	151-159
R.A.F. Tree of Command	43
R.A.F.V.R., Daily Rates of Pay	13
R.A.F.V.R., Daily Rates of Pay, Commissioned Branches	18
Semaphore Signals	113
Slang, R.A.F.	37
Slide Rule, Principles	116
Sound, Light and Wireless Waves, Velocity	122
Terms Used by R.A.F., Definitions	119-120
Titles and Terms, Abbreviations	74
Trigonometrical Functions	148
Trumpet Calls, R.A.F.	70
Units and Equivalents, Physical	140
V.C.s, Air, 1914-18 and 1940-41	32
W.A.A.F., Daily Rates of Pay	58
W.A.A.F. Ranks	59
Wind Force, Beaufort Scale	118

The Publishers are glad to invite contributions to the

ROYAL AIR FORCE BENEVOLENT FUND

Patron: HIS MAJESTY THE KING

Chairman of Council: The Right Hon. Lord Riverdale, G.B.E., LL.D., J.P.

THE ROYAL AIR FORCE BENEVOLENT FUND was established in October 1919, to commemorate the work of the Flying Services during the War of 1914-18. The object of the Fund is to assist all ranks, past and present, of the Royal Air Force, Auxiliary Air Force, Royal Air Force Reserve and the Woman's Auxiliary Air Force and their dependants. It must be prepared to help:

The disabled, and dependants of those killed while flying
Other casualties and their dependants
Sufferers on account of sickness and general distress

The decision of the Serving Personnel of the R.A.F. to give a regular voluntary subscription to the Fund promises to make good the loss of the proceeds of the Empire Air Day. The enormous expansion of the Service, however, and the inevitable steep rise in the expenditure on relief, demand unremitting support for the Fund.

Cheques, which will be gratefully acknowledged, should be sent direct to the Rt. Hon. Lord Riverdale (Chairman), or to Bertram T. Rumble, Hon. Secretary, Appeals Committee, R.A.F. Benevolent Fund, at:

1, SLOANE STREET, LONDON, S.W.1

Lightning Source UK Ltd.
Milton Keynes UK
UKHW020153240519
343228UK00007B/35/P